W9-AHA-098

Village on the Edge

Village on the Edge

Changing Times in Papua New Guinea

Michael French Smith

University of Hawai'i Press
Honolulu

© 2002 University of Hawai'i Press

All rights reserved

Printed in the United States of America

07 06 05 04 03 02   6 5 4 3 2 1

Library of Congress Cataloging-in-Publication Data
Smith, Michael French.
Village on the edge : changing times in Papua New Guinea / Michael French Smith.
p.   cm.
Includes bibliographical references and index.
ISBN 0–8248–2521–7 (cloth) — ISBN 0–8248–2609–4 (pbk.)
1. Kairiru (Papua New Guinea people)—Social conditions.   2. Kairiru (Papua New
Guinea people)—Economic conditions.   3. Kragur (Papua New Guinea)—Social
conditions.   4. Kragur (Papua New Guinea)—Economic conditions.   I. Title.

DU740.42 .S66   2002
995.7'5—dc21
2002017304

University of Hawai'i Press books are printed on
acid-free paper and meet the guidelines for permanence and
durability of the Council on Library Resources.

Designed by Janette Thompson (Jansom)

Printed by The Maple-Vail Book Manufacturing Group

To Jana,
who egged me on

Contents

WHEN I LEFT ALL MY FRIENDS BEHIND
TO GO TO THE WHITEMAN'S PLACE
I STOOD AND PLAYED MY GUITAR
ON THE PROW OF THE *TAU-K*

I THOUGHT IT WOULD BE A VERY GOOD TIME
BUT THE WIND AND THE RAIN THEY CAME
TOSSING AND TURNING THE *TAU-K*
AS IT ROUNDED POINT URUR

[TAIM MI LUSIM OL PREN BILONG MI
MI LAIK GO LONG PLES WAITMAN
MI SANAP LONG PAITIM GITA
LONG POHET BILONG TAU-K

MI TING SE GUDPELA TAIM TRU
TASOL WIN NA REN I KAM
WILIWILIM TAU-K
LONG POIN BILONG URUR]

—A song from the north shore of Kairiru Island

Acknowledgments

First of all, my heartfelt thanks to the people of Kragur for the outstanding hospitality and generosity they have always shown me.

I also wish to thank: Jana Goldman for her unflagging support and sound counsel; Peter Black and Barbara Webster Black for their valuable comments on an early version of this book; Pamela Kelley for her advice and encouragement; my anonymous reviewers for the University of Hawaiʻi Press for their useful suggestions; Simon Waibai, Stephen Umari, and Diane Buric for their mapmaking skills; Barbara Folsom for her expert copyediting; Suki Panchit for helping me make the most of my photographs; Kathleen Barlow for making my 1998 trip to Kragur possible; Theodore Schwartz for introducing me to anthropology in Papua New Guinea; my colleagues at LTG for serving as a focus group and enduring my progress reports; Harry French and Walter Elieson for stirring my imagination with their South Sea tales; Elsie Elieson for helping put a roof over my head; Rosalyn Goldman for dog sitting and other gracious assistance; and Victor and Margaret Smith for their inestimable contribution.

Introduction

"MICHAEL SMITH CAME FROM AMERICA.
HE REALLY LIKED THE PEOPLE OF KRAGUR."
(MICHAEL SMITH I KAM LONG AMERICA.
EM I LAIKIM TUMAS OL MAN BILONG KRAGUR.)
—From a song by a Kragur villager, 1976

This book is about a village in Papua New Guinea, how its people live and how life there has changed since I first went there at the end of 1975, the year in which Papua New Guinea became an independent country. The village is called Kragur and it lies on the north coast of Kairiru Island in Papua New Guinea's East Sepik Province. I first went there to conduct research for my doctoral dissertation in cultural anthropology, arriving in November 1975 and staying until December 1976. I have had the good fortune to be able to go back, even if only briefly, three times since then: for three weeks in 1981, for two days in 1995, and for five weeks in 1998, twenty-two years after my first visit.

The East Sepik Province's principal town, Wewak, is the usual point of departure or arrival for travel between the mainland and Kairiru. Weather permitting, you can see Kairiru's high volcanic outline from several points along the coast in and around Wewak. Mushu Island lies between Wewak and Kairiru, but Kairiru's dark bulk often obscures Mushu's lower, flatter silhouette. A boarding high school for men, St. Xavier's, and a small Catholic seminary, St. John's, are located on the comparatively flat ground of Kairiru's south side, where a dirt road links them with several coastal villages. In 1998, this was still the only road on the island, and St. Xavier's and St. John's still owned the only motor vehicles. All other land travel is over well-worn but often rugged footpaths that pass through secondary forest and groves of coconut palms along the coast and thick primary forest in the interior. There are about fifteen villages on the island, most scattered around its coastline. (I say "about" fifteen because maps differ and not everyone agrees on which inhabited places should be counted as distinct villages.)

To reach Kairiru's north coast and Kragur from Wewak, one travels about 35 to 45 kilometers (about 22 to 28 miles) (Map 1). The distance depends on whether you circle Mushu to the east or the west, a choice that depends on the condition of the sea. Kairiru is about 13 kilometers (8 miles) long and 5.6 kilometers (3.5 miles) wide at its widest point and rises to about 940 meters (3,083 feet) at its highest point. It looks especially tall when viewed from a small open boat running close beside the more precipitous stretches of its coastline as you round the island headed for Kragur.

The main part of the village sits atop a cliff that drops 30 to 40 feet to a narrow, rocky beach. The beach is unprotected, and even in mild seas landing or putting a boat or an outrigger canoe in the water between waves without grinding the bottom on the rocks takes skill and teamwork. Most of the village's eighty or so houses and other structures climb from the top of the cliff toward the surrounding forest on irregular terraces separated by rough walls of volcanic stone. The walls look more like they grew than were placed there. Built of hand-hewn timbers, thatched with sago palm leaves and walled with light but strong sago leaf stalks, the houses, too, blend with the landscape. In 1998, five or six corrugated metal roofs dotted the scene, glinting in the sun.

I returned to Kragur partly out of scientific interest. As the world grows smaller it is ever more important to try to understand people different from ourselves in their own terms, not as imperfect versions of ourselves or incomplete members of some homogeneous world culture that, some people say, may soon encompass everyone. It is especially important to try to understand how people are adapting to a world that is not only growing smaller, but doing so with increasing speed. I am especially interested in how Kragur people, who made sustained contact with the Western or European world only around the turn of the twentieth century, are coping with the momentous changes that ensued—in particular, the imposition of central government and the advent of Christianity and a radically new kind of economy.

Kragur people have not only endured all this, they have often seized eagerly on new experiences and new ideas. In 1975–1976, when I first conducted research in Kragur, villagers were keenly interested in changing the way they lived. Pessimists thought Kragur had to change in order simply to survive; optimists hoped that change might allow Kragur to flourish. Pessimists and optimists alike were interested in both moral and material change. They wanted more money, better housing, a more reliable food supply, and easier ways to travel to the mainland; they also wanted to be good people, or even better people. Villagers, however, often did not make a sharp distinction between moral and material issues. At the very least they saw them as intimately interrelated.

I went back to Kragur in 1998 in part to look, with the eyes of a social scientist, into how such issues were sorting out. My interest in Kragur and the Pacific Islands, however, also has a strong romantic side, with roots in my childhood. I grew up hearing stories of my grandfather's travels as a roving carpenter in the early 1900s and studying his collection of postcards from the antipodes with captions such as "Fijian Natives in Dancing Costume," "Maori War Canoe," and "Bullock Cart,

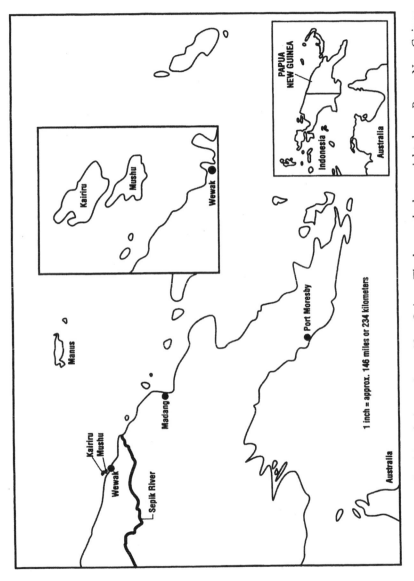

Map 1: Kairiru Island in relation to Papua New Guinea. The box at the lower right shows Papua New Guinea in relation to northern Australia and eastern Indonesia. The box at the upper right shows an enlarged view of Kairiru and Mushu in relation to the mainland. (Map by D. Buric)

Ceylon." I am not sure if I actually remember him reciting lines from Kipling's *Mandalay*, with a faraway look in his eyes, or if I merely imagine this:

> On the road to Mandalay,
> Where the flyin'-fishes play,
> An' the dawn comes up like thunder outer
> China 'crost the Bay!

One cannot see China from Kairiru, but "flyin'" fishes are plentiful in the surrounding waters and the dawn comes up with a speed and power unknown north of the Tropic of Cancer. Whether this particular memory of my grandfather is real or false, I know romantic images of the tropics accompany me when I go to Kragur, despite my anthropological training.

Since I doubt I can ever eradicate my romantic tendencies, I can only try to keep them in check. Romanticizing things exaggerates their negative as well as their positive qualities. So travelers' tales often swing from one extreme to another. Accounts of danger, discomfort, and human misery alternate with celebrations of striking beauty, exotic pleasures, and the triumph of the human spirit. A romantic view tends to ignore the mundane and the ambiguous, even though most of human life is mundane and ambiguous.

The better one gets to know people, however, the harder it is to regard them simply as objects of scientific study or actors in one's private adventures. Without leaving science or adventure aside, the more I go to Kragur, the more I go to see people I think of as friends, although I know that both they and I are frequently uncertain of the rules of our cross-cultural friendships. My relationships with Kragur people, however, may differ from my relationships with my fellow Americans more in degree than in kind, since all human relationships are cross-cultural to some extent.

Perhaps as hard to bridge as cultural difference is the class difference that separates me from Kragur villagers. Although I am not part of the economic or political elite in the United States, by the standards of village Papua New Guinea I am very wealthy and privileged. Even as a graduate student on a tight budget in the 1970s, I had much, much more money at my disposal than any villager. I bought canned mackerel by the case and rice by the 25-kilo bag, and I had a conspicuous wealth of possessions, including a camera, two tape recorders, a portable short-wave radio, two spare pairs of shorts, and several spare shirts. Unlike Kragur villagers, over the years I have been able to travel the immense distance between their country and mine several times. Research grants and consulting contracts, not personal wealth, have paid most of my expenses, but access to such opportunities is as much a part of my comparative privilege as a higher income.

Some Kragur people have only vague ideas about why I come to their village, but they accept me cordially anyway. Some may prefer that I not come at all; but, if so, they politely keep this to themselves. Others, however, understand and approve that I am chronicling aspects of their history and way of life. Virtually everyone in Kragur whom I have asked to help me in this endeavor has done so graciously.

A few villagers have given me a place in Kragur by calling me by one or another of the many Kairiru terms for designating kin. Depending on their age, they usually call me *taik* (sibling of the same sex), *luk* (sibling of the opposite sex), or *mam* (father). As of 1998, I also qualified in some cases as *bum* (meaning grandfather, and pronounced like "boom"), and a few young people used the English term "uncle." In 1998, more than one villager told me that I was no longer merely a visitor to Kragur but, using the English word, a "citizen." Again, both they and I continue to fumble with what this means in practice. Nevertheless, to be called a kinsman or a citizen is a high compliment, even though, as a rather shy person of undemonstrative northern European Protestant heritage, I probably do not wear it as gracefully as I might.

This book is in part a sequel to *Hard Times on Kairiru Island,* which was based on the research I conducted in Kragur in 1975–1976 and 1981. I intend it, however, to stand on its own. I describe a few aspects of Kragur society and culture in a slightly different way here than I did in *Hard Times,* owing some of my improved understanding to the fact that in 1998 Kragur people spoke with me more freely about some topics then they had in the past. I think that our years of association have fostered greater trust, and, as some villagers made plain, I was much too young in 1975–1976 to hear of some matters. When I sat with learned graybeards in 1998 I did not look nearly so out of place. Some of the things they told me I cannot reveal in concrete detail because of their magical importance or their implications for local politics in Kragur. Nevertheless, even hearing about matters I have to keep confidential has helped me to understand certain general issues better.

I wrote *Hard Times* primarily for an audience of anthropologists and anthropology students. I hope that there is something of interest to anthropologists in this volume, too. I also hope that a much wider audience will find it interesting, so I have not assumed that my readers have any knowledge of Papua New Guinea or anthropology. Although throughout the book I use information from various studies and draw on the work of other anthropologists, I have omitted traditional note references. Interested readers will find my sources in endnotes following the text, keyed to chapter and page numbers.

I assume that some Kragur people themselves will be part of my audience. In 1998, a larger number of them than ever before were literate in English, including both resident villagers and those living and working in urban areas. A number of them had read all or part of *Hard Times* and liked the idea of a new book about a more contemporary Kragur. I doubt that this is exactly the book they would have ordered, but I do present villagers' own voices as honestly as I can, and do not claim that my views and interpretations are the last word.

This book is primarily about Kragur, but it also concerns Papua New Guinea in general. Kragur is distinctive in many ways, but it is also very much like many other Papua New Guinea villages and faces similar problems. I describe some of the country's economic and political problems here because they form the context of village problems. The country, as well as its many villages, is seeking a new direction. But villagers may have to work out their own paths without much help from, or even in opposition to, the choices of national leaders.

There is also a lot in this book about myself. When people who are not steeped in anthropology ask me about Kragur they often are as curious about how I came to go there and how I lived there as about how Kragur people live. They sometimes want to know what doing anthropological research is like. What did people think of me? How did I observe life in Kragur without annoying the villagers to distraction? Kragur people, too, often ask me why and how I came to Kragur on different occasions, and why to Kragur and not somewhere else.

People often ask me what language Kragur people speak and how I communicate with them. There are, it is said, some eight hundred or more distinct languages in Papua New Guinea. The native tongue of Kairiru islanders is one of these, and speakers of that tongue call it either *Leiny Kairiru* (Kairiru language) or *Leiny Tau* (Tau language). Tau is another name for the island. Some islanders say that Kairiru is really only the name of the lake in the extinct volcanic crater at the top of the mountain. The lake itself takes its name from a powerful supernatural being who, it is said, created the lake and still lives there. In the distant past, the supernatural being Kairiru came from Wogeo Island, about 6 kilometers (approximately 16 miles) northeast of Tau/Kairiru, after an argument with his brother Trogup. He is said to have the body of an immense snake and the thickly bearded head of a man.

The Kairiru or Tau language also is spoken on the small nearby islands of Karesau and Yuo, in parts of Mushu Island, and in a few coastal mainland villages. In the mid-1970s, there were about thirty-five hundred Kairiru or Tau speakers, living both in the language area itself and elsewhere.

Like the majority of Papua New Guineans, Kairiru and Kragur people also speak a lingua franca called Tok Pisin, sometimes known in English as Melanesian Pidgin, or just Pidgin. "Melanesia" denotes the broad cultural and geographic area of which Papua New Guinea is a part. It includes the Indonesian province of Papua (called Irian Jaya until late 2001), Fiji, the French colony of New Caledonia, the Solomon Islands, and Vanuatu. This widely used name originated in a division of the Pacific Islands proposed by the French explorer Dumont D'Urville in 1831. He divided the region into Polynesia (meaning "many islands"), Micronesia (meaning "little islands"), Malaysia (meaning "Malay islands" and denoting island Southeast Asia), and Melanesia (meaning "black islands"). Many anthropologists question the usefulness of this hoary terminology, but it lives on. D'Urville was also one of the earliest Europeans to pay much attention to Kairiru, which many maps once designated as D'Urville Island.

There were lingua francas or trade languages in parts of Papua New Guinea prior to the colonial period, and trading partners or neighboring peoples often could speak or understand each other's languages. Tok Pisin was born of the need to communicate across language barriers on plantations and in other colonial situations where speakers of many indigenous languages came together with speakers of colonial languages, principally German and English. Because Australia was the dominant colonial power for the longest time and most recently, much Tok Pisin vocabulary is taken from English.

It is not safe to assume, however, that a Tok Pisin word that sounds like an English word means precisely the same thing. For example, depending on context, *bihain* can mean "behind," "later," or "after." And the *as* (pronounced like *ass*) of something is its base, basis, or foundation, not its buttocks. Tok Pisin grammar, like that of other lingua francas or creole languages, is relatively simple, but it is based more on the grammars of indigenous Papua New Guinean languages than on English. Simplicity of grammar, however, does not keep Tok Pisin from being a highly expressive and flexible language.

English is the language of formal education in Papua New Guinea. By 1998, many Kragur villagers had gone to high school or beyond and some had good command of English. Nevertheless, I heard villagers speak English among themselves only very rarely.

I speak and understand only a little of the Kairiru language. I can engage in characteristic village small talk, giving and recognizing compliments, asking and answering questions about people's comings and goings, and taking part in the nearly constant give-and-take surrounding betel nut and tobacco. My limited knowledge of Kairiru often lets me know what people are talking about but not exactly what they have to say about it. Some villagers chide me for not having learned to truly speak Kairiru, and there are many things in Kragur I would understand better if I had done so. I am fluent, however, in Tok Pisin, so I can converse at length and in depth with villagers in that language. Also, villagers themselves frequently speak in a mixture of Kairiru and Tok Pisin. This helps me to follow many conversations and public discussions and allows me to foster a false impression of my fluency in Kairiru by lacing my Tok Pisin with Kairiru words and phrases.

English quotations from Kragur people in this book are translations largely from Tok Pisin, except where otherwise noted. Sometimes I include the original Tok Pisin statement as well as the translation for the benefit of those who speak Tok Pisin, and to give those who do not some sense of it. A guide to pronouncing written

Tok Pisin is included in the Glossary. In reading Tok Pisin, it also helps to remember that the singular and plural forms of nouns are the same.

I have never tried to conceal Kragur's location. It is easy to find, even though it does not appear on many maps. In *Hard Times,* however, I did try to disguise the identities of individual villagers. Except when referring to deceased persons of historical significance, I gave villagers pseudonyms. Most of these were the names of their dead ancestors. Prior to the coming of the Catholic Mission, a Kragur villager was usually known by a single name; but for decades people have had Christian names (like Andrew, Clara, Stephen, Agnes, Benedict, Anna, Michael, and Julie) as well as their indigenous names. Many also now use their fathers' indigenous names as surnames in the European manner, sometimes using their own indigenous names as middle names. Some villagers probably have Kairiru nicknames, but I am only familiar with Tok Pisin and English nicknames like Hap Saksak (Piece of Sago), Willy Tinpis (Willy Tinned Fish), Four Xs, and Colonel Three Mistake.

I used indigenous rather than Christian names as pseudonyms in *Hard Times* and I follow the same practice here. Since remote ancestors did not have Christian names, this provides a larger pool of pseudonyms from which to choose. In a few instances, having run out of names of appropriate deceased ancestors, I used names of living Kragur people who were absent from the village in 1998. People who appeared previously in *Hard Times* appear here under the same pseudonyms.

Particular indigenous names are loosely associated with particular families in Kragur. Even without the clues provided by the pseudonyms, Kragur people reading this book will probably be able to identify many of their compatriots. A few of the Kragur people mentioned have such distinct identities that assigning them pseudonyms is almost pointless, but I have done so anyway for the sake of consistency. The pseudonyms, however, will conceal Kragur people's identities from those who do not have an intimate knowledge of the village. Many Kragur people probably would have no qualms about appearing in this book undisguised, and some may even be disappointed that I did not use their real names. Nevertheless, not having discussed the issue with each person affected, I preferred to err on the side of caution.

Nostalgia, Dreams, Progress, and Development

"I THINK KRAGUR HAS STAYED THE SAME FOR ABOUT A THOUSAND YEARS."
(*KRAGUR I STAP OLOSEM ATING TAUSEN YIA.*)
—A Kragur villager, 1998

"IT'S NOT THE WAY YOU WROTE IT ANYMORE."
(*EM I NO MOA I STAP OLOSEM YU BIN RAITIM.*)
—Another Kragur villager, 1998

I began writing this book in April 1998, a few weeks after returning to my home in Silver Spring, Maryland, from about eight weeks in Papua New Guinea, five of which I spent in Kragur. This was my seventh trip to Papua New Guinea and my fourth visit to Kragur. By the time I got home, the thirteen-hour time difference, abetted by loss of sleep on night flights in the comfort of economy class, had knocked all my biological rhythms out of synch and set my internal clock completely at odds with my surroundings. This always takes several days to shake. On this occasion it took me a little longer than usual because, as I eventually discovered, I was teetering on the brink of a malaria attack. After the malaria came out in the open and I treated it, I finally started to adjust.

Malaria parasites aside, I carried the last vestiges of the physical experience of living in Kragur in my suitcase. Clothes last washed in the clear stream at the eastern edge of the village smelled musty and smoky. My visit to Kragur fell in the middle of an unusually soggy rainy season, coming on the heels of a severe drought, and on most days it had been too wet to hang clothes outside to dry. Mashish, who did my laundry, hung my things in her family's house, where they dried only imperfectly and, like everything else in a Kragur house, picked up the scent of the open cooking fire.

Once out of its natural environment, this aroma of wood smoke and tropical damp fades rapidly. So, too, does vivid awareness of the physical sensations of village life. This already had begun to pale by the time I boarded the Air Niugini flight from Wewak to Port Moresby—frequently called simply Moresby or, in Tok Pisin, *Mosbi*—the capital of Papua New Guinea and my point of departure from the country. It faded still more on my overnight stay at the Granville Motel in Port Moresby, which provided crisp white sheets, fluffy towels, and a private indoor toilet and shower. The air-conditioning in the Granville is not a high-performance system and a few mosquitoes disturbed my dinner in the open-walled dining room, so the contrast with village life could have been more dramatic. The polished, softly lit, thickly carpeted, and climatically sealed atmosphere of the airport hotel in Hong Kong, however, strenuously denied the existence of punishing equatorial sun, insect bites, mud, dust, clothes damp with sweat, and nature in general.

I enjoy these stark contrasts as I travel home, but the novelty of technological comforts wears off as quickly as the memory of the physical irritations of the rural tropics. I then can grow nostalgic for the sensations of life in Kragur. The temperature on Kairiru ranges between 25 and 35 degrees Celsius (75 and 95 degrees Fahrenheit), and yearly rainfall is from 300 to 380 millimeters (120 to 150 inches). In addition to the heat and humidity, there is the way in which getting around in Kragur differs from locomotion along city sidewalks. Making your way around the village requires picking your footing among the outcrops of volcanic rock and constantly either climbing up or carefully descending stony escarpments. The sensations of life in Kragur also include the rough comfort of sitting cross-legged on a ribbed floor of split palm or bamboo, stretching out for a nap on the same with your head pillowed on the well-worn timber that edges a verandah, crunching a thick green betel-nut husk between your teeth, splashing through the sheets of water that pour through the village and plunge over the terrace walls during a heavy rain, bending your head and stepping over the high threshold to enter a house, and, for the relatively tall and unwary, thumping your head on one of the low beams in the dim interior.

The aromas of the village are those of earth and vegetation, wood smoke, strong homegrown tobacco, occasional pig droppings stewing in the sun, and, near the edge of the cliff, warm ocean waters. Sounds are of babies crying, squabbling dogs, wrangling spouses, chance hostile encounters of dog and pig, and chickens and pigs foraging beneath the houses, which stand level over the uneven ground on thick, irregular wooden posts. Transistor radios are still scarce and the rare distant hum of an outboard motor is the only traffic noise. Guitars accompany the singing at Catholic religious services and young men sometimes idle on verandahs strumming guitars and ukuleles. But these instruments have not replaced the hourglass-shaped wooden hand drums with heads of monitor lizard skin that accompany traditional singing and dancing. The drums produce a taut, penetrating pulse, audible throughout the village and beyond. Villagers only bring them out, however, for special occasions.

Frogs croak loudly at night during the rainy season, and in all seasons you can lie awake in the dark and hear the state of the tide and the sea from the sound of the waves on the beach. Roosters begin crowing well before dawn, mixing their cries with the morning calls of more exotic birds in the forest that rises up the mountain-side behind the village.

There are no electric lights in Kragur, so on moonless nights darkness is complete. You can place the palm of your hand against your nose and still not see it. Disembodied voices, kerosene lanterns, and the glowing tips of homemade cigarettes float along the paths. But when the moon is full on a clear night one enjoys its undiminished effect. Villagers sit outside in the cool pale light talking, smoking, and chewing betel nut until the small hours. Of course, day or night, the rain frequently patters on the sago-palm-leaf thatch and, as any travel brochure would have to note, the coconut palms rattle and whisper in the breeze.

As evocative as such memories are, you could experience all of this and come away ignorant of much that is central to village life. One cannot fully appreciate the nature of life in Kragur, or anywhere else, without such immediate sensual experience; but in itself it tells one little about the social drama of life, and many different dramas could be enacted on the same tropical stage. In Kragur, the drama of change is what has interested me most.

In the Eye of the Beholder

I first came to Kragur at the end of 1975, just two months after Papua New Guinea had become an independent nation, and stayed until the end of 1976. In 1998, twenty-two years later, the physical sensations of my life there were deeply familiar, and when approaching Kragur from the sea or walking through the village little evidence of change immediately met the eye. A two-day visit to Kragur in 1995 had left a similar impression. Although I knew this impression could be deceptive, it was also a mild relief. Over the years a recurring dream had disturbed my sleep. In the dream I had returned to Kragur only to find bulldozers hard at work leveling the terraces, scraping away the volcanic boulders, the coconut palms, hibiscus, croton, coleus, and papayas and some of the houses themselves, turning the village site into a smooth dirt plain, ready for paving or putting up drab new prefabricated buildings. I was able to find a few villagers lingering about, but none of them recognized me. In one version of this dream, I not only found the village under the bulldozer blade, I came across a Kragur family I know well living in a bleak cramped apartment in Wewak because they had sold their land on Kairiru and could not go back.

The dreams were troubling. Kragur people themselves would certainly consider dreams of losing their land as nightmares. Some villagers, however, probably would not object to heavy machinery taking the rough edges off their surroundings or to trading their timber and thatch dwellings for homes of more permanent materials. Some (but not all) would also like a bulldozer to carve out a road linking them to the landward side of the island. But the dream image of bare earth where houses, footpaths, and domestic clutter once had been suggested not just physical change but the decay and death of Kragur as a community. This was something no one would welcome. For my part, I also did not like the idea that all this had gone on without my knowledge and that no one recognized me. Kragur owes me nothing, but in the dream it hurt to be completely forgotten.

In 1998, however, Kragur sounded, smelled, and looked much as I remembered it, despite a few obvious changes since 1975–1976. In particular, it was easy to see that the village was larger, and a few narrow white PVC pipes running along the ground also stood out. These brought water from stream-fed tanks on the slope just above the upper row of houses to six taps scattered around the village. Yet villagers themselves did not agree on just how much Kragur had changed.

When I sat down to talk with Mowush for the first time in many years, he immediately launched into a rather gloomy monologue on the lack of change in Kragur. Mowush himself had changed in appearance. A man in his mid-fifties, he was still sturdy and muscular, but his hair was graying and he had been reduced to crushing his betel-nut mixture in a small hand-held wooden mortar. Betel nut, when chewed with lime—made by incinerating shell or coral—and the catkin of the betel pepper, is a mild intoxicant and stimulant. It is the coffee, tea, beer, and whiskey of many Papua New Guineans, and the bright red spittle created by chewing the betel mixture stains mouths, teeth, and spatter patterns on the ground throughout much of the country. When people's teeth give out with use and age, they resort to preparing their betel in a betel mortar—often elaborately carved—before placing it in their mouths. Mowush had not lost his teeth to age but to an accident in which he fell face first on a boulder. He managed to get to Port Moresby to have false teeth made but they had never fit quite right; so, he said, holding up his mortar, "This is my teeth." He had adapted well to this misfortune, but he was not happy about what he saw as Kragur's failure to change. "Moresby changes every day," he said, "but I think Kragur has stayed the same for about a thousand years. Why?"

I also encountered Taram one weekend when he was in Kragur for a brief visit with his family. Taram grew up in Kragur and went to St. Xavier's High School and the University of Papua New Guinea in Port Moresby. He then served in the Australian air force and completed a law degree at the University of Melbourne. He had recently moved back to Papua New Guinea and started a law practice in Port Moresby. More than anyone in his generation he had led a life very different from that in the village, but he was disappointed with how little Kragur itself had changed over the years. "So many things have stood still," he told me, in English. "Things that people debated in the 1970s are still debated today. This is a matter of sadness for me. I would have thought we'd have moved on."

But others seemed to see things differently. Manup was in his forties in 1998, living with his wife and children in the village after many years of work in urban areas. As we sat on the split-palm floor of his verandah one dark night he commented on my return to Kragur, saying, in English, "I think you see a lot of changes." Benau, also in his forties and also a man I knew from years past, seemed to agree. *"Plenti senis i kamap,"* said Benau in Tok Pisin in one of our first conversations that year—that is, "A lot has changed."

Many villagers wanted to talk about change in Kragur, and some wanted to make sure that my view of the village was not stuck in the period described in *Hard Times on Kairiru Island.* Schooling in English became available to Kragur people in 1959, and each generation since has been more literate in English than its predecessor. A few copies of *Hard Times* were circulating in the village and in the libraries of St. Xavier's and other schools in the Wewak area, and a few villagers in their twenties had read all or part of it. Some of my readers had a lot to say about the picture of Kragur painted in the book. The villagers most literate in English, however, had been only infants in 1975–1976, so they could not judge the accuracy of my observations on the basis of their own experience. They could, however, comment on the difference between Kragur as I had described it and Kragur in 1998.

One of my readers, Foin, had been about a year old in 1976. By 1998 she was a teacher in the primary school in the nearby village of Bou that served several communities on Kairiru's north coast. She had a house at Bou but often came to Kragur to visit her family. I noticed her because she was the only woman in Kragur who wore glasses, the result, she later told me, of the habit of reading until late at night by the light of a kerosene lamp. I first spoke with her at the house of her sister and brother-in-law, who had invited me for an evening meal. Foin did not, of course, remember me. But she had heard of me and said she had expected me to be much older. I would like to credit my youthful appearance, but she probably was surprised that I was not completely decrepit simply because at her age twenty-two years seems like a very long time.

Foin did, in fact, seem to regard the era of *Hard Times* as both distant and significantly different from the present. She had come across the book in the library of her alma mater, Kaindi Teachers College, located just outside Wewak, when she was looking for information on Kairiru to use in preparing an essay for one of her classes. She found the Kragur portrayed in *Hard Times* familiar but somewhat antique. "Yes," she reported saying to herself, "we lived like this once."

Nuor and Satap were in their late twenties in 1998. They were students at Bou school in 1976 and remembered seeing me from the windows of the school as I ran along the coastal trail in red surfing trunks, as I often did, exercising and providing amusement for those I passed on the way. (Kragur adults do not run along the trails except in emergencies.) Nuor and Satap each went on from Bou to complete high school and several years of study in Catholic seminaries, and they each had read at least part of *Hard Times.* Like Foin, they handled English well, but as we talked we slipped back and forth between English and Tok Pisin. Nuor gave me good marks for the accuracy of *Hard Times,* but he thought it described something that no longer existed: "What you wrote was accurate for that time [i.e., 1975–1976]. It's not the way you wrote it anymore." (In Tok Pisin: "*Wanem samting yu bin raitim i stret long dispela taim. Em i no moa i stap olosem yu bin raitim.*") Satap also cautioned me against assuming too much: "Don't think the village is the same as before. A lot has changed." ("*Nogud yu tingim ples i wankain olosem bipo i stap. Bikpela senis i kamap.*")

Either a truly striking transformation of village life or a complete absence of change would have provided a ready-made theme for this book. Unfortunately, to my eye the situation was not so clear-cut. On one hand, the village population was significantly younger, more numerous, and better educated. Kragur people were becoming involved in campaigns for national political offices, some villagers had taken up controversial new religious practices, and money was playing a more prominent role in daily life. On the other hand, as Taram suggested, many villagers were still pondering issues that had preoccupied them in the 1970s: How could they pursue money more successfully? How could they do so without violating traditional moral standards or their understanding of Christianity? What was the place of school education in village life? How could they pursue the new knowledge gained in schools without weakening the authority of traditional leaders?

Perhaps most familiar were villagers' concern with whether Kragur could remain a cohesive community—this despite the increased numbers and youthful vitality of the population—and their keen interest in changing their lives for the better. As they had in the 1970s, villagers spoke without prompting about their fear that Kragur was coming unglued and their perceptions of how it was either changing or failing to change. These two issues—cohesion and change—still lingered in close company in 1998 because part of what most villagers still wanted from change was to preserve Kragur in some familiar form.

Change, Progress, and Development: Some Words of Caution

Although cultural change may seem like a straightforward topic, one has to talk about it with great care. For one thing, it is important to remember that human cultures are never static. The pace of change varies and change is not necessarily beneficial, but it is the natural state of culture and is not in itself pathological. Even people's "traditions" are seldom stable and unchanging because, often unwittingly, people everywhere revise their legacies from the past to make them useful or relevant to the present. What people consider traditional today is often not what was traditional yesterday. (Nevertheless, I sometimes resort to the word "traditional" to describe aspects of Kragur life that I believe predate European contact.)

Caution is also required because the people of affluent industrialized societies often find it hard to think about change without thinking about progress. They tend to think of their world as a good example of the fruits of progress and to consider its ways as the best path to progress. The more successful people have been in that world, the more they seem to see things this way. It is, of course, very satisfying to think of oneself as one of the best people from one of the best places.

Such attitudes show up almost anytime people in affluent industrialized societies talk about the Third World, "underdeveloped" countries, and so on. I saw some good examples of this in 1998. An invitation from the American Museum of Natural History to accompany a group of some thirty well-to-do Americans on a commercial tour under the auspices of the museum made possible my return to Papua New Guinea in that year. My role was to give a few scheduled talks on things Papua New Guinean and be available to comment and answer questions informally along the way.

The American Museum tourists were interested in change in Papua New Guinea, but their interest pulled them in two contrary directions. On the one hand, some had been lured to Papua New Guinea by promises that they would see a place that had *not* changed much for a very long time. The tour brochure promised that participants would see "people and traditions that have changed little over the centuries" and places that "even today, have had little contact with the western [*sic*] world." The tour itself was titled "Papua New Guinea: Journey to the Last Unknown." On the other hand, as they traveled through the country and saw bad roads, barefoot people in badly worn clothing, the effects of a major drought, and the absence of electricity, modern plumbing, and medical facilities, many expressed the hope that Papua New Guinea *would* change, making the people's lives more comfortable and secure.

Some tour members wanted to know what kinds of changes I had seen since I first came to Papua New Guinea, but I found it hard to answer some of their questions. "Has there been any progress?" one woman wanted to know. Questions about "progress" are loaded, even if well meant. Papua New Guinea villagers are often poor, most lack adequate health care, and illness and inadequate nutrition shorten many lives. But talk of progress often implies more than greater prosperity and improvements in health and longevity. It frequently implies that all societies can be measured against a single standard in spheres more subtle than level of income, the prevalence of infant death, and the length of life. And, more problematic, it often implies that the world's affluent industrialized societies—in particular, those that embrace capitalism most fervently—have already set the standard and mapped the best route to meeting it.

This is not necessarily what the tourists who asked me about progress in Kragur had in mind. Some understood that Papua New Guineans could have ideas of the good life that were hard to evaluate in strictly American terms. A few, however, illustrated the importance of speaking of progress with great delicacy. For example, one tour member, in tones more of concern than condescension, pronounced the villagers we met to be "childlike" in their understanding of money and business. One can read too much into metaphors, but this metaphor strongly implies that human societies can be ranged on a single continuum of achievement and that those at one end, the "childlike," should strive to become like the mature adult societies.

"Development" is also a word that is hard to keep out of discussions of change, especially change in the non-Western world. Anthropologists, however, find development as heavily loaded a term as progress. Some want to avoid it completely because, they argue, it almost inevitably implies becoming more like Western capitalist societies. But it is probably too late to expunge the word from our vocabularies. It is also too late to call it back from its diffusion around the world. As it spreads, however, it often takes on distinctive local meanings. David Gegeo, for example, reports that the Kwara'ae people of the Solomon Islands use the term *diflopmen*. But what the Kwara'ae mean by *diflopmen*, says Gegeo, is "different from what 'development' implies in Anglo-European societies" and embodies a characteristically Kwara'ae vision of the good life. Kragur people, and many other Papua New Guineans, speak in Tok Pisin of *divelopmen*. But it is not safe to assume that one can easily understand what they mean by it.

What Does Kragur Want?

In 1975–1976, change was much on Kragur people's minds. In public meetings and private conversations villagers often spoke, in Tok Pisin, about the need to *sensim pasin bilong yumi* (change our ways), *kirapim ples* (improve the village), or bring *divelopmen* (development) to Kragur. When Kragur people used the term *divelopmen* in those days they often were speaking of access to new kinds of material goods and technology and successful participation in the money economy. This sounds a lot like what "development" implies in "Anglo-European" societies, but these apparently simple material aspirations were only one facet of a more complicated set of ideas about the good life and how to attain it. In addition, a longer, more careful look revealed people who were uncertain what direction they should take and who were as deeply involved in debating and defining goals for change as in struggling to achieve them.

For decades, under Australian rule, Kragur villagers had dutifully followed most of the colonial government's advice. They planted new crops to sell for money, took part in local elections and other novel governmental activities, and sent their children to school. But they were still poor; making a living was still a matter of heavy lifting and sore muscles and joints, and they still could see no clear bridge between their poverty and the comparatively affluent lives of foreigners in Papua New Guinea and the small urban indigenous elite. Villagers did not simply want to share in that material plenty, they wanted to be on a more equal social and political footing.

The social, political, and economic grade that separated Kragur villagers from affluent and privileged elites, both indigenous and foreign, was steep, and there had been nothing like it in the precolonial world. In that world, differences among villages in strength or prosperity had seldom been dramatic or enduring. Within Kragur, some villagers had enjoyed greater authority and prestige than others, but they had not formed a separate class. Everyone had enjoyed access to the means of making a living and everyone had labored to produce food and shelter. No one had looked down on anyone else because they knew only village ways.

All this had changed by the time I first set foot on Kairiru. Sometimes Kragur villagers saw their position near the bottom of the new social hierarchy as a stark injustice; sometimes they wondered if perhaps they did not deserve any better. Either way, many felt the situation called for trying harder to improve their lot.

The recent advent of independence helped to account for the fervent interest in change I found in Kragur in the 1970s. Many villagers viewed independence with considerable trepidation and did not see how it was going to improve their lives. Some even feared that the Australians were taking away with them the knowledge the country needed to survive and prosper. Many feared they could not trust Papua New Guinean leaders to care about those who were not of their own ethnic groups. Some also were concerned that the civil order imposed by the colonial government might now collapse and that it would not be long until they had to "take up the spear" again. Many felt more exposed and vulnerable than independent.

Both the frustration of Kragur's marginal social and economic position and the new and still rather shapeless challenge of independence called for renewed efforts to strengthen the village both morally and materially. Many Kragur people felt that becoming more unified and cohesive was the key to coping with both new and old difficulties. And many feared that their comparative poverty itself could eventually drive young people away and weaken the ties among those left behind. If they did not move forward, pessimists feared, they would drift apart.

But although villagers were often harshly self-critical, they did not seek wholesale change. They did not want to become exactly like the Australians who were leaving, or even the new Papua New Guinean elites. They wanted to change so they could fulfill familiar aspirations: to endure as a community, to be secure and prosperous, and to be able to meet other people as equals. The world taking shape around them, however, operated according to different principles than those of the village. So they were faced with the problem of how to take a respected place in that world without abandoning much of what made Kragur what it was.

Many were plainly confused about the specifics of where they wanted to go and how to get there. Some degree of vagueness, confusion, and inconsistency is part and parcel of culture. In fact, people everywhere often spend a great deal of time arguing about what their culture is or should be. The ongoing disagreements within a human group are often as characteristic of its culture as are the things on which people agree. (Of course, people cannot even argue unless they have a certain amount of culture in common.) The rapid pace of change in Papua New Guinea in the twentieth century contributed a great deal to Kragur people's uncertainty in the 1970s. Yet seeking social change anywhere is likely to be fraught with uncertainty. Even when plans do not simply go awry, the visions they serve, though often potent and colorful, are frequently indistinct. People must fill in the gaps as they go along, and the results are sometimes surprising.

By 1998, Kragur people were no longer in the grip of the intense feelings that had surrounded the coming of independence. They were, however, still disagreeing, experimenting, and wondering about the right direction to take. A prominent scholar of development, Norman Long, commented in 1992 that at the heart of development anywhere is "a struggle over images of development and 'the good society.' " The story of change or development in Kragur is certainly as much a story of people seeking direction as it is a story of their struggle along a chosen path.

In 1998, I found much about this search in Kragur very familiar. But I also found that, even as villagers argued and speculated, Kragur was drifting toward a kind of life quite different from that which I had once seen. It was also different from what many Kragur people once had wanted and many wanted still. To tell this story, I will have to talk about religion, economic life, social organization, and politics, and to do that I will have to discuss ghosts, magic, myths, and ancestors as well as bookkeeping, tourism, the World Bank, and the Holy Spirit. To begin, we first have to go back to 1975–1976 and what Kragur was like then, or at least what it looked like to me.

Finding Kragur

" 'AVE A CHIP, MATE! YOU'RE GOIN' UP TO THE EAST SEPIK!
IT MAY BE THE LAST CHIP YOU EVER 'AVE!"
—A bearded Australian in a bar in Port Moresby, November 1975

My acquaintance with the East Sepik goes back to 1973. I probably saw Kairiru for the first time that year, although I do not remember the occasion. I was a graduate student in anthropology at the University of California, San Diego, in 1973 and spent the summer working with one of my professors, Theodore (Ted) Schwartz, and two other graduate students, Edwin Hutchins and Geoffrey White, in what many still called the Manus District of the Territory of Papua and New Guinea. The Territory became self-governing Papua New Guinea that same year, in preparation for full independence from Australia, but the old designations lingered. I had not yet decided where I wanted to conduct my doctoral research, but those three months in the islands of Manus fired my interest in Papua New Guinea so, at Ted's suggestion, I decided to scout for a future research site on the way home.

I think Ted also suggested that I stop in Wewak on my way south from Manus to Port Moresby and have a brief look at the East Sepik District. The East Sepik and the neighboring West Sepik take their names from the Sepik River, which twists and turns and doubles back for about 1,100 kilometers (about 700 miles) from its headwaters in the West Sepik, across Papua New Guinea's only land border (with the Indonesian province of Papua), back into the West Sepik, and across the full length of the East Sepik to the north coast of Papua New Guinea and the Bismarck Sea.

I must have looked out to sea as I walked around Wewak my first day there, and I must have seen Mushu and Kairiru, but I would not have recognized them. I may even have considered visiting some of the islands my map showed located within easy reach of Wewak. My first evening in Wewak, however, I met an Australian oil prospector at the outdoor bar of the Wewak Hotel, where I was quietly converting South Pacific Lager into perspiration. He offered me a ride on his company's helicopter to a drilling site on the far side of the low mountain range that runs between the coast and the swamps and grasslands of the Sepik River basin. This was an opportunity to go into the interior quickly and cheaply, so I showed up at the airport early the next morning to take advantage of the oilman's invitation.

I spent three days visiting villages within a few kilometers of the oil company camp. My requirements for a research site were very broad: a village that would have me, that was not within too easy reach of one of the country's few towns, but that was nevertheless becoming involved with such relatively new institutions as the cash economy and formal schooling. The villages I visited, Kupiwat and Tau, met at least these last two requirements, but so did most of the thousands of other villages in Papua New Guinea, leaving a great deal to my own discretion.

Returning to Wewak

It took me two years of considerable uncertainty to find funds and obtain permission from the appropriate government agencies to return to Papua New Guinea. This was a great leap forward, but it was still only a prelude to actually conducting the field research, or fieldwork, as anthropologists usually call it. Cultural anthropology has its own literature, jargon, professional associations, and academic departments. Perhaps above all, it has fieldwork. The literature and theories of anthropology are all ultimately based on observations of human beings going about their lives on their own turf. Anthropology holds that to understand a way of life or any of its parts it is necessary to comprehend, as far as is possible, the whole, and to learn—again, as far as it is possible—what the world looks like through people's own eyes.

Ideally, one pursues these objectives while living with people for a long time at close quarters. This requires accommodating to many, though not all, local ways; but it also requires preserving a certain intellectual distance. One needs this distance not only from the people you seek to understand but also, if you go far from home, from your own immediate reactions to things that are unfamiliar and confusing and to the frustrations and discomforts of daily living in a novel environment.

Anthropologists do not confine themselves to fieldwork among people on the far edges of the industrialized world. Anthropological approaches to understanding human societies and cultures are just as relevant to urban Europeans or small-town North Americans, like those among whom I grew up. I, however, was predisposed —for scientific as well as romantic reasons—to seek out something completely different. Pioneering American anthropologist Clyde Kluckhohn argued that it is useful for anthropologists to study people who are dramatically unlike themselves because there is too much in one's own surroundings that one does not notice because it is too familiar. That is, to learn about culture, it helps to observe it where it is relatively easy to see. As Kluckhohn put it: "Ordinarily we are unaware of the special lens through which we look at life. It would hardly be fish who discovered the existence of water."

There was plenty of scope for this in Papua New Guinea. There was also ample opportunity to study one of the social and cultural differences that interested me most. Having lived all my life in a society in which most people took capitalism for granted, I wanted to see what life was like in a society in which it was still a novelty and not yet like water to fish.

I arrived in Papua New Guinea in November 1975 both thrilled and scared, for your first major solo fieldwork is a rite of passage as well as a scientific endeavor. My first stop was Port Moresby, where I was able to stay at what was then the New Guinea Research Unit of the Australian National University. This was located a short walk from the campus of the University of Papua New Guinea (UPNG), which had opened in 1967. The main item on my agenda in Port Moresby was deciding in which province to look for a research site. One anthropologist at UPNG suggested that West New Britain Province might be a good place to consider, but someone else told me that the main airfield there was flooded and closed indefinitely. None of the anthropologists, geographers, and others I consulted, however, could think of any reason not to go to the East Sepik Province, as it was now called. So, I secured a letter of introduction to the provincial government from the Institute for Papua New Guinea Studies—the organization then charged with overseeing foreign researchers —and set off for Wewak.

Wewak was a rather sleepy place in late 1975. Arriving by air you could easily find yourself becalmed at the tiny single-story terminal if you had made no advance arrangements for transportation. There was no public transportation and the private trucks and minibuses licensed to carry paying passengers—called PMVs (Public Motor Vehicles)—that plied the roads did not frequent the airport. Fortunately, one of my fellow Air Niugini passengers, a Protestant missionary, offered me a ride with the colleagues who were meeting him. There was very little automobile traffic of any kind on the road leading to town. Pedestrians walking along the side of the road were usually barefoot. They moved at an unhurried pace, making steady progress but giving due respect to the heat of the sun and the distance yet to be traveled. Whites seldom walked outside the center of town and did not seem to like to see others of their kind doing so. On several occasions in the months to come, white motorists whom I had never met would stop to offer me rides when they saw me making my way along the roads on foot.

It was three or four miles from the airport to Wewak's commercial center. The two-lane road ran west along the shore, passing the long, low wooden buildings of the hospital at Boram and the settlement of timber and thatch houses and the out-door market at Kreer beach. Here a secondary road continued along the shore to the main shipping wharf, but most traffic jogged inland. After passing a steep turn-off to the provincial government offices on Kreer Heights, the road skirted the Catholic Mission headquarters at Wirui before returning to the shore again by the residence of the brothers of the Society of Mary (often known as the Marists) and, close beside it, the Windjammer Motel. From the Windjammer the road followed a long curving stretch of sandy beach, lined with coconut palms, to the town center.

Most of Wewak's retail businesses were located along a single street, called The Centre, which cut across the narrow neck of Wewak Point. The point itself was a high knob with good ocean views, occupied by the town's best residential area and a few offices and commercial establishments, including the Wewak Hotel and the Sepik Motel. The outdoor market sat at the edge of the water at one end of The Centre. On market days, vendors from area villages laid out their goods on concrete tables beneath two long metal roofs and on the surrounding bare ground. At the opposite end of The Centre was a small wharf, usually called the post office wharf because it lay across the street from the post office. Small boats from coastal and island villages came and went from this wharf and the adjacent beach. On my infrequent trips to town during the coming year I often would find Kairiru people sitting beneath the nearby casuarina trees waiting for a boat back to the island.

The Sepik region in the 1970s has been called a frontier, and in 1975 Wewak had some of the look of a frontier town. None of the buildings on the main street rose above two stories and some were simple wooden structures. The street was paved and large trees shaded stretches of the sidewalk, but the street's surface had seen better days and the roots of the shading trees lifted and buckled slabs of the sidewalk's cement. The town as a whole had a population of about nineteen thousand, most of them indigenous Papua New Guineans. The rest were expatriates engaged in business, religious missions, or government, for some former members of the Australian administration were temporarily filling roles in the new public service.

There was also a small community of overseas Chinese, born and raised in Papua New Guinea. They were primarily engaged in business. In addition to some more substantial enterprises, these businesses included several general stores on the main street. The "Chinese stores," as many called them, stocked rice, canned mackerel, and other staple foods and a wide variety of dry goods, hanging from the ceilings and crowding the neatly packed shelves and counters. Villagers usually shopped at the Chinese stores when they came to town, seldom entering such establishments as the pharmacy, the Wewak Christian Book Shop, or the small supermarket operated by Burns, Philp and Co., Ltd., one of the oldest trading firms in the Pacific Islands.

The Chinese stores, with their plethora of goods suited to village budgets and village life, were good places to shop for a stint in the bush. What was bush (*bus* in Tok Pisin) depended on where you stood. For villagers, the bush was the uncultivated forest from which they carved their villages and gardens. But to most foreigners living in town, villages themselves, especially those inaccessible by road, qualified as bush.

I was exhilarated to have a definite destination when I left Port Moresby, but in Wewak I was once more adrift as I confronted the problem of where in this wide province to set up shop. Reading the journal I kept that year reminds me that I felt rather adrift much of the time. My brief stint in Manus had taught me some of what I needed to know about making my way in Papua New Guinea, but I still had a great deal to learn. In addition, I was chronically anxious about my ability to conduct successful solo field research and sometimes dismally homesick. For all the blue ocean, bright sun, tropical color, and anthropological riches spread at my feet, I started many days with mixed feelings about my great adventure.

In Wewak I was staying in a barren apartment rented out by a Protestant mission organization, Christian Missions in Many Lands. I filled my first long evening there reading a copy of Evelyn Waugh's *Black Mischief*, which I found nesting incongruously in a pile of religious tracts in the closet, and studying topographic maps of the East Sepik I had obtained in Port Moresby. The map of the area around Wewak showed several islands not too far offshore, and I decided to find out more about them.

On my first full day in Wewak, I made my way to the main government offices on Kreer Heights and introduced myself to the Provincial Commissioner, Tony Bais, an indigenous Papua New Guinean and a graduate of the young national university. During our brief conversation he mentioned the current ill repute of anthropologists among Papua New Guinea university students. I had already run across this in Port Moresby, where I spent several evenings drinking beer, eating pork-chop sandwiches, and talking with other patrons of the sparsely furnished bar called "the club" on the university campus. For example, one young Papua New Guinean woman who had just finished an undergraduate course in anthropology at the university told me that she and most of those in her class felt that anthropological fieldwork was "very hard to justify," and that anthropologists took much and gave back little to the people with whom they worked. Others at the club told me that many of the university students from Manus were unhappy that Margaret Mead had scrutinized their society in books, articles, and films. That such sentiments were abroad was not news to me, but the conversations at the club were a sharp reminder. Bais was polite and helpful, but he emphasized the importance of dealing squarely with people wherever I settled.

Bais also suggested that some of the villages along the coast west of Wewak might be suitable sites for my work. The village councillors—elected village leaders under a Local Government Council system initiated by the Australian administration in the 1950s—from two such villages, Boiken and Dagua, were in Wewak on business, and Bais thought I should meet them. The Deputy Commissioner drove me back to the center of town where he thought we could find the two councillors.

It turned out they were not expected for two or three days. I did not relish the prospect of hanging around Wewak waiting to see them and, in any case, I was averse to working in villages like Dagua or Boiken because, according to the map, they lay directly on the coastal road.

Meeting Missionaries and Finding Kragur

Eager to keep moving and still interested in islands, I asked a provincial official how to get to Mushu or Kairiru. He told me to go down to the post office wharf and ask around until I found a boat going in that direction. This I did, and I soon located a small boat from St. John's Seminary, on Kairiru, due to leave for Kairiru and Mushu the next day. At the time, I found Mushu the more attractive of the two islands simply because, according to the map, the Catholic Mission had a smaller presence there.

My desire to avoid areas of strong Catholic Mission influence was rather misguided, because Christianity was ubiquitous in Papua New Guinea and an integral part of the social and cultural change I intended to study. Just a few years later, in 1980, the Pacific Council of Churches would report that 85 percent of all Papua New Guineans considered themselves Christians. Catholicism was the dominant denomination in the East Sepik. German Catholic missionaries of the Society of the Divine Word entered the Sepik region in 1896, just a dozen years after the German New Guinea Company began the first sustained European effort to establish a commercial presence in the region. In Wewak itself, the mission headquarters at Wirui was a local landmark. It was the seat of the bishop of Wewak and headquarters of a diocese that covered most of the province and was staffed by approximately 227 priests, brothers, sisters, and lay personnel. Most of these mission staff were from overseas. Nevertheless, Catholicism was clearly a significant part of the local scene.

Many anthropologists have seriously neglected the importance of Christianity in Melanesia. Perhaps, like some tourists, they have been looking for "the last unknown" and have found Christianity insufficiently exotic. Whatever the reason, they have often failed to recognize the extent to which Melanesians have made Christianity their own. I harbored some personal prejudices against Christian missionary activity. Raised in a liberal, church-going Protestant family, I acquired a stern Protestant Christian conscience—enough in itself to account for an aversion to churches —but I failed in my efforts to believe in God in more than a terminally abstract sense. I also found the idea of going around the world denouncing indigenous beliefs and raising the specter of eternal damnation—as many Christian missionaries have done in Papua New Guinea and elsewhere—extremely distasteful.

I had little firsthand knowledge of Christian missionaries in the Pacific. One of my uncles, however, had been sent to Australia as a Mormon missionary in the first decade of the twentieth century, when he was only seventeen years old. He had left school before he was ten to help support his neglected branch of a polygamous family and, as he told the story, he set off on his mission ignorant, illiterate, and reluctant. He left the Mormon Church long before I came to know him, and the stories he told of his misadventures in Australia were very funny and portrayed the missionary endeavor in a most unflattering light. Told that God would put words in his mouth, he had received no such assistance and had, he claimed, turned more people against Mormonism than any missionary before or since.

Fortunately, despite such prejudices and influences I managed to keep a somewhat open mind. This allowed me to learn as the year progressed that Catholicism was very much a part of the local culture in Kragur and that there was no simple way to describe or evaluate its contribution. Kragur villagers' own understanding of Catholicism tended to encourage the kind of painful self-doubts colonialism often sows. Kragur people also, however, had found ways to use Catholicism to assert their independence and moral worth. Looking too sharply askance at Catholicism in Kragur would have made it very difficult for me to understand life there in general.

Keeping my anti-mission bias in check also let me accept, without feeling too hypocritical, the considerable assistance and hospitality that mission personnel offered me. This began with a free passage to Kairiru on the St. John's Seminary boat, a small, hard-used inboard with an ungainly open wheelhouse. We arrived late in the day at St. John's, where the staff offered me a hot shower, a clean-sheeted bed for the night, a cold bottle of good homemade beer, and a seat at the dinner table. Such hospitality took some of the edge off my prejudices.

The St. John's boat was going to Mushu and back the next day and again a day or two later, so I could go across and have a sure way back. Talk at dinner of a long-running dispute between islanders and the mission station on Mushu over the mission's right to the land it occupied also, in my still jaundiced view, recommended a visit. I spent two days and nights on Mushu, finding it a reasonable site for my research; but I decided I should have a look at what Kairiru had to offer before making a decision.

When I got back to St. John's, I asked for directions to the more isolated far side of Kairiru. I learned that the main trail going up and over the island started just behind St. Xavier's, which lay a mile or so down the dirt road. Like Wewak, St. Xavier's had a long, low silhouette. Single-story, concrete-block classrooms and dormitories sat, widely spaced, on grassy grounds between the ascent of forest and the passage separating Kairiru from Mushu. The only taller structures were the simple church and the brothers' residence, where one could sit on the second-floor wooden verandah and look out toward the oceanfront.

The first person I met when I reached the school was Brother Pat Howley, the headmaster. He thought that a visit to the north coast of the island was a fine idea. In particular, he thought I should visit a village called Kragur. Apparently Kragur had sent an impressive number of students to St. Xavier's, and some of them had been exceptionally successful in their studies and their careers. Brother Pat attributed this in part to what he called the "good attitude" of the students and their parents, that is, the value they placed on education and their open and cooperative disposition.

I set off for Kragur almost immediately. Brother Pat asked a St. Xavier's student who was going home to visit his family in Kragur to take me along. This was Taram, the same Taram I met again in Kragur in 1998. The trail started at the edge of the forest and went up and over the mountain directly to Kragur, climbing and then descending almost a kilometer (about a half-mile) in altitude in the space of about 5.5 kilometers (about 3.5 miles). It was steep in many places and treacherous in a few, but occasional switchbacks cut by the Japanese military forces who had occupied Kairiru, including Kragur, for much of World War II made it superior to most bush tracks. The trail snaked its way through the shade of dense tropical forest up the south side of the mountain, passed through stands of sago palms in the moister upper reaches, and descended the north side at a steeper angle. Here the forest cover broke more frequently, revealing spectacular views of the sea far below and slash-and-burn gardens clinging to almost perpendicular slopes. We occasionally crossed clear swift streams, which Taram assured me were potable and which proved to be so. Just before entering Kragur, Taram took me along a path to where I could bathe in a rocky, waist-deep pool of clear, cold rushing water.

Kairiru's freshwater streams are one of its most memorable features. In 1999, Tetsuo Watanabe, a surgeon in the Japanese navy during World War II, sent me a copy of the book he wrote about his wartime experiences in New Guinea, including his life on Kairiru Island. To escape the notice of Allied planes, he and his comrades had to hide "in the deep jungle where the sunlight could not penetrate" and "[mold] grew on our clothes and foods." But, he adds, "One of the few advantages of the island was that we could wash our bodies daily with abundant clear water. . . ." However, the fact that they had to wash at night in order to avoid "the very sharp-eyed enemy" diminished their pleasure. Allied air patrols regularly bombed and strafed any Japanese troops they could spot, sometimes with tragic consequences for islanders.

Brother William Borrell, a science teacher at St. Xavier's in the 1970s, speculated that the steadily flowing streams were evidence of an artesian system that brought water from the coastal mountains on the mainland. One of the stories called *nikanik* in the Kairiru language, roughly meaning "legend" or "myth" in English, provides a different explanation. According to this account, when the supernatural being Kairiru (called a *masalai* in Tok Pisin) settled on the island, he chose a valley near the top of the mountain and sang a magical spell until it filled with water. There he made his home, and from there he controls the water of the streams. If a village angers him, he can stop its streams by placing his tail in a hole in the bottom of the lake. He seldom, however, resorts to this.

On arriving in Kragur, I was given one of two rooms in the Shewaratin *haus boi,* a small house built by members of one of the village's major kinship groups, Shewaratin, for the use of its young men when they came home from work or school on leave or holiday. Literally, the Tok Pisin term *"haus boi"* means "boys' house" and comes from the condescending colonial term for plantation laborers' quarters; but villagers used the term for young men's dormitories like the Shewaratin house or as a euphemism for a men's ceremonial house. I spent the rest of that day sitting on the narrow verandah with several Shewaratin men, explaining my intentions to them as best I could. Only their demeanor might have told me just how important some of these men were, for their clothes were as shabby as those of any other villager, their faces were as weather-beaten, and their hands as hardened from work.

The village councillor, Lapim, was among my visitors. He told me that there would be a gathering that night at which he could ask the assembled villagers how they would feel about my staying in Kragur for a year or more. I was not invited to the meeting, but well after dark I could hear the indistinct sound of public discussion coming from the clear space in the center of the village. The next morning Lapim told me that they had agreed I could settle for a while in Kragur if I wanted to. I told Lapim that I would gratefully accept the offer.

In retrospect it seems that we all made our minds up rather quickly. Some months later, a few villagers told me that they had been against allowing me to stay, but now saw that things had turned out all right. I know I was eager to hang my hat somewhere. I was impressed by the village's ample supply of fresh water; I also slept comfortably through the night without a mosquito net. The steep terrain on Kairiru's north coast allows for little standing water in which mosquitoes can breed, the bare ground of the village affords them few hiding places, and the ocean breeze helps keep them at bay. Kragur also suited me in other ways. Separated from the south coast by the mountain, the village was moderately isolated from Wewak, but I still could get to town occasionally to buy supplies or get medical attention if necessary.

Returning from Kragur, I spent a couple of days at St. Xavier's, waiting for transportation to Wewak on the school's boat, the *Tau-K.* The *Tau-K* was a flat-bottomed landing craft that made the trip to Wewak and back twice a week, weather permitting, to transport St. Xavier's staff and students, supplies for the school, and Kairiru villagers, who paid a modest fare. In the 1970s, many people on both sides of the island depended on the *Tau-K* for transportation to the mainland. Like most other Kairiru islanders at the time, Kragur people had outrigger canoes but no power boats, so the easiest way for them to reach the mainland was to walk over the mountain early in the morning and take the *Tau-K.*

Back in Wewak, I got in touch with a new acquaintance, a young Australian plumber with whom I had shared some South Pacific Lagers, who had offered me the use of his truck. (He also introduced me to a Papua New Guinean family who invited me to stay with them in government housing just east of town whenever I came in from the island, an offer I took advantage of on several occasions during the coming year.) With the aid of the rather decrepit truck I assembled my supplies. Rice, canned food, navy biscuits, kerosene, kerosene lanterns, a single-burner kerosene cooker, a thin foam mattress, sheets, flimsy cotton blankets, soap, towels, matches, and a couple of plastic buckets accounted for most of these. Much of my canned food was mackerel, known in Tok Pisin as *tinpis* (tinned fish). I also acquired a sheet of plywood to use as a tabletop. Kragur carpenters can make almost anything, but I knew a flat, smooth writing surface would be hard to come by in the village. On Kairiru, the brothers at St. Xavier's would lend me two metal folding chairs to complete my furniture shopping. While in Wewak I also let the Provincial Office know that I was going to be living in Kragur. A week after coming back to Wewak from Kairiru, my new acquaintances drove me and my gear to Cape Wom, west of town, where I caught the *Tau-K* back to St. Xavier's.

I chartered the St. John's boat to take me around the island to Kragur, but I had to wait at St. Xavier's for a couple of days before it was available. The sky was bright and cloudless and the sun was blazing when we finally left, but even in the St. John's boat we moved fast enough to generate a cooling breeze. The sea was flat and calm all the way to Kragur, where tiny waves slapped limply on the beach. Fanauk, whom I did not know yet, made a couple of trips between beach and boat in his canoe to offload my gear. Hot and sweaty from standing in the sun watching this procedure, I went over the side and swam ashore, making a poor show of it by slipping and stumbling on the rocky uneven bottom when I reached shallow water and tried to get to my feet. It was not so much a welcoming committee as a loose knot of the curious that came forward to shake my hand as I stood dripping by my heap of supplies. This done, a few villagers shouldered my boxes and other baggage and I followed the small procession to the Shewaratin *haus boi*, where I was to stay until a house of my own could be built.

Despite my naïve desire to keep a distance from mission influence, in the end I allowed a Marist Brother from Australia—Pat Howley—to direct me to a research site. This did not escape my attention, but Kragur's obvious advantages made it easy to loosen my grip on my biases. Also, the staff at St. Xavier's quickly gained my good opinion. As I passed through St. Xavier's on occasional trips to and from Wewak that year, the brothers provided hot showers, good meals, cold beer, and liqueurs flavored with Kairiru's own flora from the school's chemistry lab. St. Xavier's usually charged travelers and the occasional tourist a small fee for overnight accommodations, and I asked at the beginning of the year if I could put my stays there on account. When I went to settle my bill prior to leaving the island at the end of 1976, the brothers declined to accept any payment.

I also saw that many of the St. Xavier's staff had no interest in imposing their own religious beliefs on their students. Largely members of Catholic orders, principally the Society of Mary, they took their religion very seriously; but they did not seem alarmed that some of their students, themselves raised in Catholic villages, asked pointed and skeptical questions about the faith.

Had I known more of either Catholicism or the mission in Papua New Guinea I would have been aware that both had changed significantly since the early years of the twentieth century. In those days, missionaries conducted mass baptisms of the living and sometimes baptized the dying by stealth and tallied the souls they thus saved. Since then, the Catholic Church and the Catholic Mission in Papua New Guinea had been moving away from emphasizing individual conversion, religious ritual, and the veneration of religious artifacts toward what some of my mission acquaintances in the East Sepik called "building Christian communities." And the daily business of many Catholic Mission personnel I met in and around Wewak was not gaining converts but running health and education programs.

I was to find that some Kragur people were not comfortable with the mission's diminishing emphasis on religious rites and were themselves rather intense in their devotion to Catholic ritual. Had I first come to Kragur only six months later I would have encountered along the way rather dramatic evidence of many villagers' deep involvement with Catholic rites and symbols: the statue of the Virgin Mary that Kragur people would erect in a broad clearing at the top of the trail over the mountain in April 1976. Villagers passing the statue on their travels often paused to stand reverently in front of it and recite the rosary.

Even without the statue, in my first days and weeks in Kragur, villagers' interest in the Virgin—or, as villagers called her, Santu Maria or just Maria—was among the most obvious features of life there. Villagers' ambivalent attitude toward money and their intense interest in changing their way of life also stood out sharply. These matters were all closely related. To explain how, I first have to describe religious life in Kragur in more detail.

The Virgin and the Ancestors

"We're number one in the eyes of the mission!"
(*Mipela i nambawan long misin!*)
—A Kragur villager, 1976

"[God] is different, because you can't see God, you can't
see his face. Your mother and father, you've seen their faces.
This is what makes it so hard [to understand]."
(*"[God] i arakain liklik, long wanem yu no lukim God,
yu no lukim pes bilongen. Mama papa yu bin lukim pes
bilong ol. Em i hat ologeta long dispela."*)
—Another Kragur villager, 1976

In 1975–1976, Catholicism seemed to permeate life in Kragur and Kragur Catholicism focused on the Virgin Mary. Two missionary priests had established chapters of the Legion of Mary throughout the East Sepik in the 1950s and 1960s and then had left. Although no other priests continued their work, the village organizations lived on, including the Kragur chapter. Kragur's four or five Legion members adamantly promoted the idea that frequent, well-attended religious observance, especially praying the rosary, was central to being good Catholics. Every evening one of their number led villagers in reciting the rosary in Tok Pisin in front of a small plank altar in the center of the village sheltering a statuette of the Virgin. The schoolchildren prayed first, then later in the evening the adults assembled. Either before or after their prayers, the adults often took advantage of these gatherings to discuss community issues and, occasionally, personal grievances. This undoubtedly helped boost attendance, which was generally healthy.

Ibor, the leader of the Legion of Mary in Kragur, presided over Sunday services in the half-walled church building at the place called Plos at the east end of the village. Unlike most of the other buildings in the village, the timber and thatch church sat directly on the ground and the floor was bare dirt. Sunday mornings, the village bell—an empty World War II gas cylinder hung from the trunk of a coconut palm—rang to tell people it was time to get ready for church and then, forty-five minutes or an hour later, to summon them to Plos. Most adult villagers attended the service every Sunday. Timbers laid in rows on the floor served as pews; women sat on one side of the aisle, men on the other, all freshly bathed and dressed in clean clothes.

Everyday dress for men in Kragur was T-shirts, or no shirts, and shorts or laplaps. A laplap is a knee-length piece of cloth worn wrapped around the waist, fastened with an artful tuck but not tied. Women wore loose blouses and skirts or laplaps, although married women with children often eschewed a blouse. Most clothing was faded, worn, and mended, and everyone generally went barefoot. On Sundays, however, villagers donned any newer clothing they had, and the gathering outside the church was often bright with colorful laplaps and tops, for neither men nor women attended church shirtless.

Ibor and one or two other men conducted prayers and services in Tok Pisin. Some early Catholic missionaries in the Sepik region had learned local languages and used them in proselytizing. That practice, however, soon gave way to the convenience of using Tok Pisin. Hymnals, prayer books, and the New Testament all were available in Tok Pisin in the 1970s, although only a few younger villagers used any of these. Most villagers sang hymns and recited prayers learned by heart.

The village celebrated several Christian holidays, including Easter, All-Souls' Day, and Christmas. In 1975, most of those who were physically able walked over the mountain to attend a Christmas Eve service at St. Xavier's, returning to the village on Christmas Day over a muddy trail, under low, dark clouds that drizzled steadily. I joined the trek to St. Xavier's but spent the night in the comfort of the brothers' house rather than camping on the concrete floors of the empty dormitories with the other pilgrims. To learn about Kragur Catholicism, as well as to be sociable, I attended Sunday service in the village every week and frequently attended evening prayers. No one minded that I often scribbled in my notebook during the services. Within a few weeks of my arrival in Kragur, people took it for granted that they would see me at Plos on Sundays and at prayers in the village center on many evenings.

The Virgin was much in the public eye in 1976, perhaps more than usual, because this was the year Kragur people erected her statue at Iupulpul, a site at the top of the trail over the mountain. Here the trail emerged from the forest in a level clearing. The statue was four to five feet tall and stood on a concrete pedestal about three feet high. A priest who had since left the East Sepik, like the priests who started the Legion, had supplied the statue. Kragur people took the lead among Kairiru islanders in seeing the project to completion. When the figure arrived in 1976, they carried sand and gravel to the top of the mountain to build a concrete base for it and organized the festivities at Iupulpul marking its dedication. I believe it was a coincidence that all this took place in the year of independence, but some villagers plainly found this conjunction significant. At a number of public gatherings that year village men held forth with feeling on the challenges of independence and spoke of the need to turn even more to the Virgin Mary than before. As they spoke they gestured toward the mountain above, where her statue stood.

Villagers also displayed their devotion to Catholicism and the Virgin in more private ways. Legion members used prayer for healing and often sat praying the rosary with the sick and their families until far into the night. Many villagers crossed themselves and said a prayer before beginning a meal, and many kept altars to Christ and the Virgin in their homes. Such an altar was usually little more than a colorful picture of Christ or Maria, displayed on a homemade wooden table, flanked by flowers and ornamental foliage in glass jars of water; but it was usually carefully tended and occupied a prominent place.

Catholicism Comes to Kragur

Although Catholicism was firmly established in the East Sepik Province by the 1970s, it had come there only relatively recently. German Catholic missionaries of the Society of the Divine Word landed in what is now Madang Province in 1896. Finding the location unsuitable, they decamped to Tumleo, a coastal island about a hundred miles west of Kairiru. There they established their headquarters and started a coconut plantation, the income from which was to help support their missionary endeavors. Turning coconuts into copra—the dried or smoked meat of the mature coconut, used to produce oil—is a labor-intensive operation, and the missionaries had to recruit local workers, some from nearby islands.

According to villagers' accounts, a mission vessel came to the north shore of Kairiru shortly after 1900 to recruit labor, and then, or soon after, a few Kragur men went to work on Tumleo. This was Kragur's first contact with missionaries and with something like the peculiar institution of wage labor. (Early plantation laborers were paid in goods such as cloth, tobacco, and steel tools as well as negligible amounts of money.) It probably was also villagers' first extended contact with whites or Europeans, as Kragur people call most light-skinned foreigners. (They apply these terms to North Americans and Australians of European descent, but not to the Japanese soldiers who occupied Kairiru during World War II and contemporary Japanese.)

Working for the mission was a major step in a process of radical social change, but it also brought significant immediate benefits. In 1976, older villagers told me that before the German missionaries arrived, their grandfathers had obtained steel knives and axes from the nearby islands of Walis and Tarawai, whose inhabitants had obtained them from Malay traders. But contact with the missionaries on Tumleo probably increased Kragur's supply of precious metal tools and other useful artifacts.

One Kragur man used matches acquired from the mission on Tumleo to flush his enemies from cover in what was probably the last major intervillage raid on Kairiru. Some time between 1905 and 1910, Kragur men joined the men of neighboring villages to raid the village of Chem, which then lay only about an hour's journey away on foot on the other side of the mountain. As I heard the story, they attacked at dawn, after dulling the senses of the still-sleeping Chems with war magic. One of the leaders of that expedition set fire to the houses with his mission matches so that the waiting warriors could set upon the startled Chems as they tumbled from their burning homes. The tactic was not new, but villagers told me that matches made it easier to execute.

Despite such unanticipated consequences, Catholic influence in the coastal region and on Kairiru itself grew rapidly. By 1920, a Kairiru islander trained to provide basic religious instruction—a "native catechist," as they were once called—built a church in the north coast village of Surai. Other catechists followed, including one who resided in Kragur for several years. By around 1930, Kragur people had abandoned the most obvious indigenous religious institution, the men's spirit cult or, in Tok Pisin, *tambaran* cult.

In common English usage the term "cult" has pejorative connotations, suggesting extreme, obsessive, or flagrantly bogus religion. Indeed, early Christian missionaries who regarded indigenous religious practices as bogus and misguided may well have been among the first to call these institutions cults. Anthropologists, however, use the term "cult" to mean simply a system of religious beliefs and practices. One could as well speak of the *tambaran* church or, conversely, the Jesus cult.

No Kragur people still alive in 1975–1976 were old enough to have taken full part in the *tambaran* institution before it was abandoned, so they could tell me little about it. If the Kragur cult was anything like *tambaran* cults elsewhere in the Sepik that survived to be described by Europeans or that still survive, its main activity was propitiation of powerful cult spirits and sacred objects, which together make up the *tambaran*. Cult spirits are often in a sense ancestral spirits, but they exist on a more abstract and elevated plane than the ghosts of the dead. The *tambaran* play a vital role in ensuring the growth and maturation of village boys and the welfare of the entire community. Being initiated into such a cult is a crucial step for males in achieving adulthood.

In 1935, Bishop Joseph Loerks, then leader of the new Jesus cult in the Sepik, moved his headquarters from Tumleo to a site close to the present site of St. John's to take advantage of the good harbor and ample fresh water there. In 1938, six priests, according to one account, visited the north coast and baptized people from several villages, Kragur among them, in a mass ceremony. In 1939, the mission built a training school for catechists, St. Xavier's, not far from the bishop's headquarters. This eventually would evolve into the present St. Xavier's High School.

St. Xavier's shut down during World War II and the Japanese occupation of

Kairiru, but not long after the war it began training catechists again, including Ibor. He served as a catechist on the Papua New Guinea mainland before returning to Kragur in 1952 to establish the first school there, where he taught basic literacy in Tok Pisin. He soon moved his school to Bou, and from this school descended the present Bou Community School, part of the national education system. Ibor himself became the central figure in Catholic life in Kragur, as well as a leader in other spheres, and helped make Kragur one of the most actively Catholic villages on Kairiru and in the Wewak area.

Why did Catholicism take such a hold on Kragur? There was no yawning chasm in Kragur culture for it to fill. Kragur people had their own ways of conceiving of the meaning of things and of more-than-human or other-than-human powers in the world, and they had a rich array of rituals and practices for coping with such powers and affirming the order and meaning of life. Their religious beliefs and practices, however, were not a closed system. Throughout Melanesia, innovation has long been a natural part of religious life. People have added new practices learned in dreams or in other altered states to their religious repertoires and have acquired complex rituals from other groups, just as they have passed more mundane products from village to village in widespread trading networks. Nevertheless, it might seem odd that villagers would have abandoned the *tambaran* cult except under extreme duress. Local politics may help to explain Kragur's early, apparently open attitude toward Catholicism.

Tambaran cults usually have several internal ranks, and men accumulate both knowledge and power as they climb up through them. The power and knowledge men gain within the cult translate into power in the community at large. Hence, the cults often serve to perpetuate the power of older men over younger men and of men over women. So, although the men's cult was in many ways a central part of life, women and younger men in Kragur would have had less to lose—and possibly much to gain—by supporting the priests and catechists who urged villagers to abandon it.

According to the accounts of villagers who were children at the time, younger men indeed were more enthusiastic than their elders about abandoning the men's cult to embrace Catholicism. I do not know what role women may have played in these events, but they also might have seen some advantage in the new religion. Although men dominated Catholic religious life in Kragur in the 1970s, the men's cult by all accounts was much more exclusionary and strongly, sometimes harshly, reinforced male dominance. In addition, male advocates of Catholicism may well have seen in it an opportunity to acquire for themselves some of the credit for a significant religious innovation. At least one supporter of Catholicism, I was told, was a man who already enjoyed considerable prestige in the existing order. Others, however, may have hoped to create space for new kinds of leaders with a new kind of

authority, circumventing the established hierarchy of high-level *tambaran* cult ini-
tiates and powerful magicians.

I do not mean to suggest that these were the only motives at work. Motives
probably were as plentiful as shades of political interest and the undoubtedly
diverse individual understandings of just what Catholicism was all about. If, however, the Kragur villagers of the 1920s were anything like those of more recent
decades, it would be difficult not to see tension between young and old and men
and women and a contest for influence and leadership here. In 1975–1976, villagers
were jealous of their claims to the rights to use or control important types of magical
or technical knowledge and quick to claim credit for innovations or accomplishments of any sort. They also gloried in the past and present accomplishments of
their close kin, pointing to the exploits of shared ancestors, the magical knowledge
of the elders, the successes of the migrants, and the progress in school of the children. Both youths and women shared pride in the stature and influence of closely
related male leaders, but the young still chafed under the authority of their elders,
and women often complained aloud about the authority and priorities of the men.

Old and young, men and women alike also may have found Catholicism attractive because they associated it with the wealth and power of Europeans. Even in
1975–1976, many older villagers had experienced the European world largely through
Catholic institutions and probably saw Catholicism as a major part of the European
world. This was consistent with the fact that, in the indigenous world, success in
almost any major endeavor required not only technical skill, physical effort, or
political acumen; it also required tapping supernatural powers through magic or, at
the least, avoiding supernatural dangers. One middle-aged man summed up con-
cisely the prevailing view on the importance of magic in productive endeavors such
as gardening, fishing, or hunting when he told me, "*Samting i kamap long maus
bilong man tasol.*" Literally, this means "Things came only from the mouths of men,"
but what the mouths of men do is utter magical spells. They also pray, and many
Kragur people saw little difference between magical spells (which are called *singsing*
in Tok Pisin, a term that also applies to nonmagical music and dance) and Catholic
prayer (*beten* in Tok Pisin), in particular the rosary (*beten korona* in Tok Pisin).

If Kragur people saw this similarity in the 1970s, they probably saw it in the
early 1900s as well. They also noted that Europeans were rich and powerful. Missionaries and other Europeans possessed kinds and quantities of material goods
they had never seen before, not only cloth and steel tools, but also such things as
large sailing vessels and steamships, metal roofing, firearms, and lumber-milling
equipment. The Europeans also were imposing their political authority on the hundreds of villages on the beaches and islands of Kragur's known world and displaying their military prowess. Kragur people must have known of this, for it was happening very close by. In one 1907 incident, German colonial officials raided Karesau

Island and the village of Seraseng, on Kairiru's south coast, and destroyed houses, gardens, and canoes to punish villagers for taking part in armed, intervillage hostilities. All this may well have recommended experimenting with the ritual system of the foreigners.

Moral Anxiety, Moral Claims, and the Desire for Change

Although early Catholic missionaries tried to put an end to many existing religious practices, and succeeded in the case of the *tambaran* cult, villagers themselves did not think they had to abandon all their familiar beliefs and practices in order to take up Catholicism. In 1975–1976, even though Kragur people prayed to the Virgin Mary frequently, carried rosary beads, and attended Sunday services, most also believed firmly that the ghosts or spirits of the dead played important roles in everyday life, for both good and ill.

They not only did not find this incompatible with Catholicism, some fell back on the dead to help them interpret aspects of Catholic teachings they found puzzling or unfamiliar. Several villagers suggested that the Catholic God had an indigenous counterpart. Moke, for example, once told me: "When the missionaries came, they talked about God. Our ancestors spoke of Wankau." But most talk of Wankau focused on the exploits of a culture hero who was the protagonist of a widely known myth. This Wankau had provided the ancestors with knowledge of canoe building, gardening, and other essential technologies, but he was rather human in many ways. The story of his exploits, for example, involves treachery, adultery, and revenge. Despite the equation of God with Wankau some villagers proposed, many others found the Catholic supernatural being troublesome. For one thing, God was a highly abstract and impersonal being in comparison with the *tambaran* spirits or, especially, the ghosts of people one had known in life. As Mowush said to me in 1976, "[God] is different, because you can't see God, you can't see his face. Your mother and father, you've seen their faces. This is what makes it [i.e., God] so hard to understand."

The ghosts of the dead had essentially human emotions, like jealously, pique, anger, and sometimes approval or compassion. To most villagers the ghosts of the dead were very real and very close. Their bodies were buried in the cemeteries at either end of the village, or—for the pre-mission dead—inside the village, beneath the houses of their descendants or where those houses once had stood. In the Kairiru language, ghosts are called *ramat shawaung*, shadow or spirit *(shawaung)* of man *(ramat)*. Many Kragur people could tell of encountering *ramat shawaung* walking abroad or hearing their footsteps outside their homes at night. I slept through at least one such episode. The next day my neighbors expressed surprise that I had not heard the ghostly, but apparently loud, footsteps passing my window.

To most European Christians this is not the stuff that God is made of, but at least some Kragur villagers succeeded in domesticating Catholicism by understanding God in such familiar terms. One middle-aged man, for example, told me that he had concluded that speaking of God was the missionaries' way of referring to the dead ancestors. Hence, each man had his own God, that is, his dead father. Maria, he had concluded, must represent a person's dead mother. Another man, finding it necessary to fit God and the dead into a single picture, had decided that when one prayed, the prayers actually went to one's dead kin, who then conveyed the message to God.

Such speculations were a way of making an imported belief, still novel in some respects after fifty years or so, more familiar and comprehensible, something villagers could own and not a foreign intrusion or imposition. This was important, because many probably saw Catholicism as a system of belief and ritual that was not just technically more efficient than purely indigenous practices but also *morally* superior. To domesticate Catholicism was to claim some of this virtue as indigenous.

Moral status entered the picture because morality and worldly achievement were closely linked in important spheres of Kragur life. This was most apparent when villagers were confronted with an immediate problem, such as poor fishing or a persistent illness. Villagers assumed that in many realms—such as growing taro or sweet potatoes, fishing, hunting, or avoiding illness and accidents—well-being depended on maintaining good social relations. In their view, anger or unresolved grievances could cause crops to fail, fishing and hunting expeditions to come home empty-handed, and people to fall ill. This could happen in several ways. For instance, a sorcerer might use malign magic to harm either an individual or the entire village in retaliation for a perceived wrong. The most common cause of material misfortune, however, was not the anger of a sorcerer but the anger of ordinary villagers.

The way Kragur people dealt with much tenacious illness provides a good example. Any closely knit community is full of opportunities for people to annoy one another, and most such friction in Kragur had few repercussions. Most villagers, however, believed that if people were angry the ghosts of their dead ancestors could take it upon themselves to attack those who had angered them. The dead usually attacked by making someone ill. If an illness was serious and lengthy, sooner or later villagers would conclude that someone's ancestral ghosts were causing it. The remedy was to discover who among the living was angry with the sick person about what and resolve the matter publicly. This was a tricky business, because the ancestors could act without the knowledge or consent of the living and often seemed to draw little distinction between large and small grievances. So, the illness could result from an incident that the parties involved had almost forgotten.

The outdoor public assemblies at which village men sought to discover the

anger that lay at the root of an illness caused by ghosts could go on for hours, sometimes for days, and touch on the patient's relations with many people. For a re-
searcher, these meetings were a rich source of information about the kinds of things
villagers thought worthy of anger. I attended them as regularly as I did church services, looking for a spot on a verandah where I could lean my back against a wall or
house post and settling in for the day with camera, notebook, betel-chewing equipment, and cigarettes.

Kragur people often addressed issues of collective prosperity much as they did
illness. In 1976, villagers were greatly concerned because the schools of a particular
kind of fish, called *konan* in the Kairiru language, that usually spawned close to
shore had been making a poor showing. One of the village leaders had performed
the appropriate magic to summon the *konan* in large numbers, but it was not working. Most villagers I spoke with agreed that the magic was probably ineffective because there was too much discord in the village. They dealt with this by holding a
series of assemblies—again, men only—to discover and resolve grievances that might
be throwing a monkey wrench in the works. Both fishing magicians and Catholic
leaders took prominent roles in these assemblies, and people spoke of the need to
regain the favor of both the ancestors and the Virgin Mary by restoring community
harmony.

Given this view of things, villagers easily could have concluded that impressive
European wealth was evidence that Europeans were exceptionally harmonious
people, and many did so. Variations on the idea that whites or Europeans lived together more cooperatively and harmoniously than Papua New Guineans did, and
enjoyed superior health and prosperity because of it, were common in Kragur in
1975–1976. As Brawaung, a middle-aged man who became one of my closest friends
and collaborators, put it, "You people of America, Australia, all those places, follow
God's laws so you don't get sick, you don't have problems. You follow the ways of
God, you can't be angry at others, fight with others. You follow a good way and so
you aren't troubled with illness and pain." Sakun, a man in his thirties, entertained
a similar image of the comparatively harmonious social life of Europeans and its
rewards. As he put it:

> At a meeting or whatever kind of social event all the men and women must be happy
> and celebrate together. When the children in school have a special event, right away
> all the parents must be there. We [Papua New Guineans] don't do things that way.
> One person thinks he's most important, another thinks he's most important; every-
> one keeps to himself. When the bell rings they stay in their houses. It's making the
> village go downhill. If you just keep to yourself in your house it doesn't make the
> village joyful, it doesn't make the village happy. You whites, if there's a special event
> anywhere, everyone will be there, celebrate, make everyone happy. That makes the
> country grow and prosper.

It was hard to convince Sakun and others that "we" whites were not necessarily all that harmonious. Most of my efforts clearly failed and, in some villagers' eyes, my own comparative wealth belied my words.

Kragur people wanted to prosper too, and that probably helped draw them to Catholicism, which many saw as the Europeans' way of achieving harmony among themselves and with the supernatural. But, while their poverty in comparison with Europeans insinuated their moral inferiority, they were not willing to concede the point entirely. Here, too, they found Catholicism useful. As I suggested earlier, by assimilating Catholicism to familiar ideas about magic and the spirits of the dead, villagers claimed it for their own. As such, it was evidence of their moral stature, not just a foreign antidote for moral deficiency. Their claim to Catholicism also went beyond domesticating its beliefs and practices. In 1975–1976, several villagers told me of how God Itself had recognized Kragur's special moral qualities by visiting the village long before the Society of the Divine Word, and the story was widely known.

It was said that one day Masos—an old man at the time, the maternal grandfather of Ibor—was sharpening his stone knife on a boulder at Sumulau, the place on the stream where I had bathed the day I first came to Kragur. Suddenly his hands stuck fast to the rock. Fearing that this was the work of a *masalai,* a powerful supernatural being, he called out to his small granddaughter—who would become Ibor's mother—to run to the village and tell people to bring food and other offerings so the *masalai* would free him. While she was gone, a voice spoke to Masos saying it was the voice of God, who lived in the sky. God told him It wanted to bless Kragur so it would prosper and gave him some instructions to convey to the other villagers. Most of these had to do with cleaning their houses and putting on new clothes. At the time this meant new bark-fiber skirts and beaten-bark loincloths. Ibor and some others, however, added that God also told Masos that they should not fight and steal among themselves, and that they should not kill strangers who came to the village but give them food and shelter.

Father Geoff Brum, serving at Wirui in 1976, told me that Kragur was not the only village he knew of that claimed to have encountered God before the arrival of the Christian missions; and fellow anthropologists have told me of at least one other East Sepik locale that makes a similar claim. But if Kragur people knew this, they were unconcerned. Their own story asserted Kragur's independent and longstanding relationship to the God of the missionaries.

Some villagers clearly implied that God came to Kragur because it already was a morally superior place whose tradition of internal harmony and compassion toward strangers stretched even further back in time than the days of Masos. Villagers often referred to this tradition in Tok Pisin as Kragur's *gudpela pasin,* that is, Kragur's

Good Way. I capitalize Good Way because in 1975–1976 it had the ring of an established ideology; it was not just any good way, it was Kragur's Good Way.

As we shall see, like many traditions, the Good Way was evolving, having roots in the past but responding to contemporary circumstances. And like many ideologies it enshrined general principles but was vague on specifics and open to interpretation. Nevertheless, even in the midst of intense interest in change, villagers could not discuss their aspirations for Kragur for long without touching on the role and shape the Good Way would take in that future. In its emphasis on both harmony and generosity, the Good Way was intimately connected with economic life. So, to understand Kragur's moral concerns and villagers' thoughts about change and the future one has to understand something about their way of making a living.

CHAPTER 4

Food, Money, and the Strangeness of Capitalism

"AMONG YOU [WHITES], IF ONE OF YOUR RELATIVES COMES
AND STAYS WITH YOU, THEY HAVE TO PAY YOU WHEN THEY LEAVE.
WE'RE DIFFERENT."
(*LONG YUPELA, WANEM KANDERE I KAM STAP WANTAIM YU,
TAIM EM I GO I MAS PAIM. MIPELA I ARAKAIN.*)
—A Kragur villager, 1976

Kragur villagers' attitude toward money made as strong a first impression on me as their enthusiasm for Catholicism. From the day I settled in the Shewaratin *haus boi* many villagers brought me cooked and fresh taro and sweet potatoes, greens of various kinds, papayas, citrus fruit, bananas, and fresh and smoked fish. Women from neighboring houses stopped by on their way to the stream with their own dirty dishes and laundry and offered to wash my things as well, an offer I gladly accepted. Those who brought me food sometimes asked if I had a little rice or canned mackerel to spare. Sometimes they asked on the spot, but usually only some hours or days later. With only one or two exceptions, however, when I offered them money for food or assistance, they refused. Several villagers took it upon themselves to explain to me that they did not buy and sell things among themselves, so if I were going to live among them it would be wrong to treat me differently.

I knew that many communities in Papua New Guinea were only marginally involved with the cash economy and that buying and selling played little or no role in most precolonial societies. I had expected, however, that villagers almost anywhere I lived would have no objections to engaging in commercial transactions with me, an outsider. In Manus in 1973, people in the villages where we lived and worked were happy to exchange food for cash or the twisted six-inch lengths of black, resinous tobacco we carried especially for this purpose.

One American anthropologist I met in Port Moresby just a few weeks before finding my way to Kragur had even counseled me to pay people for interviewing them in the course of my research. Ted Schwartz, however, had advised against this. It also would have been difficult to square with the informal way I went about most of my own work. I spent a lot of time observing public events, chatting with the other onlookers, hanging out with work groups in the village or the bush, and striking up conversations with people resting on their verandahs. Often, I also arranged in advance to meet with people to discuss particular topics, such as their wage work experience, their life histories, their views on particular village events, or some topic of which they had special knowledge. But we treated these meetings more as social occasions than as business transactions. They were only loosely scheduled, for villagers seldom designated meeting times more specific than "morning," "afternoon," "after dark," or simply "tomorrow." When people came to my house, I usually offered tea, cigarettes, and betel nut if I had any on hand. When we met at their houses, they often offered me cooked food and I usually brought betel or tobacco. Wherever we met, I also was good for some rice or canned mackerel in the days and weeks to come.

Even if I had wanted to pay villagers for information and interviews, it would have been impossible. In fact, my efforts to pay for things seemed to embarrass people. Village leaders also rejected my offer to pay daily wages for building a new house so I could move out of my small room in the *haus boi*. They decided that my house should be built in the same way as other village houses. It would be a communal project, and I, as the owner of the house, would provide a large share of the food for the communal meals that marked the end of each day's work.

Some villagers made it clear to me that refusing to buy and sell things among themselves and to engage me, a visitor, in commercial relations was very much a part of Kragur's special Good Way, its unique brand of solidarity and generosity. The Good Way had religious roots, but to understand its economic dimension we also have to look at the nuts and bolts of making a living in Kragur and the ways in which economic life there differed from that in a capitalist society.

Village Livelihood

Given Kragur's circumstances, cultivating a principled disdain for money was not a bad idea, for villagers had very little money and few opportunities to earn any. Most of their cash income came from selling copra produced from their own modest stands of coconut palms. I did not gather good income data in 1975–1976, but when I returned to Kragur for a few weeks in 1981 I estimated that villagers' income in 1980 from copra sales and a few other minor sources—sales of local produce in the Wewak market and some sporadic wage work in Wewak—amounted to only about 20 kina per capita. The kina, divisible into 100 toea, is the principal unit of Papua New Guinea's currency, introduced with independence in 1975. In 1980, 20 kina was equivalent to about US$20, and even by Papua New Guinean standards this was not very much. The minimum legal wage for urban laborers in 1976 was around 20 kina every two weeks.

Kragur people working for wages and salaries in towns sometimes sent money home, but I do not know how many kina came into the village this way. I do know that some villagers blamed their lack of cash on the fact that they had no kin working in towns or complained that their migrant kin were shiftless and unemployed. It appeared that migrants usually sent money home for special purposes—such as mounting a feast commemorating the dead or paying school fees for younger kin—rather than as regular contributions.

In 1975–1976, low and falling prices were damping villagers' enthusiasm for producing copra. According to the Papua New Guinea Copra Marketing Board, prices had dropped by more than 50 percent in the preceding two years, substantially reducing the rewards for what can be backbreaking work. Kragur people usually worked communally to process coconuts into copra, although individuals received their cash returns in proportion to the number of bags of the leathery, smoked meat of the coconut that came from their own trees.

Women gathered the dry mature nuts fallen to the ground and carried them on their backs in bulging string bags, leaning into the narrow handles straining across their foreheads, to where the men broke the nuts open with heavy bush knives and removed the meat. The thick, white meat was laid on wooden racks over a smoldering fire in a thatched smokehouse. Men usually tended the fire, eyes watering from the smoke, replenishing it with the loads of wood women brought from the bush. When the coconut meat had turned to gnarled brown copra it was packed tight in burlap sacks. At this point, men occasionally strained their backs when they shouldered the heavy sacks and carried them down the steep path to the beach. From here they ferried the sacks by canoe to a power boat moored offshore—either the regional Local Government Council's diesel work boat or a local charter—for the trip to Wewak. In Wewak, Kragur villagers paid to have their copra trucked to the Copra Marketing Board warehouse to be sold.

Villagers needed money to pay the 10-kina-per-adult yearly tax to the Local Government Council; to pay school fees for children attending Bou or St. Xavier's or one of the high schools on the mainland; to make rare purchases of tools (axes, bush knives, fishing hooks) or household utensils (kerosene lamps, aluminum cooking pots, enameled metal dishes); or to make equally rare purchases of clothing (usually secondhand). A transistor radio to bring in Radio Wewak was nice if you could afford it and keep it supplied with batteries. Money also was useful for paying the *Tau-K*'s fare to Wewak or buying rice and canned mackerel to supplement one's own gardening and fishing. Villagers could buy canned mackerel, rice, newspaper for rolling cigarettes from their homegrown tobacco, batteries for flashlights and radios, bars of soap, and a few other items at a small one-room store Ibor operated, and two other villagers sold rice and canned mackerel from their homes. Villagers called such a small retail business, in Tok Pisin, a *tred stoa* (trade store) or *kentin* (canteen).

There were many other things Kragur people could do with money if they had it. Bringing beer from Wewak on special occasions, for example, was an infrequent but popular indulgence. Nevertheless, villagers could and often did get by for long periods of time without any cash on hand. They built their own houses from timbers and other materials from the forest, fashioned their own outrigger canoes, made fishing nets and string bags from handmade cord, and shaped their own wooden handles for axes and other metal tools. Men sometimes filled odd moments by carving bamboo combs or weaving small palm-frond baskets in which they carried their tobacco-smoking and betel-chewing paraphernalia. Chinese-made metalware was gradually replacing carved wooden plates, but many people still used the home-made wooden plates, especially when contributing food to a collective event of some kind.

Most important of all, villagers produced almost all their own food. The backbone of welfare in Kragur was the productivity of the gardens. The staple crops were taro and sweet potatoes, which villagers cultivated in slash-and-burn plots on the steep mountainside. They cleared the trees and undergrowth with ax, bush knife, and fire and used the larger timbers to form low erosion barriers. When the fertility of a garden plot began to decline, it was left to lie fallow for a few years and return to secondary forest. Gardeners in Papua New Guinea can tell by the kinds of trees and other vegetation growing on a piece of land once used for gardening if it is ready for cultivation again.

Taro—with broad, heart-shaped leaves rising from the dense knob of its edible root—was by far the most valued food. Sago was less popular than either taro or sweet potatoes but was an important food when garden produce was in short supply. Sago is a starchy powder extracted from the pith of the sago palm by breaking the palm open, laboriously pounding the fibrous pith, and separating the starch by repeatedly rinsing the pounded pith with water. The Kragur pounding tool was an adze-shaped wooden handle tipped with a piece of lead pipe. The apparatus for rinsing the pounded sago pith was an elegant structure built from various parts of the sago palm itself. Rigid sago-palm-leaf stalks supported a porous sago bast fiber sieve over a basin made of the flexible barklike lower portion of the leaf stalk. It was constructed on the spot and left to decay and return to nature when the work was done.

Sago palms typically do best in wet lowlands, but on the north side of Kairiru they grow best close to the streams near the top of the mountain. Kragur villagers usually prepared sago powder or flour to eat by mixing it with hot water to create a glutinous gel. This they formed into globules that they garnished with grated coconut, fish, or boiled greens. Villagers gathered several kinds of greens in the bush and grew small amounts of a few introduced vegetables, such as green onions, tomatoes, and pumpkins. Tobacco was an important garden crop, and bunches of drying tobacco leaves hung in rows from rafters inside many houses. Villagers also tended stands of tall, slender betel-nut palms.

Fish provided most of the animal protein in the Kragur diet in 1975–1976, but there was less of it than villagers would have liked. Prime fishing season is roughly from May through October, when the southeast trade winds blow and the sea is relatively calm. Villagers mounted extensive magical and religious efforts that year to bring in large schools of *konan,* but the results were disappointing. Aside from this, only a few men fished very often, usually dropping deep-sea lines from canoes far offshore. Women sometimes fished with hook and line from rocks along the shore or gathered shellfish.

Many people claimed that their parents and grandparents had fished more avidly than they did. They sometimes said that new kinds of work—copra work or the village hygiene and maintenance work organized by the village councillor—had sapped time and energy once devoted to fishing. With the little money villagers earned they occasionally bought canned mackerel; but when people contributed a plate of food to a public event, they preferred to use fish from Kragur's own waters, smoked or freshly cooked, to crown the plate of taro, sweet potatoes, or sago they had prepared.

Only two men, those with licensed shotguns, ever hunted the wild pigs that roamed the bush. There were only two more-or-less domesticated pigs in the village, bristle-backed creatures captured in the bush when young. A few men occasionally trapped or hunted small marsupials.

Bananas, mangoes, papaya, pineapple, and a variety of other fruits—including breadfruit and custard apple or soursop—were often plentiful. With the exception of hard cooking bananas, however, Kragur people usually ate such foods only as snacks during a long day of work, for they took no regular midday meal. Most fruits required little active cultivation and could literally be plucked from the trees. Producing the staple foods of Kragur life, however, required hard and heavy labor and was far from a tropical idyll.

Some villagers were especially skilled in one essential activity or another, such as building canoes or houses, processing sago, or making string bags. No one, however, specialized in one kind of activity to the exclusion of others. Virtually every adult possessed to some degree all the skills appropriate for an adult man or woman. The principal division of labor was between men's and women's work, but even this was not absolute. Men and women each had parts to play in virtually all major aspects of making a living. Women, however, spent more time producing food than men did, from 40 to 50 percent more hours per week, according to my observations that year. Women also spent more than ten times more hours per week in household tasks, such as cooking, gathering firewood, and washing dishes and clothes. In addition, they had primary responsibility for child care, which went on twenty-four hours a day. For their part, men spent more time than women building things, mostly houses and canoes, and engaging in moneymaking activities, such as culti-vating coconuts and processing copra. Men also spent approximately twice as much time as women taking part in various kinds of public meetings and ceremonies, including many hours attending assemblies for curing the sick.

Meetings and ceremonies involved a great deal of sitting. The sight of men, un-encumbered by children, doing so much more sitting than women did give the im-pression that women worked harder than men. Kragur women noticed and com-mented on this. It is only fair, however, to point out that many women also regarded such activities as important, and many men thought of them as tedious necessities.

The Novelty of Commodities in Kragur

Life in Kragur provided plenty of physical labor for everyone but precious few of the things that money could buy. There were good reasons for villagers to be inter-ested in making more money; but not only were opportunities to do so limited, little in their precolonial experience had prepared Kragur people to feel comfort-able buying and selling, and contemporary village life had little room for commerce.

Households—parents, children, and the occasional in-law or other relative—provided most of their own food but shared surpluses with kin in other house-holds. Most such sharing was spontaneous, but if provisions were short you could ask your kin if they had any food to spare, as long as it did not become a habit. A kind of exchange was involved here, because villagers expected that eventually they would receive more or less as much as they gave, and it was bad manners and bad politics in the extreme to take continually without giving. People also shared money with their kin if the need was pressing. But in 1975–1976 no one ever, to my knowl-edge, exchanged food or anything else for money within the village except when purchasing goods at the trade stores, and even there informal credit was rampant. Sharing was, some said, "the law of our ancestors and up to today we follow it."

A great deal of food, tobacco, and other goods also could change hands on cer-tain formal occasions. The most notable of these, which I have never seen, were large feasts called *warap* in the Kairiru language. The heir of an important leader would give a *warap* to commemorate the dead leader and validate the heir's claim to leadership. I was told that a *warap* given for a prominent leader also served to commemorate the leader's deceased kin of lesser importance. To mount such an event the sponsors of the feast had to call on a network of supporters to amass the large quantities of food to be given to their guests, many of whom came from other villages. The guests themselves brought gifts of food, which the sponsors distrib-uted to their supporters. In the long run, no one came out richer or better-fed than anyone else, but the sponsors confirmed and increased their status, and all of those participating in the acts of giving and receiving confirmed and strengthened their social ties and mutual obligations.

When I came to live in Kragur, the village's decision to take me into the gift-giving system and not to take my money complicated things for me. I had read of economies in which buying and selling were absent, but had had no experience as a participant. It was, in fact, a new situation for everyone. I was the first white or European to stay in Kragur for more than a few days. I was not a familiar kind of outsider like a priest, brother, or government officer, and I was not there to do business. Most important, I was not a member of anyone's family. If I had been, kinship relations would have prescribed roughly what was expected of me and what I could expect from others. As it was, I had to improvise. I developed closer relationships with some families than with others, and this channeled much of the flow of my reciprocal giving. I gradually learned that I could give away most of my supply of rice and canned mackerel and depend on gifts of fish, game, sago, and garden produce to keep me fed.

Adapting to life without buying and selling also complicated my efforts to deal fairly with villagers in our daily relations and transactions. Even where people habitually buy and sell goods and services there is room for them to feel that they have been treated unfairly. In Kragur, I was often at sea. Since I was very wealthy by their standards, some villagers undoubtedly thought I was rather stingy. But there were others who worried about holding up their end of the relationship. I had been concerned that simply buying food for those who built my house was not enough, but Sogum, an older man, worried that I was not going to use the house long enough to get full value from the money I had spent on fish and rice. "It's not like you're going to stay here ten years or something," he said. "You'll spend your money and then go back to America. Who will give you your money back?" Sogum, however, was being overly generous. It would have cost me much more to build the house if I had paid the workers wages. Although I did reciprocate by contributing food when villagers built other houses that year, I contributed only token labor.

In Melanesian societies, many people still do not depend for their livelihoods on selling things, including their labor, in order to buy other things. They produce much of what they need themselves. When they do exchange things with others, the practice is often not sale and purchase, or even barter. Rather, it is what anthropologists often call gift exchange or sociopolitical exchange. The term "gift exchange" tends to obscure the fact that people do expect to get something out of these exchanges, if not immediately then eventually. The term "sociopolitical exchange" emphasizes that in these exchanges people are frequently more interested in creating or maintaining social and political ties than they are in acquiring particular goods.

Much sociopolitical exchange in Melanesia takes place on prescribed special occasions—associated with events like marriage, birth, and death—between prescribed persons. There is also often a great deal of less formal daily give-and-take among kin. In addition, in a society in which most exchange is sociopolitical, people do not work with others in exchange for wages but to fulfill social obligations, usually reciprocal obligations among kin.

One side of all this is the effort to keep up with and control the obligations that receiving gifts creates. I was in Kragur long enough to learn that sometimes it was best to avoid a gift if you could because it put you under obligation to the giver. And the relationships that gift or sociopolitical exchange creates and maintains are not necessarily relationships of warm camaraderie and equality. Gift giving can also be used to dominate and shame others.

But gift giving goes beyond creating, meeting, and maneuvering obligations. Papua New Guineans and Melanesians in general put a great deal of themselves into producing food and may even feel that the spirits of their ancestors permeate the food that is produced on ancestral land or with the ancestors' magical assistance. This, as Bruce Knauft puts it, "makes a gift of food a gift of oneself in a fundamental way." So, people may regard sharing food as creating a bond of bodily and spiritual substance. The obligation to share is part of kinship in Melanesia, but—in a way—sharing food also makes people kin.

The opposite of an economy in which gift or sociopolitical exchange dominates is a commodity economy. In a pure commodity economy virtually everything —including human effort, defined as a commodity called labor—can be bought and sold. Exchange is an impersonal, one-dimensional social relationship, not part of a larger relationship with kinship, religious, political, or other dimensions. In most societies, one finds neither pure gift nor pure commodity economies. There are few places, however, where commodity exchange is as dominant as it is in Western capitalist societies, and few places where gift or sociopolitical exchange is as important as it is in Melanesia.

It has been quite easy in recent decades to find Papua New Guineans apparently throwing themselves enthusiastically into capitalist economic activity, but even here a closer look may reveal something contrasting. Andrew Strathern, for instance, describes the Melpa people's vigorous interest in using the new economic system to make money. However, he observes that they use a great deal of this money to give ceremonial gifts and mount dance displays with the aim of achieving "integration between groups of people" and with "the realm of the sacred." The meaning at the bottom of their economic activity, he argues, "is about as far removed from the capitalist mode of production as it can be."

Anthropologists continue to debate to what extent precolonial economic practices throughout Papua New Guinea resemble those of modern capitalist systems, where commodities clearly rule. Some differences in descriptions of indigenous economic practices in Papua New Guinea may dwell in part in the eye of the beholder. On one hand, anthropologists sometimes revel in discovering ways of living that contrast sharply with those of their home societies. Another kind of distortion sometimes occurs because people born and raised in a capitalist system find it very easy to interpret the behavior of people everywhere in the familiar terms of market calculation, profit seeking, and continuous accumulation of wealth. It also is easy to overextend the metaphorical use of concepts like money, markets, and supply and demand to the point where the metaphor clouds one's vision. It could be tempting, for example, to describe Papua New Guineans' use of material wealth to forge and maintain social relationships and proper relations with the sacred as a way of increasing "social capital" or even "sacred capital." But to do so risks misapprehending a way of life that is truly different in important ways.

In 1975–1976, gift or sociopolitical transactions, not buying and selling, certainly predominated in Kragur. Villagers sometimes told me that "food is our money; you white people have money and we have food," but they were acutely aware of many of the ways in which food and money were different. They knew, as one young man put it, that you could not take a string bag of taro to the Air Niugini office and buy a ticket to Port Moresby, and they knew that white people did not hand out money to relatives and visitors the way villagers gave away food. And even though they had used the currencies of every foreign power that had ruled in the region— Germany, Japan, and Australia—some villagers still seemed to find money rather mysterious. Many were curious about where and how it was made, and some seemed quite sure that it had supernatural origins.

Well into the colonial era, Kragur people were still taking part in an overseas trading circuit that linked it with villages on Wogeo Island, about 12 kilometers (60 miles) northeast of Kairiru, villages along the mainland coast southeast of Kairiru in the Murik Lakes area, and villages between Murik Lakes and Wewak (Map 2). The core of the trade was in specialty products from each area: tobacco from Kairiru, galip nuts (sometimes called canarium almonds or Tahitian chestnuts) from Wogeo, strong and highly decorative baskets from Murik Lakes, and low-fired pottery from the other coastal villages. By the 1970s, no one could give me a detailed description of this trade. Older villagers did say that Kragur participants traded with specific partners on Wogeo and in the other points on the circuit. A Kragur man and his partner assured each other of safety and hospitality in their respective villages, and partnerships could be passed on from generation to generation.

Ian Hogbin observed this trade from Wogeo in the 1930s. Here is how he described the transaction involved:

> The transactions can hardly be called barter as the goods are not exposed and examined, but the returns expected are rather more rigidly fixed than is usual in pure gift exchanges. Thus, if a man hands over a parcel of nuts and requests that he be given tobacco he definitely expects a bundle of a certain size. . . . It is true that if he considers the return gift inadequate he has no direct redress, but in the future he will avoid this particular [trading partner] and make an agreement with someone else.

This is different from the giving and receiving of food in Kragur but still unlike buying and selling in pursuit of profit within a system in which supply and demand set prices. In addition, although Hogbin described this practice only briefly, it appears

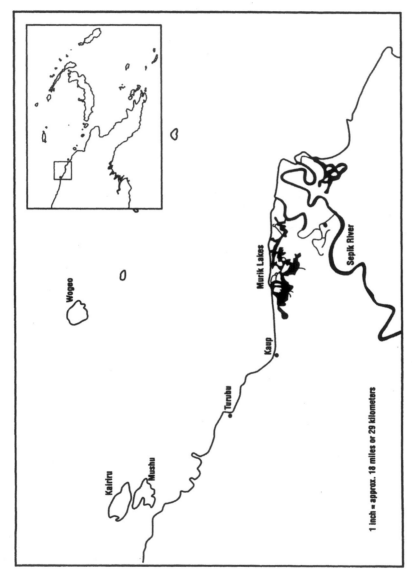

Map 2: Principal places on Kragur's overseas trade route. Regular sea trade among Kairiru, Wogeo, Murik Lakes, Kaup, and Turubu ended long before the time of my first visit to Kragur in the 1970s. (Map by D. Buric)

that, once traders returned home, they distributed the goods they had acquired in accord with the principles of sociopolitical rather than commercial exchange.

The Importance of Land

Kragur's economic life differed from capitalism not only in the forms of trade and exchange. Kragur, like all indigenous Papua New Guinean societies, lacked one key feature of modern capitalism and still does: the separation of producers from the means of production. This separation creates a class of people whose labor is a commodity they must sell to survive. Such is not the case for Kragur people, or most others in Papua New Guinea, because they retain a tight grip on the primary means of production.

The primary means of production in Papua New Guinea were, and still are, the land on which people garden, hunt, and gather, and the reefs and waters of the sea. Although Kragur people make use of the sea, they pay much more attention to land, and, as elsewhere in Papua New Guinea, rights to land depend largely on kinship. That is, they depend on one's relationship to others through descent from a common ancestor or through marriage. In Kragur, when people speak of rights to land they eventually speak of the ancestor who originally cleared, planted, or settled a plot of ground. In defining social affiliations or group membership Kragur people emphasize descent through males (patrilineal descent), so the firmest rights to land are based on direct descent through males from the males who originally cleared, settled, or otherwise used the land in question.

Villagers sometimes speak of the living male descendants of a common male ancestor as though they collectively hold rights to land, but this can be misleading. Such closely related men do not use land collectively; no central authority within such a group allocates rights for gardening plots or other land, and more than one person can have a claim to use a particular plot. Some claims, however, are stronger than others, depending on such factors as degree of relationship to the original user, who has used the land for what and for how long, and some measure of need for land, such as household size.

Descent through women also is relevant to land rights. Although Kragur people place much greater emphasis on descent through males than on female links, one can make a legitimate claim to use land based on, for example, descent from the sister of an ancestral male. Households also may obtain rights to use land from the wife's natal family, provided no one chooses to exercise stronger claims.

In many Papua New Guinean societies people do not treat all land in the same way. As Ann Chowning has written, "It is not uncommon to find distinctions made between gardening land, village land or house sites, and bush land, with different systems of rights applied to each, not to mention the rights that relate to sacred places, grave sites, paths, water supplies, sago swamps, and fishing areas." Further, rights to use trees or other resources on the land may be separable from rights to cultivate a garden or build a house. People also often distinguish between rights to temporary use, such as using land for gardening for a few seasons, and rights to longer-term use, such as cultivating trees that may take years to mature and remain productive for many years more.

Indigenous Papua New Guinea systems of land and resource rights do not provide everyone with equal access to every type of resource. But these so-called customary systems do generally manage to balance access with need, and virtually no one is completely excluded. I can write about indigenous or customary resource rights and tenure systems in the present tense because most land in Papua New Guinea—as much as 99 percent by one estimate—still falls within such systems, guided by unwritten principles and orally transmitted knowledge of the complex histories of particular tracts of land.

There are also, of course, national and provincial laws pertaining to land, but national and provincial governments have limited power to intervene in customary land matters. Under early colonial law it was possible for land to be removed from the customary system to become the object of absolute individual possession, sale, and purchase. Under Australian administration and since self-government and independence, however, land law has tried to guard against removing land from customary tenure while also providing for ways for customary landholders to use land in business—for example, as security for loans—and means of making land available for use by noncustomary investors.

Under current Papua New Guinea law, land held under customary tenure cannot be alienated (that is, removed from the customary system through sale or lease) except to the state. The state, however, must determine that the land "is not required or likely to be required" by the customary landholders, for example, for subsistence. The state has the power to acquire land by compulsion—for example, for public works—but relies largely on agreements with the landholders. One problematic feature of Papua New Guinea law, however, is that the state claims ownership of mineral and petroleum deposits underground. Landowners are entitled to compensation for damage to land or other losses resulting from exploiting these resources, but what constitutes adequate compensation is a question usually fraught with controversy. Still, the overwhelming portion of the country's land remains under customary tenure. This allows people to take part in the capitalist economy —migrating to work for wages or growing crops to sell—without it completely absorbing them.

Money, Time, and the Strangeness of Wage Labor

In my experience, Kragur people do not look at land as impersonal dirt and rocks or as they view the few crops they produce on it for sale. Land for them is not only an economic resource. Clearing land and planting and harvesting crops make concrete villagers' ties with deceased ancestors, with living kin, and with descendants still to come. This is very different from working on a plantation for wages.

Enduring rights to land and other resources have kept the necessity of wage labor in Kragur within narrow limits. In the 1970s, most adult men in Kragur had had some experience in working for wages on coconut or cacao plantations, in gold mines, as construction workers, and in a variety of other capacities, but they were not part of a working class. Wage labor was not an absolute necessity because they still could produce most of the basic necessities of life on their own land and in their own seas, and could earn a few kina producing copra or selling garden produce in the market. They exchanged unpaid labor with their kin when tasks required more labor than a single household could muster.

After decades of sporadic involvement in wage labor, many Kragur men, and the few women with wage-work experience, still found working for money in the European or white man's style rather peculiar, and in some important respects repellent. In 1975–1976, I made a point of talking with as many villagers as possible about their experiences as wage workers and asking them how wage work differed from the work they did in the village. I did not have to prod them to expand on this theme. Many spoke with distaste of how strictly regimented most wage work was, how the boss was always telling you what to do, and how in many jobs you did the same thing all day, day after day. On plantations you also had to do everything on a strict schedule, marked by the sounding of the plantation bell: get up in the morning, eat breakfast, start work, break for lunch, finish work.

The fact that Kragur people did not have to sell their labor had a lot to do with their characteristic indifference to time and their dislike of being pressed into rigid time schedules. When leaders in Kragur occasionally complained, usually to no effect, about wasting time, they had to do so in Tok Pisin. There is no noun analogous to the English noun "time" in the Kairiru language. In Kragur, people had always organized their activities by reference to the passage of the sun and other natural phenomena, and in 1975–1976 most still did so, even though a few wore wristwatches. Most villagers did not think of labor in terms of time or of time in terms of money, and it would have been difficult to propose that equation in the Kairiru language. People in industrial capitalist societies tend to take this equation for granted because they are long accustomed to buying and selling labor—for most of us, selling it—and to the detailed means of measuring and organizing labor time that have spread from the workplace into life in general.

When working in the gardens, the sago stands, or the village, even in communal endeavors, Kragur people tended to begin tasks or stop to rest as they pleased, each person working at his or her own pace. Leaders sometimes complained loudly and publicly that people were not working hard enough or even that they were "wasting time," but this never went down well. On one such occasion, some of the men and women who had assembled to begin a day of communal work in response to the summons of the village councillor began to grumble quietly as the councillor's deputy carried on rather too long with complaints that they had not come promptly when he rang the village bell that morning. Finally, Brawaung, never a shrinking violet, burst out loudly: "This is wrong! We're not pigs! We're not dogs! We know how to work!"

These words crossed my mind during tedious executive monologues at many staff meetings during my corporate years, and I longed to sling my ax over my shoulder, turn my back on the meeting, and stride off up the mountain, as Brawaung had done. But I had little to fall back on if I lost my job. In Kragur, there were ways to exert social pressure on those who did not pull their weight in communal endeavors, and powerful magicians, if angered, could damage crops. No one in Kragur, however, had the power over another villager's livelihood that the boss of a factory or an office worker in Australia or the United States has over an employee. When Kragur people talked about change, this aspect of life in so-called developed societies —that is, the great vulnerability of the employee completely dependent on his or her pay—never entered their visions, and some would have found it difficult even to imagine.

Kragur villagers' attitudes toward time and their independence in work were possible because land and labor were not commodities to be bought and sold. Instead, land, labor, and the products of labor were deeply enmeshed in a system of noncommercial exchange that both shaped and expressed their ongoing mutual obligations. What distinguished this way of life from capitalism was not just a different system for distributing goods or allocating rights to resources, but a different conception of the moral significance of material goods and resources. It was these moral issues that truly complicated villagers' relationship with the ways of the European world.

Money and the Moral Puzzle of Prosperity

"Money makes you a man. If you have nothing, like
me, you'll be rubbish forever. If you have a hundred
or a thousand in the bank, then you're a man."
(*Mani i mekim yu man. Yu stap nating, olosem mi,
yu stap rabis yet oltaim oltaim. Yu gat handet, tausen
samting i stap long beng, em yu man.*)
—A Kragur villager, 1976

"This money isn't something you can take and show
to God and he'll say you can enter heaven!"
(*Dispela mani i no samting yu kisim yu go soim
long God em i tok yu kam insait long heven!*)
—Another Kragur villager, 1976

In 1975–1976, Kragur villagers' deep roots in a world in which few things were bought and sold did not mean that money and business had no place in their emerging ideas about the good life. Their significance, however, was far from settled. By the 1970s, European colonization, Catholic missionaries, and the growing influence of capitalist economic institutions had raised unusually pointed questions about the nature of the good life. Villagers were especially troubled by their poverty in comparison with whites or Europeans. Given a homegrown tendency to assume that material wealth was evidence of virtue, their comparative poverty raised many questions in Kragur people's minds. Were Europeans better people than they were? Were the principles of business a new kind of morality? Was Catholic morality a way to make money? Would making more money make them better people? Could they find a place in the new world of money and business and still remain good people in any familiar way?

Villagers' talk usually focused on less abstract issues like how to organize copra production, why a charter-boat business had failed, or whether they should buy and sell betel nut or tobacco among themselves. Behind these more specific questions, however, loomed larger quandaries. Kragur people were not alone in this. For decades, throughout Papua New Guinea people have felt ever-increasing tension between the possibilities they see in the money economy and the pull of familiar forms of social and economic relations based on kinship and noncommercial exchange. This tension is, as Bruce Knauft puts it, "currently at the heart of cultural contestation" in Melanesia in general. The possibilities that Melanesians see in money, however, often have moral as well as material dimensions.

Questions about money, business, and morality in Kragur were not only complicated, they were also highly controversial. I am sure many people sat alone and pondered them, but they also argued with each other loudly and publicly. These disagreements were not as simple as contests between old and new ideas and values. Kragur people were attracted to new ways in part because they saw in them means of pursuing familiar and honored values—in particular, their Good Way. But common allegiance to Kragur's Good Way could not forestall disagreement and debate, because the Good Way had no precise, authoritative definition. People agreed on the importance of some very general values—especially social harmony and generosity. But precisely what these values meant in specific instances was open to disagreement, just as in the United States virtually everyone would say he or she values freedom and democracy, but much of our politics is a continuing debate about what these ideas actually mean in practice.

There was a contrapuntal theme in Kragur people's attitudes toward money that became more evident the longer I stayed in the village. People who, on one occasion, would wax eloquent on their indifference to money, on another would complain bitterly of how hard it was to obtain any in Kragur. A few questioned me intently about stories they had heard of magical means of obtaining money, and there was a constant rumble of interest in finding a way to earn cash that was more reliable and less onerous than copra production.

It was impossible, however, for villagers to think about money for long without considering how it fit in with the values of generosity and social harmony. These values carried a great deal of weight in Kragur, but contact with the European world had deeply influenced the form they took in the 1970s and had opened them to new interpretations. To complicate things further, disagreements about the proper role of money in Kragur had pronounced political dimensions.

Generous People

Over the years, villagers had observed that Europeans not only had a great deal of money, they were not very generous with it. Such lack of generosity violated an important Kragur value. To give things away, ostensibly without thought of return, was known in Tok Pisin as *givim fri* (to give freely) or *givim nating* (to give [expecting] nothing). According to some villagers, Kragur people had been giving things away in this fashion since long before they heard of dollars or kina. Villagers' allegiance to generosity, however, was not a simple thing.

I could never say that Kragur people were not generous, for they have shown me outstanding hospitality. Nevertheless, the indigenous gift-giving system drew some of its strength from self-interest and fear. Generosity brought respect and could enhance prestige, but failure eventually to return the generosity of others could be downright dangerous. As I listened to public disputes and efforts to discover the grievances that had brought down the wrath of an ancestral ghost it was very clear that failure to fulfill others' expectations of generosity—for example, not distributing the fish one caught to those who felt they deserved a share, or not contributing to a feast given by someone who had contributed to your feast—was a good way to anger people.

Nevertheless, villagers sometimes liked to claim that Kragur's economic practices flowed from pure springs of compassion. When explaining to me villagers' aversion to buying and selling, one strong proponent of the noncommercial ethic said, "We don't sell things for money; we just try to help people." Often, Kragur villagers seemed to strain to etch the boldest possible contrast with Europeans. Several villagers, for instance, told me they had observed that Europeans would not even give food and shelter to their own siblings without asking for money in return.

Elaborating such contrasts made Kragur look like a "pure" gift economy and Europeans seem almost pathologically impersonal and obsessed with money. Several factors could account for this claim of radical difference. Nicholas Thomas has observed that when Pacific Islanders encountered Europeans' novel economic practices and relations—for example, when working as indentured plantation laborers or migrant wageworkers—they were able for the first time to see their own practices as they might appear from the outside and in contrast with a truly different system. In representing their own practices, they then tended to emphasize those aspects that differed most radically from their new point of comparison. (Thomas calls the understandings of their own cultures that Pacific Islanders have created in this way "neotraditional.")

I think that another process was also at work in Kragur. While the European colonial hand did not rest as heavily on Papua New Guinea as it did on Africa, the Americas, or even other parts of the Pacific, even a comparatively mild colonial rule assaults a colonized people's feelings of self-worth. Many Kragur people probably felt the need to assert their moral equality with Europeans, even their moral superiority to them. Exaggerating the contrast between indigenous and European economic practices and finding indigenous practices morally superior might have been one way to do this.

It also might have been a way to claim some virtue *within* the dominant European world, for many villagers thought that too much concern with money was incompatible with the religion of the Europeans: Catholicism. Some told me that missionaries had preached to them that God favored the poor and that excessive concern with wealth was sinful. Ibor himself often preached that preoccupation with money could stand in the way of salvation; but just how much was too much remained an open question, and Ibor himself was more deeply involved in monetary endeavors than most of his fellow villagers.

There were other complexities as well in this already rather convoluted scene. I am quite certain that some villagers suspected that being good Catholics by not pursuing money might in the long run bring them even greater material rewards. I think some believed that the final reward for being loyal Catholics would be knowledge of the magical secrets that had made the Europeans themselves so wealthy. The idea that European wealth had magical origins was consistent with the indigenous assumption that achieving prosperity required having good relations with the supernatural. Achieving prosperity also required good social relations among living men and women; but just as the encounter with the European world had influenced ideas about generosity, so it had complicated ideas about social harmony.

Prosperity and Harmony

In the 1970s, Kragur villagers often spoke of their desire for such things as a more reliable food supply, better health, more durable houses made of concrete and corrugated iron, piped-in water, electric lights, and more money. But any ambitions for raising cash incomes or participating more successfully in the market economy presented problems. Although Kragur is not far as the crow flies from Wewak, transportation between the north coast of Kairiru and the mainland was poor, especially during the monsoon season when high winds and rough seas could force small boats to lie ashore for days at a time. In addition, most adult villagers were only marginally literate or numerate and knew little of how to run a business. They had experimented with a variety of small business ventures other than copra production, but most of these had been ephemeral. I examined the written records of a few of these businesses and found them haphazardly kept. The proprietors could not have known if they were turning a profit or losing their shirts.

Ambitions for material improvement and better health, however, were not all. Kragur people wanted other things as well. In particular, many wanted to live together in greater harmony. They valued social harmony in itself, but they also believed that they had to live together more harmoniously in order to achieve health and prosperity. In turn, it appeared that many villagers valued health and prosperity in part because these states encouraged social harmony, and they seemed to feel that social harmony was difficult to achieve in the absence of shared material well-being. Unfortunately, this description, sufficiently complicated as it is, probably distorts reality by breaking a seamless ball of aspirations into discrete parts. Kragur people often acted and spoke as though there were no such clear distinctions.

What I observed in 1975–1976, however, was not an unaltered precolonial culture. The advent of Catholicism had probably encouraged the concern with social harmony. Laura Nader has argued that the form of Christianity that spread along with European colonial empires may have helped to create ideologies of social harmony that anthropologists later would encounter and "attribute to the natives." In Kragur, villagers probably took an active part in such a creation. If they suspected that the religion of the Europeans was the path to mastery of all things European, it would have exacerbated the tendency to meld issues of morality and prosperity, and endowed teachings of Christian brotherhood and compassion with special meaning and appeal.

The deep concern with social harmony that I found in Kragur in the 1970s also may have derived some of its energy from the village's history of involvement in what have come to be known as "cargo cults." As with the *tamabaran* institution, it is less prejudicial to speak of "cargo religions" or "cargo movements" rather than cargo cults. These are a kind of religious belief and ritual, common in Papua New Guinea, that promises access to supernatural sources of wealth, deliverance from injustice and hardship, and communion with the ancestors. In the colonial era, the wealth that believers sought was the cargo (*kago* in Tok Pisin) they had seen ships and planes deliver to the Europeans; and they believed that with access to the cargo would come political and economic equality with Europeans. Cargo rituals often address dead ancestors, who it is thought can deliver the cargo if properly approached. Participants often believe that the success of the ritual depends on their demonstrating to watching supernatural beings their unity of purpose.

By 1975–1976, cargo rituals and theologies had been part of Kragur's world for decades. A 1946 Australian government patrol report spoke of a group led by a Mushu Island man, Lalau, who allegedly committed suicide in order to visit the dead and hasten the delivery of the cargo. Kragur people also were aware of at least two more enduring movements: the Yali movement, centered in the neighboring province of Madang, and the Peli Association, centered in the mainland East Sepik Province. Kragur people themselves had taken part in only two instances of cargo activity of which I knew. In one of these, prior to World War II, a number of young men from Kragur are said to have joined ritual marching in imitation of European soldiers in another north coast village. Villagers also told me that many of them took part in rituals in Kragur in the early 1970s, meeting in the cemetery to say the rosary and petition their deceased kin to send the cargo. Not everyone took part, and the rituals petered out when some became concerned that they might have caused an outbreak of illness in the village. Villagers were seeking the help of the dead, but they knew that the dead could also be dangerous and unpredictable.

Why did Kragur people indulge in this kind of activity? In some ways it was not too great a departure from normal practices, for both magic and the goodwill of the dead were important to routine food production. Many anthropologists have emphasized that cargo beliefs take this and other common Melanesian cultural patterns to the extreme, and have argued that the stresses the social disruption of colonialism placed on Melanesians probably helped to precipitate this extremism.

Christianity also helped to nurture cargo religion in many instances, as it apparently did in Kragur, where people prayed to the Virgin Mary and the dead in tandem. Belief in the millennium, when Christ will return to overturn evil and rule for a thousand years, has played an important part in the history of Christianity. Any hints of that in early mission teachings might well have encouraged a colonized people to seek their own millennium. The German missionaries who first brought Christianity to the Sepik undoubtedly preached about the glorious rewards to be found in heaven. I do not think, however, that Kragur people had an indigenous notion of reward or punishment in an afterlife. In the 1970s, despite decades of hearing about heaven and hell, villagers still encountered the ghosts of the dead haunting the precincts of the village. As one man put it, "If they have somewhere to go, then why don't they go there?" It should not be surprising that some Kragur people sought their salvation and reward in the here and now.

There is an irrational element in cargo beliefs, especially when belief in the imminence of salvation persists in the face of repeated disappointments. But the social and cultural upheaval that helps to precipitate cargo activity does not go away when hopes are dashed, and, as Ted Schwartz suggests, the excitement of it all may be its own reward for some believers. It is not fundamentally more irrational, however, to hope for glorious supernatural rewards during one's lifetime than it is to hope for the same after one dies, although in the former case, of course, more people will notice if you are mistaken. And though the details of cargo religion are vividly Melanesian, what are sometimes called millenarian, millennial, or messianic religious movements have appeared all over the world throughout human history. Supernaturally flavored visions of America are found in some Melanesian cargo beliefs; but this is only fair, for, as theologian Harvey Cox points out, Americans themselves "have always had a stronger than average dose of millennialism in their veins."

Observing the zeal with which some Kragur people pursued regimens of Catholic worship and ceremony in 1975–1976, I suspected that at least some worshippers still cherished the hopes that had drawn them to pray and petition the dead in the cemetery a few years before. I also suspected that the concern for harmony villagers so often expressed might rest in part on the hope that either Maria or the dead ancestors would approve and send the cargo.

It was clear that several influences shaped villagers' concern with harmony in the 1970s: indigenous beliefs, Christianity, the extreme promises of cargo religion, and the hopes and fears aroused by independence. But the basic assumption that many of life's problems have their origins in human discord had deep roots, even if many streams had watered them in the colonial era. Villagers were neither averse to public arguments nor timid about expressing their feelings, but they feared the anger that smoldered and lay hidden. I heard this fear expressed in many quiet conversations around cooking fires and saw it in the anxiety many villagers showed when engaged in some activity that might, if mishandled, make others angry.

It is hard to write about Kragur beliefs about social harmony and material well-being without seeming to emphasize people's concerns with wealth and health. I should stress again that villagers valued good health and material plenty partly because these conditions made it easier to live in comparative harmony with each other. Much of living harmoniously in Kragur had to do with meeting obligations to share food with kin or contribute to feasts marking such important events as marriages and deaths. Plenty of fish or garden produce meant people could meet such obligations easily. Prosperity and good health also showed that the village was relatively free of dangerous and antisocial hidden anger, reducing fear and suspicion in daily life and making it easier to smile upon one's neighbors.

Muddying the Waters

While Kragur villagers shared a general assumption that people had to cultivate good social relations in order to enjoy more general well-being and vice versa, there was often plenty of room for disagreement on exactly what constituted good social relations in particular cases. When they gathered to cure illness, for example, village men not only had to determine who was angry about what, they often had to debate the finer points of social conduct and obligation. Some points were not so fine. For example, there was wide agreement in Kragur that villagers should cooperate with each other, and both village leaders and their followers used similar language to praise and advocate cooperation. It was obvious, however, that rank-and-file villagers had different ideas than their leaders about what this meant in practice. Leaders, for instance, regarded heeding *their* demands as a defining feature of a cooperative village, while many of the rank and file thought the leaders themselves sometimes failed at cooperation by placing their personal ambitions ahead of the collective welfare. Such a circumstance, of course, is nothing unusual. Years later, I recalled this form of Kragur disagreement vividly as I sat in corporate staff meetings listening to company executives call fervently for "teamwork." To these company executives, teamwork usually meant doing what *they* asked without question or complaint.

I first lived in Kragur in an era when questions of correct conduct had become especially complicated. Decades of involvement with European government, business, and religious institutions had exposed Kragur people to new ways of organizing social relations and to novel ideas about what good social relations are. Villagers also had seen that Europeans enjoyed a remarkable material standard of living. It was hard for many of them to avoid concluding that there must be something especially good about the European way of living together.

Over and over again—in public meetings, private conversations, and casual remarks—I heard villagers invoke the need for greater harmony, cooperation, or unity when they spoke of what it would take to make Kragur a better place to live. I also observed their preoccupation with what they saw as their inferiority to Europeans in this regard. For example, some told me that whites or Europeans settled their disputes more readily than Papua New Guineans, were less prone to jealousy over women, were more moderate in their drinking, and cooperated spontaneously in work and business in ways Papua New Guineans could not. For example, villagers observed that the authority of the "boss" kept workers in line on the plantations and in the mines where they had labored for Europeans. But some assumed that when Europeans worked with other Europeans, their punctual and coordinated efforts were the spontaneous result of their harmonious spirit. This habit of seeing Europeans as more cooperative and harmonious complicated the speculation and debate about the means and the propriety of entering more deeply into the world of money and business.

By 1975–1976, there had been much experimentation with small business in Kragur. It was one of several Kairiru villages that had combined in the early 1960s to invest in a boat to carry passengers between the islands and the mainland, but this venture had failed. Several villagers had opened small stores, although when I first arrived in late 1975 there was only one. Two more opened in 1976, but by the time I returned in 1981 both had closed: the owner of one had died and the other store had gone broke. In 1976, a small group of kin was planning a piggery, financed by a migrant relative, but by 1981 little had been accomplished. In 1981, someone had started selling kerosene, also with financial backing from a migrant relative, and a few men were talking about getting a license to sell beer. In the 1970s, villagers initiated at least two village-wide business efforts: a village development fund and the Village Development Youth Club. The latter had obtained a government grant for a boat to carry garden produce to the mainland for sale. These efforts were still alive but dormant in 1981. According to correspondence with villagers, within a few years the fund was dissolved and the youth club existed in name only.

As I noted earlier, there were plenty of reasons for business ventures in Kragur to fail. Nevertheless, Kragur people often explained these failures as the consequence of inadequate social harmony. As some put it, "We aren't unified yet," "We don't have good cooperation," and—in the English of a returned migrant—"People are still wild." Many also clearly assumed that whites or Europeans were more successful in business in part, perhaps a large part, because they *were* unified and cooperative. Needless to say, this assumption bathed the grittier realities of life in a society dominated by money and capitalist markets in a deceptively rosy light. It also heightened rather than diminished interest in attaining greater social harmony, and it threw into the ring new ideas, drawn from European examples, of just what social harmony entailed.

To live in harmony with others in indigenous terms was, among other things, to give generously to your kin, meet obligations to give on formal occasions, and help your kin to meet their gift-giving obligations. It also meant helping your kin with their work and contributing your labor to the many tasks undertaken communally. To fail to meet such obligations or to be stingy with your kin was very bad manners. It was also dangerous, because it could arouse anger and tempt illness or other misfortunes. Yet villagers were well aware that European life (some Catholic Mission personnel excepted) revolved around money and buying and selling goods and labor.

The importance of money in the contemporary world was impossible to ignore; it was at the core of a new kind of prosperity. Given the prevailing tendency to associate prosperity with living in harmony with both other people and the supernatural world, villagers' lack of money was a nagging suggestion that they were not as good as they might be. True, the rampant commercialism of European society was at odds with long-standing Kragur notions of the right way to live; but the association of buying and selling with a novel and impressive degree of prosperity seemed to give it moral luster in some villagers' eyes. To cloud things further, the European example itself was not consistent. Catholicism seemed to advocate a kind of generosity and lack of concern with money that Kragur people found very similar to their indigenous notions; but secular European institutions were dramatically different.

All of this was the source of considerable perplexity. The confusion one young man ascribed to others was evident in his own words. Even as he advocated changing village economic practices, he paid tribute to potentially contradictory moral standards. "We young people should do as the Australians do," he told me. "When someone comes to the village we can't just give things to them. They should pay rent and things like that. We Kragur people are good people, we're generous and helpful. I think the people of my village are good people, but they're a little mixed up too." On another occasion, in a public meeting, a middle-aged village leader showed similarly mixed feelings. He spoke forcefully for curtailing the generosity to visitors on which many villagers prided themselves in favor of finding cash markets for their surplus garden produce. In the midst of his plea, however, he could not resist pointing out Kragur's moral superiority to other villages precisely because of its people's gift-giving habits. "It's a good way!" he declared. "This way is only found in our village, not in other villages! They've all changed completely! But it doesn't work. . . ."

The Politics of Money

Villagers' judgments of differing views of the good life and how to attain it had long-term consequences for everyone. They also had immediate political significance in contests for prestige and influence. It would have been hard to understand much of the advocacy and argument I heard in Kragur if I had not recognized this political dimension. For example, by the 1970s all Kragur people considered themselves Catholics, but some had carved out small spheres of influence practicing and promoting Catholic prayer and ritual. In some cases they had attained levels of influence probably closed to them in other areas of endeavor. Of these people, some worried that too much concern with money could distract people from Catholicism. They did not say so, but growing interest in money also could have undermined their own stature and influence.

Some villagers clearly sought influence as vocal advocates of business. Talk in public meetings often turned to the lack of money in Kragur, and some men often rose to suggest that they would do better to sell whatever garden produce, betel nut, and tobacco they could spare rather than giving gifts to visitors from other villages and sharing with fellow villagers. Some periodically proposed that Kragur establish a regular market at which people from Kragur and neighboring villages could buy and sell things. At the time, nothing came of these proposals. But anyone who could have put more money in people's pockets by implementing such measures might have gained considerable prestige and influence.

The average woman may have been less inclined than the average man to cast her lot too decisively with the money economy. Some women made it clear that they regarded relying too much on money as a threat to the food security their gardens provided. For instance, one woman—suggesting distrust of men as well as markets—told me that life in town was harder than life in the village because in town you had no garden and only the husband worked for money. "When [the money] is gone," she asked, "where do you get your food?"

Generational conflict also entered into the controversy over the role money should play in village life, a controversy to which my own presence in Kragur contributed. I had been in the village for several months before one youth told me that he and a number of other young men would have been happy to accept my offer to pay wages for building my house but the leaders had ruled against it. The leaders he referred to, all middle-aged and older men, could have had a number of motives. They were more steeped in the norms of a nonmonetary society and an indigenized version of Catholicism than the younger generation. Even had they self-consciously calculated the best way to exploit me as a resource, they would have been inclined to do so in an older, nonmonetary way by enmeshing me in a net of reciprocal obligation. Ruling out the wage option, however, also kept the situation firmly in the hands of the older leaders and reminded the young of their elders' power.

The fact that Kragur people could turn to no single definitive example of the proper way to deal with money left ample room for rhetorical maneuvering on the village political stage. Buying and selling among themselves violated long-standing norms, yet it apparently contributed to the material well-being of Europeans, suggesting that it had something to do with social harmony and moral merit. Even so, some Catholic teachings and practices seemed to support the virtue of the old ways. One could invoke the virtues of unity and harmony to both advocate and oppose pursuing money more energetically.

It was apparent that many villagers were ambivalent about and some opposed to expanding the role of money in Kragur. But interest in doing so would not die. The desire for money seems quite natural to people of societies where money economies are well established. In Kragur, money was still relatively unfamiliar and, for many, carried the taint of unseemly and dangerous selfishness. It also, however, had many uses and was clearly an attribute of social standing in the larger world that was encroaching on Kragur. In that world, as one villager put it, "Money makes you a man." Add this perception to villagers' tendency to associate monetary wealth with a new kind and degree of moral achievement—perhaps a new and better kind of social harmony—and you have a potent mix. This mix fired intense interest in money even as it kindled debate and confusion about the nature of the good life and what kind of future to pursue.

To Papua New Guinea for the World Bank

"Poor Papua New Guinea."

—A Kragur villager (in English), in the 1990s

When I finished my dissertation and received my degree in 1978, academic jobs for people with Ph.D.s in cultural anthropology were drying up and disappearing like dust-bowl farms. I did find a university teaching post, but it was part-time and temporary. I hung on in a series of such jobs until 1983, when I reached the absolute nadir of my career and enrolled in a master of business administration program at a large Midwestern university. I tried hard to get into the spirit of the thing, but it was not my cup of tea. Long before I could complete the program, a public policy consulting firm offered me a job and I took it, even though my first impression of the firm was rather surreal. Arriving for an interview, I encountered such a spectacle of fat pompous men in gray suits, waited upon by deferential underlings, that I nearly bolted for the open air.

I worked at the consulting firm for almost ten years, but the job and I never came to comfortable terms. It was interesting to observe life in business and government circles and compare their customs with those of the academic world. (I can report that all are equally peculiar in their own ways.) Upper management at the firm, however, loved too much the trappings of corporate hierarchy and suffered from a nagging fear that their employees were not working hard enough.

Discontent with this atmosphere and scarce employment options drove me to seek escape by spending my weekends writing *Hard Times on Kairiru Island*. Concern that the work I had done in Papua New Guinea not go to waste and a desire to leave a modest mark on the anthropological landscape also pushed me along. The book finally came out in the spring of 1994. I had married—again—just before finishing the book, and just after it came out I resigned from my job and moved to the Washington, D.C., area, where my wife was employed and I was going to look for more congenial work.

Getting Back to Wewak

Since returning from Papua New Guinea at the end of 1976 I had kept an eye open for opportunities to go back. In the eyes of some of my friends who had never been bitten by the anthropology bug, this did not show the best judgment. Wracking bouts of malaria followed me home from Manus in 1973, and I had returned from Kragur when I did in 1976 partly because repeated bouts of dengue fever—leaving in their wake deep, intractable skeletal aches and chills—had exhausted me.

I managed a brief trip to Papua New Guinea, including a visit to Kragur, in 1981 in connection with a conference sponsored by the Papua New Guinea Institute of Applied Social and Economic Research. A consulting assignment for the U.S. Agency for International Development in 1989 took me to Papua New Guinea and several other Pacific Island countries. I came tantalizingly close to Wewak, but it was impossible to arrange a detour. After finishing *Hard Times*, I was especially keen to visit Kragur again, but I doubted that this would coordinate easily with making a living.

To my surprise, the first work I found in the Washington area called for experience in the Pacific Islands. This was a temporary position in Conservation International's forest conservation programs in Papua New Guinea and neighboring Pacific countries. Working at Conservation International put me in regular touch with news from Papua New Guinea, and the news was not good. Industrial logging was tearing out irreplaceable tracts of rainforest at a frightening pace. (This was transpiring even though by law no such logging can take place without the approval and participation of the indigenous landowners.) In addition, the government was teetering on the edge of bankruptcy and was negotiating an Economic Recovery Program (ERP) loan from the World Bank.

More through dumb luck than skillful networking (a chance connection to a member of the bank staff through a friend of a friend of my wife's), shortly after leaving Conservation International I landed a consulting assignment in Papua New Guinea for the World Bank. My job was to put flesh on the bones of a plan to provide grants to nongovernment organizations (NGOs) engaged in rural development activities. The term NGO referred to a variety of nonprofit organizations, ranging from branches of worldwide organizations, such as World Vision International or Conservation International, to national religious organizations, such as Catholic Health Services, to organizations of more local scope, such as a community theater group in Madang Province, a women's council serving the East Sepik Province, or even groups representing single communities. The program was not part of the bundle of actions that the Papua New Guinea government was required to undertake to qualify for the ERP loan. In fact, the bank wanted the program to be as independent as possible from government agencies, and NGOs themselves were to take a large role in its administration. My job was to talk with NGOs in Papua New

Guinea about the proposed program, gauge their interest, solicit their ideas on how such a program might be administered, and prepare a draft design.

In Papua New Guinea in 1995, government support for programs to improve rural living standards had virtually disappeared in many areas. The bank staff I worked with hoped the NGO grant program could help NGOs fill some of the gaps left by the failure of government assistance. Some at the bank undoubtedly also hoped that giving money to NGOs would have public relations benefits, since many NGOs were among the most vocal critics of the ERP loan conditions. Nevertheless, it looked like a reasonable idea in itself.

I had a lot of freedom to plan my itinerary in Papua New Guinea. Fortunately, Wewak was the home of some NGOs worthy of a visit, so I would at least have a chance to see Kragur people living in town. If I was lucky, I might be able to make a quick trip to the island. This was a happy thought, but I also was acutely aware that this opportunity to revisit the site of *Hard Times on Kairiru Island* was the result of the hard times then afflicting all of Papua New Guinea.

Gloomy Independence

It was a distressing irony that in 1995, as Papua New Guinea looked abroad for urgently needed aid, the country was celebrating the twentieth anniversary of its independence. Papua New Guinea had attained independence less than one hundred years after formal annexation by foreign powers. The entire island of which Papua New Guinea now occupies the eastern half is often called New Guinea, sometimes making descriptions of shifting colonial and national boundaries a bit confusing. The Netherlands claimed the western half of the island in 1828 as part of the Dutch East Indies. (This is now the Indonesian province of Papua, formerly Irian Jaya.) No foreign power, however, laid a claim on any part of the eastern half until Germany declared the northern section, also sometimes known simply as New Guinea, a protectorate in 1884 and allowed the German New Guinea Company to administer it in the company's commercial interests. The same year, Great Britain declared a protectorate over the southern section of the eastern half of the island, known as Papua. In 1888, Great Britain made Papua a Crown Colony, and in 1899 Germany made its New Guinea protectorate an imperial colony.

Britain soon handed its colony over to Australia—in 1906, only five years after Australia's own confederation—and it became the Territory of Papua. When war broke out in 1914, Australia took over German New Guinea, later receiving a League of Nations mandate to administer the former German colony. Until the outbreak of World War II, Australia maintained separate administrations in Papua and New Guinea. Japan invaded and occupied large parts of coastal New Guinea in 1942, and Australia consolidated administration of its remaining territory under a single military government.

After the war, in 1946, Papua and New Guinea became the Trust Territory of Papua and New Guinea, governed by Australia as trustee of the United Nations. The trusteeship called for Australia to prepare the territory for self-government and independence and to promote the economic and social welfare and advancement of the people. Both the United Nations and indigenous political activists soon began pressing Australia to move toward granting independence. Indigenous political agitation, however, came nowhere near constituting a mass movement. In the words of Stephan Pokawin, a Papua New Guinean scholar, "Independence for PNG . . . was not the result of national consensus. The majority of Papua New Guineans were either not concerned, against, or not committed. . . . Many people were not sure of what independence would bring for them and the country." Papua New Guinea became self-governing in 1973, with Australia retaining authority over its foreign affairs, and fully independent on September 15, 1975.

In 1995, as the country prepared to celebrate the anniversary of its independence, not only was it having to turn to the World Bank to help it out of its financial difficulties, but there seemed to be little to show for twenty years of self-rule. Prime Minister Julius Chan, in a speech marking the occasion, made the less-than-inspiring assertion that the situation was "by no means . . . unsalvageable," and Sir Michael Somare, who had led the push for self-rule and become the country's first prime minister, stated flatly that its people were "worse off than they were at the time of independence."

Unfortunately, by some measures he was correct. A number of crucial aspects of health status, for example, were stagnating or deteriorating. The infant mortality rate declined dramatically between 1966 and 1980—from 150 deaths per thousand live births to 72—but rose again to 84 deaths per thousand live births by 1994. Malaria had become a more serious problem since independence. Average life expectancy at birth in 1970 (49 years for men and 51 years for women) was significantly higher than it had been just after World War II (when it was estimated at 32 years for men and 31 years for women), but it hardly improved at all from 1970 to 1990, when it was estimated at 52 years for men and 51 years for women. Such average life expectancies at birth, in part the result of high infant mortality, were significantly lower than in a number of other Pacific countries. The whole sorry health situation was in large part the result of the decline of rural primary health-care services. In 1994, the minister of health announced that the nation's health infrastructure had collapsed and that as many as 60 percent of health facilities in the provinces were closed or without staff, medicines, or equipment.

The problems with health services were part of a larger failure of rural public services. Public employees themselves complained that they did not have the resources to serve rural areas, but some observers felt that they were rather too comfortable with their situation. John Connell, an Australian scholar of Papua New Guinea's "struggle for development," concluded that "bureaucrats have sought their personal development by becoming 'desk jockeys' in the urban centres and the public service has increasingly tended to service itself rather than the public." Many rural people I spoke with shared this dim view.

How the country came to this point of economic crisis is not a simple story of heroes and villains. Virtual withdrawal of the government from the countryside, bureaucracies isolated from the people, and desperate reliance on foreign assistance were certainly not what the leaders of the fledgling country had intended two decades before. In the years just preceding and following independence, planners, politicians, and public figures tried to articulate development goals that were tailored to Papua New Guinea and that would help it avoid some of the worst features of development in other new countries. Such unfortunate features included neglect of the rural masses, increasing inequality, and growing foreign control of the economy. What happened?

The international balance of political and economic power is often unfriendly to struggling new countries. Some scholars have argued that this international environment has been at the heart of Papua New Guinea's failure to thrive. Others argue that successive Papua New Guinea governments have had opportunities to shape an economy less vulnerable to external forces but have ignored them. Independent Papua New Guinea inherited an economy heavily dependent on mining and petroleum production. But it seems plain that after independence the returns from these industries were not used to promote other sectors of the economy in ways that would have spread the wealth and made the economy more stable. Hence, falling prices for the country's key exports and the closure of the massive Bougainville copper mine shook the economy at the beginning of the 1990s, starting the slide to crisis.

John Connell observes that, like the lopsided development of the economy, independent Papua New Guinea inherited other unfortunate trends. Colonial rule in Papua New Guinea had been relatively benign and left the indigenous economy largely intact. Yet it also did little to extend modern infrastructure into the hinterlands or build new national economic and political institutions. In addition, the Australian administration set the pattern for the postindependence tendency to concentrate public investment and public services in urban areas, more accessible rural areas, and regions already enjoying greater prosperity. It also set in motion a tendency for development programs to favor individuals already more successful than their fellows in the new economy.

The increasing inequality that such policies helped foster is one of the most depressing aspects of postindependence Papua New Guinea. Women have fared especially poorly. The nature of both indigenous and colonial societies placed men in a better position to take advantage of new opportunities to gain wealth and influence in the colonial and postcolonial eras, and indigenous cultural values have impelled them more strongly than women to do so. Some observers blame contemporary discrimination against women—including a serious problem of violence against them—almost exclusively on the effects of colonialism. This position, however, disregards the patriarchal nature of many indigenous societies and its manifestation in the attitudes of many contemporary men.

Other forms of growing inequality owe much to the colonial era, but they thrive on the willingness of more fortunate Papua New Guineans to perpetuate them. It was not very long ago that white colonial administrators lived in a world set starkly apart from the world of "natives." But many Papua New Guineans who have taken over government, moved into the professions, and become successful in business have all too easily replicated the same pattern, maintaining and increasing their distance from the mass of the population. In 1995, the speeding new car that enveloped in dust the pedestrians along the Port Moresby roadside usually carried members of parliament or Papua New Guinean business elites, not colonial officials or foreign planters.

Papua New Guinea Welcomes the World Bank

The traveler arriving in Port Moresby in mid-1995 would have seen little obvious evidence of the severity of the country's problems. Jackson International Airport looked no worse than usual. Efforts to repair streets and clean up roadsides to charm the foreign dignitaries coming for Independence Day celebrations even had the town looking a bit tidier than usual. Evidence of one growing problem, however, did stand out. Everywhere, high fences and security guards holding large, fierce-looking dogs on strong leashes illustrated concern with the rising crime rate, a phenomenon most pronounced in urban areas.

A chain-link fence draped with bougainvillea and razor wire surrounded the grounds of the Islander Hotel, the town's most posh hostelry, which housed the World Bank's Papua New Guinea offices and most of its foreign staff. Security instructions for all visitors were the same as those I had received when staying in Port Moresby in 1989: do not leave your hotel at night except by car, in a group, and traveling directly to and from your destination. Near the equator, darkness falls early and suddenly. Going about Port Moresby late in the afternoon, as the sun began its swift descent, you felt a rising sense of urgency, as though you were in Transylvania and had to hurry back to an inn draped in garlic.

Some members of the World Bank mission who were not familiar with the country were a bit nervous about going abroad even during the day. Given not only the prevalence of both petty and serious crime but also the outright hostility toward the World Bank in some quarters, this was not entirely unreasonable. In July, as many as four thousand students and others had marched on parliament to protest the bank's policy demands, protesters burned several government vehicles on the campus of the University of Papua New Guinea, and there had been large, angry demonstrations in the town of Wabag, in the Western Highlands Province.

The national coalition of NGOs (the National Coalition for Socio-Economic

Justice) that had formed to oppose the World Bank's loan conditions did not have any difficulty finding stinging criticism of the bank's role in other countries to use in its campaign. There are many accounts of the social costs of World Bank structural adjustment programs, and many volumes arguing that the bank's lending policies strengthen an international economic order that serves the interests of wealthy and powerful countries and transnational corporations. World Bank policies usually focus on achieving economic growth through increasing exports, liberalizing trade, and providing a favorable environment for foreign investment. The bank prefers solutions to economic and social problems that rely on market mechanisms and private enterprise rather than state intervention. It is a standard free-market capitalist vision, and it is very fair to ask if it really *is* best for everyone, especially in a country to which it is, in many respects, so very novel.

The ERP loan conditions for Papua New Guinea also included plenty of specific measures that aroused concern and anger. For instance, devaluation of the kina had raised the prices of imported goods, including such urban staples as canned mackerel, and thousands of public employees were to be laid off. Yet, as tough as such policies were, taken one by one there was room for argument about their merit, and Papua New Guineans themselves were divided in their views of some measures.

True, the currency devaluation raised the price of imported canned mackerel; but some pointed out that the price had been inordinately high to begin with because there was a 100 percent duty on canned fish, imposed to protect Papua New Guinea's only domestic cannery. Yes, public employees who lost their jobs would face hardships, and so might many of their relatives who benefited indirectly from their cash incomes. Several years later, a World Bank evaluation of its own program for Papua New Guinea judged that, given the many problems with the administration of public services, it had been "inappropriate" to focus on reducing public service employment. Yet a great many rural people without the good fortune to have close kin in good government jobs cried no tears for public employees, because for some time they had seen very few public services.

There were also loan conditions designed to encourage more careful husbandry of forest resources and improve ineffective—in some instances, corrupt—government regulation of the logging industry. While some NGOs and government functionaries approved of these, there were those in government and the private sector who wanted to keep logging regulation nice and loose.

Probably the most incendiary issue, however, was the bank's alleged effort to change the land system in Papua New Guinea. Before I left for Papua New Guinea in August 1995, I was aware of the charge that the bank's loan conditions for Papua New Guinea included a program that would "effectively dismantle customary land tenure and commodify the land, in order to make industrial logging and mining easier," as an electronic mail bulletin I received from one conservation activist put it. The same bulletin contained the text of an "Action Alert" from the Australian organization Aid Watch, which charged that one of the loan conditions was a "plan to drastically change the present system of customary land ownership so foreign corporations can operate more easily in the country."

In fact, these charges were off the mark, as I ascertained before beginning my work for the bank. The bank at one point had included support for something called the Land Mobilization Program (LMP) in the loan package, but this had been removed from the draft loan conditions around two months before the July demonstrations. The LMP was a program begun in the 1980s that tried to address some of the difficult issues surrounding the use of customary land in business ventures. It was not a program for eliminating customary tenure, although it did raise the issue of land registration, that is, formal means of determining and documenting land rights. Devising means of land registration that do not do serious damage to the flexibility of indigenous land systems is a daunting undertaking. In the East Sepik Province in particular, legislation regarding voluntary land registration has taken steps toward addressing some of the problems involved. But the issue remains both complicated and controversial. In brief, that is why the LMP was taken out of the loan negotiations.

By the summer of 1995, however, the official status of the LMP was irrelevant. In politics, the more shocking the allegations the more easily they seem to flourish. The outcry over the LMP was also less than entirely spontaneous. Allegations that the bank wanted to dismantle customary land systems were a splendid weapon with which to attack the ERP loan conditions in general as well as the sitting government.

Alien Government, Unfamiliar Nation

Many Papua New Guineans probably were easily convinced that the World Bank was up to no good because they had no faith in their own government, which had sought help from the bank. In fact, many private citizens I spoke with in 1995 distrusted the Papua New Guinea government even more than the World Bank. They mistrusted not just the current government but the government as an institution. The staff of local-level government organizations expressed deep distrust of every level of government above their own, and some village representatives to these local bodies did not trust the staff. People in provincial towns spoke with disdain of the "people in Moresby," the capital, who were "living in a different world," as one activist put it. Activists in rural areas sometimes made the same complaint about those in the provincial towns. As a representative of a rural women's organization in the East Sepik Province told me, "the bigshots in Wewak" did not understand what life was like still farther afield.

Such criticisms might sound familiar almost anywhere, but mistrust of government has a special flavor in Papua New Guinea, and this distinctive and pungent mistrust provided fertile ground for the reaction to the bank's ERP policy prescriptions. In light of conditions in 1995, many Papua New Guineans felt that the government—not just the sitting government, but every government since independence—simply had not proven itself. Many also felt that the elite Papua New Guineans who ran the government treated the citizens of the country unfairly and unequally. Europeans working in Papua New Guinea or reporting on events there often complained of corruption in the higher circles, but they were no more vocal on this issue than rank-and-file Papua New Guineans themselves.

Many Papua New Guineans probably also distrusted the government because they still saw it as a foreign entity. Papua New Guineans had taken the tiller at independence, but the boat itself was built on the European model. The electoral and parliamentary political system was nothing like precolonial political systems, and these differing systems were only awkwardly coordinated.

Above all, the idea that the people of Papua New Guinea were all members of a single nation and that this identity transcended narrower affiliations—with family, kinship group, village, and speakers of the same language—had not taken hold. There had been no prolonged, popular struggle for independence in which disparate groups throughout the country might have forged a sense of unity or acquired a stake in new national institutions. The nation, too, was an unfamiliar concept to many. Indeed, some Papua New Guinea peoples did not regard themselves as having ceded their autonomy and accepted subordination to the greater power of the state. In fact, to some the state appeared positively menacing. In the 1990s, Papua New Guineans caught up in Christian revival movements in parts of the country associated the state with the Antichrist.

What About Kragur?

In Kragur just after independence, at least some villagers were very uncertain about the meaning of independence and uneasy about its prospects. As one said to me, "We have independence, but we don't understand. The men in the House of Assembly talk about it, but we don't understand. We just go along. What's independence? What's self-government?" Some villagers thought that the country had been in too much of a hurry. According to Councilor Lapim: "Papua New Guinea isn't doing this right. Independence is coming first and understanding is coming behind." Brawaung had lamented, "We're not ready yet!"

Some such early fears had proven to be justified. However, one can get too carried away with cataloging Papua New Guinea's failures and travails. Near the end of the 1990s, John Connell wrote: "Papua New Guinea is experiencing similar problems to those of other developing countries in the post-independence era, but in an unparalleled array that matches the diversity of the country and the recent establishment of modern institutions. . . ." This hardly minimized the country's problems, but it was a reminder that they were not simply a manifestation of the darkly exotic qualities often attributed to Papua New Guinea in news stories and travel literature. Of great importance was the fact that neither the colonial era nor the post-colonial quest for development had destroyed rural systems of food production. These ways of making a living were neither easy nor utterly reliable, but they provided a time-tested floor of security. In fact, as of the late 1990s, real rural incomes —that is, monetary incomes plus the goods and services that never entered the cash arena—were higher in Papua New Guinea than in much of the South Pacific and some parts of Asia.

As my travels for the World Bank finally turned me toward Wewak, I had to wonder just how Papua New Guinea's national problems were affecting Kragur. I could easily imagine that villagers were disappointed, for the trepidation with which many had greeted independence had been mixed with cautious hope. Many certainly might be angry, and some might be worried that the government's and the World Bank's alleged cure for the country's problems would be worse than the disease. But it was not at all certain that the material circumstances of their lives would have deteriorated. I knew that their lands were intact, and if Kragur was receiving fewer public services and less government attention than it had in the 1970s it had not had much to lose.

Kragur has a so-near-but-yet-so-far quality. Although only seemingly interminable water and sky stretch away seaward from the cliffs of Kragur, Kairiru is easily visible from the mainland and in good weather a fast boat can reach Kragur from Wewak in an hour. But there is no regular boat traffic, most boats that ply these waters are not very fast, the weather is not always good, and the last twenty yards or so that bring one safely across the rocks can be tricky. The trip to and from Kairiru's gentle landward coast is much easier, but to reach Kragur from there you have to cross the mountain. Wrapping up my work in Madang Province and preparing to leave for the East Sepik, I wondered if the obstacles separating Kragur from the comparative bustle of the provincial capital also had kept it aloof from the effects of the national crisis that was bringing me back to Wewak.

Weekend on Kairiru

> "WE'RE JUST LIKE A CITY NOW."
> (*MIPELA I STAP OLOSEM WANPELA CITY.*)
> —A Kragur villager, 1995

> "THE GOOD SPIRIT IS STILL THERE."
> —A Kragur man living in Wewak (in English), 1995

To prepare for my work for the bank in Wewak, I contacted several NGOs there by letter and telephone from Port Moresby and Madang. I also wrote from Moresby to a few Kragur people in Wewak and some friends in the village to tell them I was coming. Pawil met me at the airport in Wewak. A native of Kragur, by the 1970s he had long since left the village to pursue his education and become a Marist Brother. We had not seen each other since 1981 and knew each other better from the few letters we had exchanged than from firsthand association. He was one of several Kragur people now living and working in Wewak whom I knew or whose parents I had known in the village.

I made it very clear that I was coming to Wewak on behalf of the World Bank, but Pawil and others did not seem to hold it against me. Most of the NGOs I had met with so far had considered the bank's ideas for an NGO funding program with open minds, and some with avid interest. A few, however, were so convinced that nothing good could come from the bank that no discussions were possible. The Kragur townsmen were suspicious of both the bank and the Papua New Guinea government, but they hoped that I could cast some light on the many rumors then circulating.

Mwairap, headmaster of Brandi High School near Wewak and the son of a deceased Kragur leader, took me to his house one afternoon and grilled me in fluent English about the World Bank loan conditions for over two hours. Like others, he had heard that some form of land registration was one condition of the loan and that its purpose was to make land available to foreign investors and, in some way, to help secure the loan. (One of the more extreme rumors going around was that land registration would enable the World Bank to use the land as collateral for the loan. If the government failed to repay the loan, the bank would then appropriate the land and drive the owners off.) Like others, Mwairap trusted the Papua New Guinea government no more than he did the World Bank. How, he wondered, could the government be prevented from wasting the World Bank loan (on "high-priced consultants," among other things) the way, he said, previous governments had wasted previous international loans? Yet while they shared many common concerns about the World Bank's involvement in Papua New Guinea, Kragur people in Wewak still extended themselves to help me, introducing me to people in business, government, and NGO circles and helping me set up appointments.

Wewak Revisited

Before getting down to work I had a cursory look at Wewak, my first since 1981. After picking me up at the airport, Pawil took me for a brief tour in the Marist Brothers' vehicle, pointing out the growing squatter settlements on the outskirts of town and the pile of debris on Kreer Heights where the provincial offices, erected in the early 1970s, had burned down. Allegedly a disgruntled political opponent of the provincial administration, who was never apprehended, had torched the building in the mid-1980s. We also passed the boarded-up studio of Radio Wewak, a government-funded station, now closed for lack of funds.

My hotel on the beach had been a fixture in Wewak for as long as I had been coming there. Years ago, it had been called the Windjammer Beach Motel, but it now sported a dual identity. Though the front desk still answered the phone "Windjammer," it was listed in the national telephone directory—one slim volume serving all of Papua New Guinea—as the Sepik International Beach Resort. It had an impressive new facade resembling a curving crocodile, a new carved wooden bar in the shape of a crocodile with gaping maw, and much higher prices. The effort to appeal to tourists was apparent, but so were the security guards who watched the high front doors and patrolled the beachfront.

All of these changes mirrored circumstances throughout Papua New Guinea: the drift of rural people to towns ill-equipped to employ and house them, the volatility of political life, the exhaustion of funds for public services, and a growing problem with violent crime. These were also major themes in the interviews I conducted in my work for the bank. The exhaustion of government funding had left church-run health services carrying an ever greater share of responsibility for rural health with smaller public subsidies; business endeavors situated any distance from the province's few main roads suffered from the decay of secondary roads, and many businesses bore the additional costs of frequent burglary and banditry. NGO activists noted that without Radio Wewak it was harder than ever to organize meetings and promote their programs.

All, however, was not in decline. Perhaps it would be more accurate to say the decline was not for all. The town's businesses still clustered around the main street that cut across the neck of Wewak Point. Many of the stores on this strip were very familiar: the Chinese stores, the Air Niugini office, the Wewak Christian Book Shop, and the two banks. Klawaung, a Kragur man whom I had last seen when he was a student at UPNG, had acquired a general store on the main street, and I often stopped there between appointments to use the telephone or get a cold drink. What really caught my eye, however, was the shiny new Papua New Guinea Motors showroom displaying imported cars. This certainly suggested a growing indigenous elite, as did my evening spent at the Yacht Club as Klawaung's guest. The club was situated on the rim of Wewak Point, and we sat on the spacious patio of the outdoor bar looking out over the harbor. The club once had been a bastion of white expatriates, but now indigenous Papua New Guinean business people and professionals, too, sat at ease at its tables.

News of Kragur

From 1981 until 1995, the only news I had of Kragur was what I read in occasional letters. These usually told me who had died, or if there was much illness in the village, and reported the occasional unusual event, such as the small tidal wave that washed away canoes moored against the cliff one year. In 1993, however, I received a letter from Pawil. His letter said (in English) that he had read my doctoral dissertation and noted that I had described the older people in Kragur in 1975–1976 as "at the crossroad." In 1993, he wrote, "they still are." By then, of course, the older generations of the 1970s were gone. Taking Pawil literally, it sounded like the generations that had taken their place were facing the same conundrums.

In 1995, Kragur people in town and on the island needed no prompting to tell me about goings-on in the village and offer their opinions. In the sketchy picture that emerged I saw variations on familiar themes. In addition to questioning me about the ERP loan conditions, Mwairap had a lot to say about life in Kragur. People in the village, he said, were now primarily interested in money and possessions. They made taro gardens, gathered betel nut, and grew tobacco primarily with an eye to selling their produce not only in the market in Wewak but also to each other. He also said that Ibor, the formerly vigorous leader of village Catholic life, who had preached against excessive concern with money, was losing influence. Mwairap spoke with warm approval of those who energetically pursued market gardening and other business ventures. He was among several townsmen who told me that villagers were now buying and selling things among themselves. Giving to friends and relatives was "withering away," he said. "Now, if you have no money you don't chew betel nut unless you can get it from your own trees. People are beginning to realize that there isn't anything you get for free, and that's a good thing." The Kragur he described differed strikingly from the one I knew. I could not help being a little skeptical, but I had to remind myself that I had not set foot in the village for many years.

On to Kairiru

After a few hectic days of work, I was able to set out for Kairiru again. On a Friday morning, Pawil drove me to the beach by the post-office wharf, where a boat from the village was waiting. Moraf, the son of my old friend Brawaung, was there with his family's sixteen-foot fiberglass boat and a borrowed outboard motor. Several other Kragur people also were there, sitting on the ground in the shade of the casuarina trees, waiting for a boat to the village. (With the help of migrant kin working in towns for money, a few Kragur villagers had by now acquired small boats with outboard motors.) I did not immediately recognize all the faces, but some were unmistakable and we exchanged greetings and shook hands all around. These villagers, however, were not going with us, because we were not going directly to Kragur. Instead, we were to go first to St. John's, where Brawaung was staying with another son, Kapiai, who worked there as a carpenter. I knew from letters that Brawaung's health had been failing. He and his wife, Misiling, now were staying at St. John's, partly to be nearer to the hospital in Wewak.

The day was bright, the sea was rolling but not too choppy, and the trip to St. John's, on Kairiru's south coast, took only about an hour. This was fine with me, because the only place to sit in the boat was the narrow edge of a two-by-four that spanned its width. I could not figure out how to distribute my weight properly and every slap of the hull against the water ground my hipbones deep into my flesh. Moraf stood relaxed at the tiller for the whole trip, keeping his balance with no effort, and his young son perched on the gunwales in apparent comfort. The gunwales were broader than my increasingly knifelike seat, but to sit there without risking going overboard if the boat hit an unexpected bump took more seamanship than I commanded.

St. John's boasts a concrete wharf in the sheltered passage between Kairiru and Mushu, so landing was nothing like the event that it is on Kragur's own beach. Brawaung's and Misiling's adult children had produced many children of their own, and several of the latter came running to the wharf to escort me to the metal-roofed house where Brawaung, Misiling, and their children and grandchildren crowded the low concrete-slab verandah. Having mastered at least some aspects of local etiquette, I had brought with me a 25-kilo rice bag filed with betel nut and betel pepper, purchased at the Wewak market the day before. My hosts praised my good manners as I handed out the betel, keeping back enough to display my good manners again when I got to Kragur.

We passed the afternoon and early evening sitting on the floor of the verandah, chatting, eating fish cooked over an open fire in the yard, and punishing the betel-nut supply. I had taken up betel chewing on my first visit to Kragur but declined the offer to join in this time. I had been in Papua New Guinea for several weeks and thought I was acclimated, but the sun and heat were getting to me that day, and I feared I had probably lost my tolerance for betel intoxication as well. Brawaung still chewed betel and smoked local tobacco with pleasure, but a combination of pulmonary and spinal problems—the latter, they told me, aggravated by an incident with a bag of copra—had rendered him unable to stand or walk. He had been to Wewak's sparsely equipped hospital several times, but apparently they could do nothing for him. I remembered him as a short, wiry man. Like most rural Papua New Guineans, both men and women, he had impressed me as remarkably powerful for his size, as well as quick and agile. Now, however, he was emaciated and frail.

Brawaung's case was extreme, but—in contrast to Americans—it is rare indeed for rural Papua New Guineans to grow fat as they grow older. Even those who escape wasting diseases tend to become thinner as they age. Misiling was still in good health, but the years had left their mark on her, too. Even more so than men, village women tend to keep working until they are utterly immobilized by age or illness. "The old women really like to work," say the young men in Kragur. Perhaps so, but the women are also keenly aware of how much the welfare of their children and grandchildren depends on the daily labor of making and tending gardens, gathering firewood, and preparing meals.

Despite his disability, Brawaung was still clearly the head of the family and directed activities with assurance from where he sat at the edge of the slab. While the light still held, we took some group photos. Later in the evening, Kapiai escorted me to the house of Father Clement, an American priest long resident in Papua New Guinea, who served Kairiru and Mushu. His own house being very full, Kapiai had arranged for me to stay in one of Father Clement's guest rooms.

The next morning, after breakfasting on fish Moraf had caught during the night, we set off for Kragur. We would stop by St. John's again on our return trip to Wewak so we left our farewells until then. Circling around the west end of the island, we were within sight of Kragur in about forty-five minutes. Pulling into the bay, Moraf circled slowly a few times before heading for the beach. He told me later that he was waiting to see if anyone had organized a greeting party, maybe with drumming and singing. But this was to be a more modest landing, although from the boat I could see a number of people making their way along the clifftop to meet us at the landing place.

Pawil's younger brother Bokim and his kinsman Kwan had prepared a room for me in Bokim's house at the place called Momosang at the west end of the village, just beyond the main cluster of dwellings. My house was long gone. After I left at the end of 1976, a village youth club had appropriated it as a meeting place. It was still standing in 1981, but it had decayed and been torn down since then.

Bokim and Kwan had organized a work party to build a new outhouse on the steep slope rising behind Bokim's house. The logs that covered the pit were still white and glistening where the bark had been stripped away and the palm-leaf thatch of the walls and roof was still fresh and green. In 1975–1976, I had shared a somewhat aged outhouse with several households. Villagers themselves sometimes said that many of these structures could stand to be replaced more often, and breezes from their direction sometimes confirmed this. Nonetheless, I think I hesitated to ask villagers to build me my own privy for fear of acting too much the white man and casting aspersions on local hygiene. In any case, the new outhouse at Momosang was a luxury.

I spent the afternoon visiting some of the older villagers I knew best, bringing them each a gift of betel nut and betel pepper. Going around the village I could see some obvious changes. One townsman had told me that the population had increased to 350 or more. I saw for myself that houses were still built of bush materials, but they were densely packed, and a few unusually large, relatively new structures were conspicuous. This and the abundance of children made significant population increase plausible. It also suggested that migration to urban areas might have slowed down and/or migrants were returning to Kragur, perhaps because of the difficulty of finding work in the towns. I also saw the new water system, paid for with a grant one of the townsmen had been able to obtain from the World Health Organization.

One of the new water taps was right outside Bokim's house, but late in the afternoon I walked to the men's bathing place on the stream, pleased to find its clear pools as inviting as ever. I did not, however, locate them as easily as before. A major landmark, the church at Plos, was gone and I could not find the once familiar path at the edge of the forest. I had to backtrack and try again more than once before finally locating the secluded glade where the men bathed.

My conversations with villagers were mostly consumed with explaining how I happened to be dropping by so suddenly, hearing of who had died since my last visit, and explaining what had become of my first wife, who had joined me very briefly in Kragur in 1976. The older people were, the less they knew or cared about the World Bank or my connection with it. Despite my curiosity about changes in village life, this was primarily a social call. The subject of money, however, did come up. One woman, well known to me and now a grandmother several times over, told me spontaneously that money was now much more important in Kragur. "We're just like a city now," she said. "We follow the customs of the town." I found this hard to picture, but I did not have time to see with my own eyes how much like a town Kragur had become in this respect. I did see enough, however, to convince me that the place of money in Kragur life was still controversial.

Money, Harmony, and National Crisis

Several of the townsmen had come out to the island that same weekend and, on my one night in Kragur, they called a meeting in the center of the village. The manner of this meeting was familiar. Men and women ranged themselves on convenient verandahs or sat on bark mats on the ground, men in the foreground, as they had done years ago. A hissing kerosene pressure lamp hung from the eaves of a house at the edge of the central clear space and cast a harsh light over the front ranks of the crowd while the rest receded into darkness. To my discomfort, however, a single wooden desk chair had been placed in the center of the loose arena formed by the assembly and I was ushered toward it. I had no desire to be so conspicuous, so I carried the chair back a few steps to within the circle of men seated on the ground.

Two of the townsmen dominated the proceedings. Each began his speech with some words of welcome for me. Mwairap even announced that he had read my book about Kragur and that it was fair and accurate, a review I greatly appreciated. They then quickly moved on to admonishing the assembled men and women that, although the village was changing, it was not changing fast enough. The principal change they seemed to have in mind was deeper involvement with business and money. One speaker, for example, waxed eloquent on what a fine thing it was to pay each other for betel nut.

Eventually, one of the townsmen called on me to say a few words. I thanked everyone for Kragur's great hospitality, then and in the past; but this seemed too terse, so I launched into more controversial waters. I agreed with the townsmen that having more money would be a fine thing, but added that I hoped Kragur people would not forget the advantages they had enjoyed for generations. Many other villages, I said, would gladly pay money for the relative lack of mosquitoes that kept malaria at bay and the superb water supply. Looking around me as I spoke, I noticed a few older men nodding in agreement.

I knew that most villagers would have welcomed new opportunities to make money, but I wondered if their interest in money had quite the same roots as that of the townsmen. Recall that in 1975–1976 many villagers appeared to think that Kragur was poor in money because the village was not united and harmonious, and they wanted money partly to demonstrate that they were good people, capable of such harmony and cooperation. Many of the townsmen, on the other hand, had lived much of their lives in such imported institutions as schools, businesses, and bureaucracies. Their interest in turning Kragur toward money may not have rested on the same strong association between wealth and social harmony that had underlain much village interest in money in years past. And if they *were* interested in money in some part because they hoped it would increase social harmony, it was possible that they understood social harmony in different terms than resident villagers past or present.

For most resident villagers in 1975–1976, harmony was impossible without generosity. No town dweller would have disputed that, but life in a world where one's livelihood depends on keeping track of one's money undoubtedly had affected urban Kragur people's definitions of generosity. I knew, for example, that some townsmen thought that villagers should cut back on traditional forms of giving so they could accumulate goods to sell in the market. Some town dwellers also had told me that their kin in the village often expected more monetary generosity than the townsmen's wages or salaries could support. Their village kin, they said, did not understand how much money it took to live in town; they could not give money away as freely as villagers distributed the fish they caught. Fish and taro, of course, could not be banked or saved. Giving freely of them was not only an obligation, it was also a prudent way to ensure that others would share their abundance in the future when one's own supplies were short.

Deborah Gewertz and Frederick Errington, who have studied village societies in Papua New Guinea for many years, have begun to observe what they call an emerging urban middle class in Papua New Guinea. This "middle class," however, is an elite with respect to the majority of the people of the country. Gewertz and Errington noted in 1996 that while members of this growing group in Wewak retained ties with their village relatives, many attempted to limit and define those ties in ways consistent with the urbanite's aspirations in the cash economy. For example, they made "stringent rules" to regulate "the demands of kin for economic assistance." They gave money to village kin to help mount village ceremonies, such as those for the dead, but they did so "largely to strengthen their future claims on ancestral land—land they explicitly referred to as an 'asset.' " To do this is not necessarily to repudiate generosity, but it gives it a particular meaning, tailored to the needs and aspirations of people who rely on their jobs and their paychecks more than they do on their relatives.

I do not know exactly what the Kragur townsmen had in mind when they addressed the assembled villagers that night, or how the villagers understood it. The vehemence of the townsmen's admonitions, however, gave the impression that their point of view still needed defending. Indeed, there also was concrete evidence that some villagers opposed both the townsmen's views on the direction Kragur should take and their efforts to assume positions of leadership. In my conversation with a young village man on my first day on Kairiru, he complained rather angrily that the men from town sometimes came to the village and told people that they should start individual businesses rather than combining their efforts. This confused people, he said, and angered the old people. It obviously did not make him happy either.

The meeting itself, as though on cue, illustrated tensions between resident villagers and educated, comparatively affluent town dwellers. After thanking the townsmen politely for coming to meet with the resident villagers, one middle-aged man told them bluntly that he would be more impressed when they did something more than show up periodically and tell resident villagers what to do.

There was tension about money among resident villagers as well as between villagers and townsmen. One of my Kragur hosts in Wewak had praised a particular young man for his energy in market gardening. On Kairiru, a young villager spoke of the same local entrepreneur with disapproval, charging that he was not thinking of the village, only of himself. (*"Em i no tingting long ples,"* he said in Tok Pisin.) But if the pursuit of money was still controversial, it did seem to be higher on the Kragur agenda and less subject to criticism than in the past. As before, however, many individuals were not of one mind on the issue. For instance, the critic who charged the village entrepreneur with lack of concern with the community had his own plans to establish a small business in partnership with his siblings.

Also, despite the apparently increasing respectability of money, Catholicism remained prominent in Kragur life. My last day in Kragur, a Sunday, Father Clement came to the neighboring village of Bou to serve mass for the people of several villages in the large open-walled church there, built since my last visit. Kragur people turned out in force for this event, much as they would have in the past. I also learned that Kragur Catholicism now came in some new varieties. In Wewak one of the townsmen had told me, in English, that some villagers were involved with "charismatic" Catholicism and "speaking in tongues." I saw none of this at the mass at Bou. Earlier, however, as I sat and visited with a village family, one of the young women had suddenly burst into tears and begun exclaiming incoherently. Everyone took this very calmly. Her brother quickly reassured me that there was nothing wrong with her and that this was simply "the movement of a spirit."

Were interest in money and interest in Catholicism more at ease with each other than they had been in the 1970s? I was to leave Kairiru with nothing more than tantalizing observations and questions about this and other issues. Did Kragur people still want *both* greater material prosperity *and* a more harmonious community, and did they feel the two must go together? However much they talked of buying and selling betel nut or praised individual entrepreneurs, even the townsmen still spoke as though Kragur people would face their future together, for better or worse. And even some of the townsmen wanted to believe that Kragur people could still boast a special kind of solidarity. As one said to me, in English, "The good spirit is still there" (using "spirit" here in the secular sense).

Deeper questions, of course, remained: How might definitions of "the good spirit" be changing? How much concern with money could it encompass, what differences in wealth, how much individual endeavor and accumulation? How much could actual social relations change and still allow people, especially resident villagers, to find in them some semblance of familiar social ideals?

I also had no answer to a more immediate and concrete question: how were the unfortunate conditions in Papua New Guinea as a whole affecting Kragur? I knew I could put little weight on my fleeting observations, but the national crisis was less apparent in the village than in town. There were no outward signs of decline, no security guards or razor wire, no squatter settlements, and no incinerated government offices. And the village was filled with people of all ages, even though tight urban job markets might have driven some of them home. Also, although there was plenty of talk about the village's slowness to change, I had heard no talk of decline from either townsmen or resident villagers, and the sense of emergency abroad in Port Moresby did not seem to stalk Kragur's paths. I suspected that if I stayed longer I would hear a great deal about disappointed hopes and government perfidy and neglect. Nevertheless, I got the impression that Kragur people remained able to take care of themselves, if—as usual—little help was available from other quarters.

Adventures with Parasites

We were to head back to Wewak shortly after mass on Sunday. At one point in the service, a local church leader read announcements of coming events, also noting "Michael Smith is with us today" (Tok Pisin, "*Michael Smith em i stap wantaim yumi tede*"). Coupled with the chair of honor offered me at the previous evening's meeting, this was more celebrity than I was accustomed to. After the service, people lingered outside the church, talking and calming cravings for tobacco and betel, the use of which was prohibited inside. Sunday is a good day for visiting on Kairiru, but—unfortunately—I had to be on my way.

Back at Bokim's house I packed the few things I had brought with me in my shoulder bag and waited for word from the beach below that the boat was ready. I was wondering again if I was too old or simply too out of shape to stand the tropical heat, because the sweat had poured off me on the short walk back from Bou and I now felt extremely tired. Bokim brought me something to eat: a thick cross-section of fish cooked on the fire and a square of *tapiok*. I had not seen the latter, made from the cassava tuber, before in Kragur, but Bokim said it was now quite common. To me on that morning it resembled in appearance, taste, and texture a chunk of very old mucilage. I have always enjoyed almost every food people eat in Kragur, but I found this fare so unappetizing I could eat only about half of the fish and less of the *tapiok*. In addition to losing my tolerance for tropical heat, I apparently also was developing a finicky palate and a delicate stomach. Rather sadly, I began to dismiss my occasional dreams of doing research again in Kragur and, feeling chagrined, looked forward to returning to hotel life.

But soon the boat was ready and I skittered down the path to the beach. After a few more good-byes, I was ushered into the boat before Moraf and his helpers pushed and pulled it between small waves out into water deep enough to drop the propeller and start the engine. Mwairap was joining us and he leaned easily against the gunwales as I balanced uncomfortably again on the edge of the two-by-four. On smooth seas we cruised around the west end of the island. We pulled into Victoria Bay and landed briefly so that I could finally see the hot springs that steamed just at the tide line on a sandy beach there, a reminder of Kairiru's volcanic heart. After that short stop, we proceeded to St. John's for a last meeting with Brawaung, Misiling, and the others. We also had to purchase enough gasoline to make it back to the mainland. We came up a bit short on the gasoline, the engine dying a little over a hundred yards from the wharf. Fortunately, by then we were running close to shore in the calm Kairiru-Mushu passage. Mwairap and I got out and waded to the beach while Moraf pulled the boat the rest of the way.

As we walked along a well-worn path toward Kapiai's house, I became completely convinced that I no longer had the resilience for field research in the tropics. The sun on my back and neck was appallingly hot and my legs felt like flaccid twigs. While Moraf went to the nearest village, only a few hundred yards from St. John's, to find some gasoline for sale, I lay down on a cot on Kapiai's verandah and tried to gather my strength. I now thought I was probably suffering from heat stroke. Brawaung's and Misiling's grandchildren brought me cool water and a green coconut to drink, and someone even produced a chunk of ice that I held against my forehead and rubbed on the back of my neck. None of this helped at all, and when Moraf arrived to say that the boat was ready to go I decided it would be best to get to Wewak before the problem got worse, no matter what it was.

The sea spray was reviving and the trip passed quickly. Instead of landing by the post-office wharf we came in to shore where a narrow channel empties into the sea alongside the Marist Brothers' residence. The tide was low, so after I splashed ashore Mwairap and Moraf had to pull the boat over a few yards of sand to enter the mouth of the channel. Once inside, Moraf could tie up the boat behind the Marist house, where he intended to spend the night.

First, though, Moraf walked with me to the Windjammer, where I checked in again. He watched with interest and told me he had never seen how someone checked in at a hotel. He had attended St. Xavier's High School and worked on a plantation in another province for a few years after leaving school, but the cost of even the more modest hotels in Papua New Guinea is far beyond the reach of most of the country's citizenry. I do not think Moraf had seen television before either, although he knew what it was. Papua New Guinea acquired television in the 1980s, but there was only one national channel. The few other channels originated in Australia. Moraf sat and watched the rolling picture on the television set in my room while I unpacked some clean clothes.

I was burning up now and hoped that a cool shower would help alleviate what I still thought was heat stroke. But as I stepped into the shower I began to shiver with cold. I changed my plans and turned the hot tap full on. It finally dawned on me that I was coming down with malaria, which accounted for my susceptibility to heat, humidity, and unfamiliar food all that weekend. That I only realized this now showed how stale my tropical living skills had become. I must have been addled from mounting fever, because I did not ask Moraf to stay and help me get medical attention. Later, I only dimly remembered bidding him good-bye before sinking into a stupor. An attack of fever does not send Kragur villagers running to a doctor and—ensconced in the hotel as I was, with money in my pocket and cold water in the minirefrigerator—I doubt that Moraf regarded my condition as serious.

Unfortunately, my natural resistance to malaria is probably nil, and drifting back into consciousness in the early evening I realized that I needed help. I had been taking the weekly preventive malarial medication recommended by the World Bank, but I was not carrying any curative medication. I had naïvely accepted assurances that the preventive medication (mefloquine, also favored in the 1990s by the U.S. Peace Corps, but new to me) would keep me from harm. I should have known better. There were only two private physicians in Wewak. One of these was a Kragur man who had been in the village that weekend and who, I knew, was still there. When I finally mustered the strength to stumble across the room to the phone, I learned from the hotel desk that the other physician was also out of town.

I was in no condition to make my way alone to the hospital. Fortunately, with the desk clerk's assistance I was able to contact one of the Marist Brothers. I knew Pawil was out of town, but I reached Brother Terry Kane, head of the Catholic Education Office in Wewak, whom I had interviewed several days before in the course of my duties for the bank. Brother Terry soon arrived at my door, bringing with him Brother Mathew Bouten, head of Catholic Health Services. Brother Mathew checked my pulse and felt my brow and pronounced the immediate need for the hospital. The two brothers half-carried me between them to their vehicle, drove me to the hospital, and made sure I received prompt attention and treatment, which included a massive injection of quinine. For the next three days they came to the hotel morning and evening to take me, still drained of strength and unsteady on my feet, to the hospital to complete my treatment. This consisted of more massive quinine injections. Feeling more alert on my last visit, I timed my final injection and found that it took nearly four minutes to squeeze the contents of the syringe into my sore buttocks.

This misfortune extended my stay in Wewak by several days. Finally returning to Port Moresby, I spent a few days there finishing my work for the bank. The flight back to the United States was luxurious. The bank's travel office had managed to get my business-class ticket—sufficiently luxurious in itself—upgraded to first class. I stopped worrying about being too old and soft, and perhaps too prone to malaria, for life in the bush and sank into hours of snoozing and eating every delicacy offered. A multitude of solicitous flight attendants proffered these delicacies; for the price of a first-class ticket buys not only a comfortable seat and good food but also prodigious deference and the skillful simulation of warm hospitality.

I looked forward to being home again, but as I took strength and encouragement from caviar and chilled vodka I also looked ahead to returning to Wewak, Kairiru, and Kragur. The original plan for designing and implementing the NGO funding program called for one or two more visits by members of the design team, and one of these might afford an opportunity to stay on for a few weeks and do more than just stop by Kragur for a bath, a village meeting, and a mass.

CHAPTER
8

Free Ticket to Paradise

FOLLOW IN THE FOOTSTEPS OF MARGARET MEAD . . .
AND VISIT ONE OF THE LAST TRULY UNSPOILED PLACES OF THE WORLD.

—From a brochure for an American Museum
of Natural History tour of Papua New Guinea

Within a few days of returning home, when I was just starting to rebound completely from my malaria-tinged jet lag, the World Bank called and asked if I could go back to Papua New Guinea in a couple of weeks to help plan some research on NGO activities and an investigation of how social networks helped alleviate poverty. The trip was short—seven days in Port Moresby and five days in transit—and uneventful. I did not try to tack on a visit to Kragur because I expected to return to Papua New Guinea within the year to help set up the NGO funding program and perhaps to work on the research projects the bank was planning.

But as its loan negotiations with Papua New Guinea proceeded in difficult fits and starts, the bank put the NGO funding program on a back burner. When the bank took it up again, it settled on a plan that did not require my services. Work on the research projects also was slow to start, and when it did begin, the bank decided to contract most of it to Papua New Guinea's National Research Institute. I spent 1996 peddling my consulting skills wherever I could. In 1997, I began working with LTG Associates, Inc., an anthropological consulting firm that has carved out a niche analyzing the cultural dimensions of health care and other social policy issues.

This work suited me well, but I could not help thinking about how to get back to Kragur for a while. My visit in 1995 had rekindled my curiosity about how life there was changing and renewed some old friendships. For years I had exchanged letters fitfully with a few Kragur people, and after my 1995 visit the volume of correspondence increased. I even received two telephone calls, but these brought bad news. Within a few months of returning home, Brawaung's eldest daughter, Bashi, twice used the telephone at St. John's Seminary to call me. She called first to tell me that her father's health was declining rapidly, and a few days later she called to tell me that he was dead. His death not only saddened me, it reminded me that many of the people I knew best in Kragur were not going to be there forever.

Late in 1997, however, I had a stroke of luck. Kathleen Barlow—a friend since graduate school at the University of California, who has also worked in the Sepik region—was scheduled to serve as a lecturer on a tour of Papua New Guinea in early 1998 sponsored by the American Museum of Natural History. In December 1997, she called me to ask if I could take her place. She was overwhelmed with work and, with great regret, had decided to forego the tour. The museum paid lecturers only a token amount, but they got a free trip to the country in return for serving as resident experts on a two-week excursion in the most comfortable circumstances Papua New Guinea's tourist industry has to offer. I was working on a project for LTG, but I was able to get away for a few weeks. My wife, Jana, could join the tour for a steeply discounted price. She had never seen Papua New Guinea, so we signed her up as well. She would return to work when the tour ended, and I would stay on for six weeks, as long as the tourist visa I would travel under would allow.

Back to Papua New Guinea and the East Sepik

For many years the glossy and colorful in-flight magazine of Air Niugini, the Papua New Guinea national airline, has been called *Paradise,* and in 1998 the national tourist board was luring travelers with the slogan "Paradise Live." This is a memorable phrase, but despite the spectacular natural beauty to be found throughout Papua New Guinea it is hard to live up to such a claim. A slogan used several years before, "Papua New Guinea: Like Every Place You've Never Been," was more modest and better captured the country's inimitable character. But journalism and travel writing about Papua New Guinea are fond of the extremes and tend to focus on things like leeches and crocodiles or, at the other pole, spectacular sunsets, blue lagoons, and people with hibiscus blossoms tucked behind their ears. In reality, Papua New Guinea is neither Paradise nor Hades, although in 1998 the country was still having its share of troubles.

Forces of nature had inflicted some of these. Cyclone Justine had battered coastal and island regions of Papua New Guinea early in 1997. While the government struggled with Justine's effects, the worldwide El Niño weather system had transformed the normal dry season into an extended drought, aggravated by killing frosts in some parts of the country's highlands. The Australian international aid agency, AusAID, estimated that at the end of 1997 more than one-third of the country's population lacked adequate food and water and thousands more were facing rapidly deteriorating conditions. Unable to deliver basic services to most of the population before this disaster, the government was now completely unable to cope and turned to Australia to lead the relief campaign. In addition to desiccating and freezing subsistence gardens, the drought damaged commercial coffee, cocoa, and coconut crops. It also shut down operations of the huge gold mine at Ok Tedi in the far west of the country, a major source of government revenue, by impeding the river transport on which the mine depends. All of this further weakened the already troubled national economy.

The tour saw much of Papua New Guinea's usual lack of Western affluence and its deteriorating modern infrastructure, but we saw little dramatic evidence of its most recent hardships. I noticed, however, that since 1995 the Islander in Port Moresby had added a new layer of security fence, enclosing the area immediately in front of the main doors. We also saw some of the effects of the drought during our few days in the Eastern Highlands Province, where we passed hillsides blackened by fire as we traveled by van to and from the tourist lodge on each day's excursion. Flying from the highlands to Timbunke, on the Sepik River, we passed over more acres of scorched earth and brown trees and what appeared to be dry riverbeds. The water in the Sepik River itself, however, was high, evidence that the rains finally had begun in earnest in the river's watershed.

The tour spent several days in the East Sepik Province, cruising down the broad Sepik River on the luxury catamaran *Melanesian Discoverer,* but we came nowhere near dear old Wewak, the province's capital. Instead, on leaving the mouth of the Sepik east of Wewak, we cruised along the coast to Madang, the capital of the neighboring province, where we caught a plane south across the width of the country to Port Moresby. The tour group paused only long enough to go through customs and board the flight to Hong Kong. I said goodbye to Jana and the rest of the tour members and took a cab to the Islander. The next day I made the flight back across the mountain ranges that form the spine of the island of New Guinea and along the north coast to Wewak. By mid-afternoon, I was walking across the steaming tarmac to the open-walled baggage-claim area and pulling my duffel bags from among the off-loaded suitcases, boxes, and oddly shaped bundles.

As I did so, I looked around for someone from Kragur waiting to meet me. Only a few people had been on the flight and they were dispersing quickly. Finally, I heard someone speaking my name quietly and realized that a young man I had glanced at but failed to recognize was Bokim. In 1995, he had had short hair and a beard; now he was clean-shaven and wore his hair in long dreadlocks. Bokim had come to the airport by bus. But he quickly spotted a small pickup truck loading other new arrivals, spoke to the driver, and secured us a ride in the back to the Marist Brothers' house, where I had arranged with Pawil to stay while I was in town. Like the brothers' house at St. Xavier's on Kairiru, the Marist house was neat but Spartan, its furnishings battered and worn, its concrete floors bare, the communal shower and toilet block a bit dank. Pawil was out of town, but the other brothers found me a room and put me at my ease.

Early the next day, Bokim and I took a bus to the center of town to buy supplies for my stay in Kragur. At the Tang Mow wholesale outlet, just across the street from the market, I purchased much of what I needed: two 25-kilo (about 55-pound) bags of rice; two 48-tin cases of canned mackerel; a case of large, hard biscuits; a case of peanut butter; a case of strawberry jam; an economical but ridiculously large bundle of toilet paper rolls; two cartons of Benson & Hedges cigarettes; and a box of filterless, six-inch cigarettes rolled in a simulacrum of newsprint and filled with dark, pungent tobacco that sears the throat and lungs. The latter, I was told, were now more popular than the sticks of black trade tobacco older villagers used to favor. We also made some retail purchases at the R. A. Seto general store: a plastic bucket, laundry soap, matches, a lantern, two towels, and a couple of empty rice sacks.

While Bokim went to buy a few gallons of kerosene, I took the rice sacks and visited the market for social necessities: a sack of betel nut and a sack of betel peppers to share with hosts and guests when I got to Kragur. Betel nut, called *buai* in Tok Pisin, hangs in large, thick-stemmed clusters just below the crown of the tall slender betel palms. Dense clusters of betel, called *rop* (ropes) in Tok Pisin, rather than loose nuts, are the best gifts, so I wandered around the market examining the offerings until I found a vendor with a good stock of healthy *rop buai*. After Bokim and I finished our rounds, we deposited all our purchases at Tang Mow. Later that day a Tang Mow truck delivered them to the Marist house, where we heaped the bags and boxes in a corner of the common room.

The next day we set out for Kragur at about 9:45 A.M. Bokim had moored his small boat in the fresh-water channel to the sea that passes just behind the Marist house. He and his one crewman loaded my gear and their other cargo in the front of the boat and covered it with a tarpaulin. Just as I was about to climb in, Bokim went back into the common room and came out with one of the wicker chairs. He placed it in the boat, up against the pile of cargo and facing the stern. This was where I was to sit. Remembering the discomfort of perching on the edge of a two-by-four in a rough sea, I settled appreciatively on the chair's soft cushion. It began raining as we headed out to sea. I pulled a corner of the tarpaulin over my shoulders, but Bokim and his mate let the rain wash over them.

Facing backward, I could not watch us draw nearer to Kairiru. But in an hour we drew abreast of Mushu, and I could see its gentle green slopes pass by and then recede as we moved across the wide eastern end of the passage between Mushu and Kairiru. The rain had stopped by now, the sun was breaking through, and as we came abreast of Kairiru the water changed from slate gray to emerald green. Now, to my right, Kairiru rose sharply from a rocky coastline. Stone outcroppings punctuate the steeply rising face of the island here, but it is largely forest, clinging to the plunging mountainside and perpetually falling away. It was obvious that the rains had begun here, too. The streams in the island's upper reaches end abruptly when the land drops away beneath them, and they now were spilling long, thin waterfalls, reddish-brown with mud. Large patches of ground had been washed away in places, leaving reddish-brown gouges in the green.

We circled wide around the tall, black volcanic rocks erupting from the ocean at Urur Point, where sea birds roost and waves foam. This is the home, islanders say, of a dangerous spirit being (Tok Pisin, a *masalai*), and thus to be traversed with care. *Masalai* or no, it was a place where conflicting currents often swirled and churned. I now turned in my seat so I could watch for Kragur, and by 11:15 I could see the coconut palms and thatched rooftops squeezed between the cliff and the mountain. I knew that there were more dwellings in the village than there had been in 1975–1976, but it still did not stand out starkly from its surroundings. The forest on all sides was lush and the green seemed to be seeping down among the houses.

As we turned into the bay, the village and its grounds became more distinct, the houses along the top of the cliff forming a clear line. We were able to approach to within a few yards of the beach, untroubled by large swells, but a group of young men waded out to hold the pitching boat steady so it would not wash up on the rocks. As I started over the side, Moraf and another man grabbed me, one on each side, and carried me ashore. This was undoubtedly less an honor than recognition of my clumsiness in boats. Whatever the motivation, I landed dry and unbruised.

There had not been enough time to exchange letters with anyone in the village about where I could stay. I did write to several villagers I knew well, telling them I was coming. It might have simplified things to contact only one family, but I could not have done that without slighting those I ignored. In the hope of avoiding confusion, in each letter I mentioned the two or three others to whom I also had written, hoping that my various friends would sort things out among themselves. That this approach was not completely successful came to my attention in Wewak.

As Bokim was helping me settle in at the Marist house, he told me that he had prepared a room for me at Momosang again and that the outhouse was still in good repair. But the next day I encountered Bash in Wewak and he immediately told me that he and his kin could look after me when I got to the village. I said that Bokim already had made ready for me at Momosang. He protested politely, and rather than pursue the issue there on the street I told him it could wait until I arrived. Perhaps I should have insisted then that I could not renege on my arrangements with Bokim. I did not want to insult him and his family; but I did not want to insult Bash and his kin either. Bash's father, long dead now, had been among my most gracious hosts and valuable teachers, and Bash's older brother, Waiwun, was one of those to whom I had written announcing my impending visit. So I left the issue up in the air, hoping that a diplomatic solution would come to me or that my prospective hosts would settle the matter among themselves.

I was not so lucky. The narrow track up from Kragur's beach reaches the coastal path midway between the main village and Momosang. Bokim's kinsman Kwan was the first to greet me as I scrambled to the top. Even as he did so, Moraf (to whom I also had written) and a few young boys were bringing my boxes and bags up from the beach. "We're going to Bash's house, right?" he said, as he and the others paused on the path. Kwan looked alarmed, it began to rain again, I dithered, the luggage began to move down the path to the main village, and I ran after it.

I followed the baggage train to a new house Bash and his older brother Waiwun had built for their younger brother, now away at school. It was divided in half and I was to have the room that made up the west end. Most village houses have virtually no furniture. This room, however, was furnished with a metal and plywood cot and a thin foam mattress, complete with mature but serviceable sheets and pillows. There was also a small homemade wooden table and a weathered, metal straight-backed chair. The window looked down the hill, over the roofs of other houses toward the ocean, and with the door open and the window shutter propped up with a stick there was a nice breeze.

The location was excellent. The house was only a short walk from the bathing pool; but it was still in the midst of other houses, so casual visiting would be easy and I could see and hear the goings on of daily life. Moraf also had organized a party to build a new outhouse for me. It stood just a few yards off the main path leading east out of the village. After I left, Moraf and his kin would use it, but during my stay I was privileged to share it only with the quick, slender lizards that sunned themselves in front of its palm-frond door.

I was still worried that I had insulted Bokim and his family. Bokim sent word that I was invited to eat with him and Kwan at Momosang that evening. They had steamed a chicken in an earth oven, cooked rice and taro, and cut up a pineapple and a papaya for dessert. I ate sitting in the cane armchair, which the luggage train to Bash's house had left behind. After our meal, I explained that I had decided to stay at Bash's and Waiwun's house because it probably would be easier for me to do my work if I lived in the central village, and I apologized for the confusion. If Bokim and Kwan were angry, they did not show it. They assured me that they understood and gave me the key to the padlock on the room they had prepared for me, so I could use it when I felt like a change.

This was reassuring, but it did not allay all of my concerns. Kragur people have forgiven me many a social misstep, assuming, I suppose, that I was too much of a European to know any better. But I worried that my choice might stir bad feeling among the villagers involved. I took comfort, however, in the thought that nothing I could have done would have satisfied everyone.

Bash's and Waiwun's house was not far from the large establishment that Brawaung's widow shared with her one unmarried son and Moraf, his wife, and their four young children. They assumed that I would take most of my meals with them. Hoping for such an arrangement, I had not brought any cooking gear. I had, however, brought a lot more canned fish and rice than I could possibly eat myself, so that there would be plenty to share with my hosts. We stored the cases of fish and the bags of rice at the Brawaung family house, and I joined the family most mornings and evenings for plates of rice and fish, greens, taro, sweet potato, and occasional delicacies like chicken or dugong (the latter tastes like beef, not chicken).

During my five weeks in Kragur, many families invited me to come to their homes for evening meals, often inviting me several days in advance and, on one occasion, even sending a written invitation. People I had known well in years past issued most of these invitations, but a few new acquaintances also asked me over for dinner. In 1975–1976 and 1981, villagers had often sent me plates of cooked food in the evening, and if I happened to stop by when people were preparing a meal they invariably asked me to sit and eat. But European-style dinner invitations had been rare. Indeed, in 1976, when Mowush had invited me well in advance to join his family for an evening meal, he had noted that this, he knew, was how Europeans did things. In 1998, a few younger villagers even spread a colorful cloth on the floor where we ate and embellished it with a glass jar of fresh flowers.

Bigman from the World Bank

All in all, Kragur people took care of me well and showed me their usual hospitality. Among small children I was even a minor celebrity. As I passed by, they sometimes giggled and chanted, "Michael Smith! Michael Smith!" Of course, some villagers undoubtedly were indifferent to my presence, and some may even have resented it. Others, however, at least took my return to Kragur as a compliment to the village. A few still spoke disparagingly of a foreign linguist who had spent several months in Kragur in the late 1970s but who, villagers said, ceased contact with everyone in the village within two or three years of his departure. I suggested that he was not necessarily "a bad man," as one villager charged; he might have become ill, he might even be dead. But I knew that when villagers provide generous hospitality to visitors they do so partly in the hope of establishing an enduring social tie, just as their ancestors cultivated links with trading partners in Wogeo, Turubu, and Murik Lakes. To some villagers, eating the taro, enjoying the crystalline water, sleeping on the ancestral ground, and then apparently forgetting Kragur was an insult as well as a disappointment.

Some also were pleased that I had spread Kragur's name abroad in a book. In any case, my status had risen considerably in the years since I first walked over the mountain from St. Xavier's. Said Benau, who remembered my early days in Kragur, "You're a real bigman now. Before, you were just a boy, but now you're a real bigman." Traditional Kragur leaders are called *ramat walap* in the Kairiru language, which translates as big *(walap)* men or man *(ramat)*. In Tok Pisin they are simply called *bikman* (bigmen or bigman).

I am afraid, however, that some of the honor and deference I received was based on misunderstanding. I am sure that at least a few people thought I had earned a great deal of money from *Hard Times*, which could not be further from the truth. "So, did they give you a few toea?" for writing the book, one old man asked me, with a knowing smile. And one townsman cautioned me that some believed I had earned big money from *Hard Times* and might expect that I was going to share it with the village.

The mistaken idea that I was making money from my association with Kragur was not new. Early in 1976, I had received a letter signed by several Kragur university students in Port Moresby accusing me of imposing myself on Kragur and using the village as a springboard to a lucrative academic career. They also demanded that I pay Kragur a rather large sum of money in compensation. I wrote back, explaining how and why I had come to settle in Kragur, my very limited means and the general financial foolishness of pursuing an advanced degree in anthropology. These critics and I eventually met, and we now get along well when we see each other in Port Moresby or Wewak.

But the impression that I am a wealthy person, not only by village standards but also in the wider world, lived on. In 1998, Kauref, a retired policeman come home to Kragur, asked me how I was able to visit Papua New Guinea so often. I told him, as I told many others, about the work for the World Bank that brought me to Papua New Guinea in 1995 and the American Museum of Natural History tour. He nodded in understanding, but added, "[People] see you go and come by airplane. I think some of them think 'Oh, Smith is a millionaire.'"

In 1998, a new misunderstanding had joined this familiar one. To many villagers, I was not just a bigman, I was a *bikpela man bilong World Bank*, that is, a bigman from the World Bank. As I visited families around the village, I explained how I had come to Papua New Guinea on this occasion and that I no longer had anything to do with the bank. But if word spread from house to house, it did so very slowly.

I am sure many villagers were disappointed that I was no longer with the World Bank. Like many other Papua New Guineans, Kragur people were suspicious of the bank. Nevertheless, some villagers were eager to tell someone they believed to be influential about their anger with the Papua New Guinea government and about Kragur's need for better transportation and health care and more business opportunities. Leaders from two other north-coast Kairiru villages also came to see me in Kragur, hoping to tell someone from the World Bank of their own communities' needs and their frustration with the government. Unfortunately, all I could do was promise to try to contact my few acquaintances at the bank and convey these messages from the hinterlands of Papua New Guinea.

Early Impressions

February, when I arrived in Kragur, is the middle of the rainy season, and this year, in contrast to the last, the rains came in full measure. During my five weeks in Kragur it rained every day, if not during the daylight hours, then at night. The water in the main men's bathing pool was sometimes so deep and turbulent that men bathed in the shallow rivulets on its margins. During the drought, garden crops had been stunted for lack of water, but by February villagers were worrying that the seed tubers they had planted would rot in the ground. The island seemed to be saturated. At one end of the village, the soaking rain had opened a narrow but deep fissure in the earth a few feet from the edge of the cliff. Villagers took pains to walk on the landward side of this threatening crack and hoped they would not lose a few more feet of level ground to the sea.

As in the 1970s, the gardens were still the mainstay of the village; but garden produce, especially taro, was currently in short supply, and villagers said the preceding year had been a hungry one. People had turned to their sago palms, but they eventually used up all the mature palms that could yield rich harvests of sago starch. Those who had a little money bought rice. But Papua New Guinea imports most of its rice and, as one villager pointed out, the devaluation of the kina had increased the cost of imported rice at a bad time.

Kragur and other parts of Kairiru, however, had escaped the worst effects of the drought because the mountain streams that supply drinking water to many villages had not dried up. Later, in Wewak prior to my departure, a Catholic Health Service administrator told me that the medical-aid post on Kairiru's south coast had not reported the steep increases in diarrheal diseases that occurred in many parts of Papua New Guinea. This was evidence that Kairiru people had not lost their source of clean water for drinking, cooking, and washing.

In my experience, Kragur people have always been lean, and on average they looked no leaner now than I remembered them. They also were plentiful. In 1995, Brother Pawil told me that Kragur's population had climbed to between 350 and 400, a large jump from the approximately 220 I found there in 1976. The village was indeed more populous. In 1997, a young village man, Muneram, conducted a census in aid of efforts to secure government food relief during the drought. His work confirmed that Kragur had about 350 inhabitants. It also showed that the population was younger than it had been in 1976. About 90 percent of resident villagers in 1998 were below the age of fifty, compared to 70 percent in 1976.

I could also see for myself that many villagers were doing just what Mwairap had reported in 1995: buying and selling betel nut. They paused on village paths to exchange coins for betel nut and betel pepper, and small children ran from house to house with handfuls of coins, seeking betel nut for their parents.

Other details also caught my eye. A few young men were wearing long pants and athletic shoes or work boots, and a few young women were wearing shorts, styles of dress I never saw in the village in 1975–1976 or 1981. Fat, cream-colored pigs, clearly descended from comfortable farm stock, had replaced the lean, dark, bristle-backed bush stock, although they still wandered freely about the village like the pigs of old. Women still carried clothing and dishes to the stream to wash, but I also saw many women washing cooking pots and plates at the water taps near their houses. And I noticed a house built of two-by-fours, milled planks, wallboard, and corrugated metal roofing, and another under construction. They belonged to townsmen with salaried jobs, keeping a foot in the village and perhaps preparing for rural retirement.

Villagers still laced their Kairiru language with Tok Pisin. Some of my acquaintances complained that the lacing was getting so thick that it was ruining their indigenous tongue. I had exercised my Tok Pisin on several trips to Papua New Guinea since my first visit to Kragur and slipped back into the language easily. One of the young men who slept in the room next to mine even reported that on my first night in the village I talked loudly in my sleep in a mixture of Tok Pisin and Kairiru. Among other remarks, apparently I announced in Kairiru that I had to urinate. This is plausible, because I did wake toward morning and step outside to relieve myself while the waning darkness still afforded some privacy.

While awake, however, I found that some of my Tok Pisin vocabulary had become archaic. I knew that in urban areas, in newspapers, and on the radio more and more English words were entering Tok Pisin. The same thing was happening in Kragur, albeit to a more limited extent. Some common Tok Pisin words were giving way to their English equivalents. For example, many villagers no longer used the words *staus* or *pekato*. Instead, they said "toilet" or "sin." Just as they objected to Tok Pisin's adulteration of the Kairiru language, so some villagers were not happy with this Anglicization of Tok Pisin. From these, I drew a few compliments on the purity of my speech, since I tended to stick with my old-fashioned vocabulary and archaic idioms.

There were many signs that villagers were now more literate than ever before. One of the townsmen in Wewak visited the village frequently and sometimes brought me a copy of the *Papua New Guinea Post Courier*, an English-language publication. As in the past, people who saw me reading the paper often asked if they could have it when I was finished. Some still valued the *Post Courier* mostly as cigarette paper; but, in contrast to the 1970s, several of my neighbors now wanted to read about what was happening in Port Moresby and the world. Strolling through the village I now saw an occasional young person reading a book or newspaper, and the doors and timbers of a few houses even sported graffiti inked in the broad strokes of marking pens. Of course, other than names and dates, most of the words and phrases were completely cryptic to me, just like most of the graffiti I see on city walls at home (in the Washington, D.C., area). I saw other evidence of increasing literacy at the first assembly for a day of council work I attended. Councillor Bokashim, a man in his thirties, presided with a clipboard in one hand and a pen in the other, consulting his notes and jotting down more notes to himself.

Kragur now had two councillors, each of whom was responsible for a different section of the village. This had come to pass partly because the village had grown so large and, some said, to help secure Kragur a more adequate allocation of food aid during the drought. So, although the village was bigger, the Monday morning assemblies for council work were smaller affairs, held near the respective councillors' houses rather than in the central open space. The village-wide evening prayer sessions were gone, too, even though, as I would learn, other kinds of Catholic gatherings were plentiful.

All of this was interesting, and some developments hinted at significant changes. Did more open pursuit of money mean that ideas of social harmony and mutual responsibility were changing dramatically? Did the councillors with clipboards and the young people reading newspapers threaten to undermine the authority of older leaders, the masters of magic and the keepers of the oral tradition? Was the graffito "666 Satan Boys" inked on a house timber a superficial prank, or perhaps a mark of rebellion against the pervasive Catholicism? Personally, I missed the council assemblies and the evening prayer sessions in the central gathering place. They had been wonderful opportunities for keeping up with village events. Evening prayers had also been occasions for relaxed socializing by moonlight, lamplight, or just the light of cigarette embers and the small fires people stoked to dry their tobacco leaves and light their smokes. But did the demise of these collective events mean anything? Was Kragur more fragmented than it had been in the 1970s? Had it become weaker even as it grew larger?

Some villagers left no doubt about their misgivings. "We've never had this kind of disunity before," one man told me in the fluent English he had cultivated in years of urban life before returning to Kragur with his wife and young children. Another young, well-educated family man used a mixture of English and Tok Pisin to tell me that things were not as I had seen them in the past. The "relationships" among people had changed, he said, using the English word. He went on in Tok Pisin to say that relationships now were not strong but "*lus lus,*" that is, very loose or weak. The old, too, saw this. Mansu, a man in his sixties, told me that "When you were here [in 1975–1976], people worked together," but things were different now.

It would be easy to dismiss such views, sincere as they were, as contemporary versions of a chronic complaint. Here, for example, is Brawaung in 1976: "Things were all right before. When the village bell rang, everyone came right away. But that's over now." And here is what another villager had to say: "Before, if we organized a *singsing* all the old men and women would come and have a good time, but not now. They don't feel like it, they don't want to come. That's a sign that the village is in trouble."

What I heard in 1998, then, sounded very familiar; and if one judged solely on the size and age of its population, Kragur appeared to be thriving. In the 1970s, many adults had worried that the young people who left Kragur to go to school or find work would never come back, repelled by the physical hardship and what the adults saw as the related social malaise of village life. Ten years from now, said one, "There won't be any young men. They go to school; they go for good. There won't be anyone to help us with the work. We'll die and it will be over." By 1998, neither physical hardship nor social disintegration had eroded Kragur's strength of numbers. Nevertheless, there were good reasons to listen carefully to what villagers had to say about the current state of social relationships. The persistence of such concerns was itself worth noting; and, if the general themes were familiar, the specific issues that troubled people might be revealing.

There was some evidence that there might be new reasons for villagers to be concerned about unity and harmony. The possibility of gold mining on Kairiru loomed in the background, and I heard rumors that prospects of big money and major environmental disruption had aroused controversy. I also heard of and saw events dramatically different from any I had observed in the past. Villagers told me that, had I come a few months earlier, I would hardly have been able to sleep because groups of young men drunk on locally distilled alcohol roamed the village at night, raising a din and threatening, even injuring, their sober neighbors with fists, stones, and bush knives.

Home brew, as the potent liquor was called, was not a problem for Kragur alone. According to the newspapers, it was popular all over the country. It could be exceedingly strong, containing as much as 80 or 90 percent alcohol, according to one story in the *Post Courier,* more than enough to dull the edge of one's judgment. But I had drunk beer and hard liquor with Kragur people on many occasions in the past, sometimes to excess, and threatening elders, fighting, and wielding bush knives had not been part of the program. To the contrary, in those days many villagers had delighted in telling me how pacific Kragur people were when they drank. I also had attended multitudes of Catholic religious services and had never seen, nor heard of, what I saw on two occasions in just a few weeks in 1998: prayer services broken up by shouted arguments and stone throwing. In fact, I had never seen any Kragur person in any context do anything more violent than shout and gesticulate angrily.

Whether dramatic incidents like fights and stone throwing were linked to larger changes was another question. A number of villagers who told me of their disquiet over violence and disunity placed at least some of the blame on particular events. A few, for example, thought that dividing the village into two Local Government Council wards had created a rift. Several also told me of a series of events in the early 1990s that had left in their wake suspicion and enmity that obviously still lingered. The details are too complex and too sensitive to recount here. I can say, however, that division of Kragur's support between rival candidates for parliament (one of them a local man), a failed business venture, the discovery of a corpse (not a local man) on the beach following an Independence Day celebration, and a fire that consumed as many as three village houses had given rise to accusations of political skulduggery, financial malfeasance, murder, and arson.

There was nothing more shocking here, either factual or alleged, than the goings-on in the small American town in which I grew up. But as small as that town was, with about five thousand residents, it still provided a great deal more elbowroom than Kragur does for people at odds with each other. It was easy to believe that the events of the early 1990s had frayed or even torn the social fabric.

Regarding the body on the beach, there had been no clear evidence of foul play, and the fire had turned out to be the result of an accident with a container of gasoline (fuel for an outboard motor) and a burning kerosene lamp. At the time, however, some villagers had found a pattern in the events that made each of its elements appear more sinister. In 1998, some villagers looked back on all these occurrences quite coolly and calmly, but an unpleasant brew of fear and recrimination still bubbled in some quarters. Episodes of schism were nothing new in Kragur, but there was a relatively new element in this one. The challenges to social harmony posed by close involvement in a hard-fought campaign in the wider, modern political arena were still novel. Parliamentary elections in Papua New Guinea seldom involve marked ideological differences. They are, however, often fraught with promises and expectations of spoils and patronage, and this is as fertile ground for faction and conflict as any disagreement about principles.

Kragur people could still taste the bitter residue of the election and the events that had been dragged into its orbit. (I noticed that the two sets of villagers who had prepared housing for me had been on opposite sides of the electoral campaign, and I wondered if this did not partly account for the absence of coordination between them.) But villagers also spoke of less dramatic and more gradual changes when they mused on the state of village unity. They spoke of weakening village leadership; a growing gap between the young and the old, those with formal education and those without it; and the increasing influence of money and its corrosive effects on social life. I heard no one speak of fear that migration would depopulate Kragur, but many were concerned that no matter how strong the village was in numbers, its people were thinking more of themselves and their immediate families and less of the community as a whole. "Kragur is becoming like Wewak," said one worried townsman. And some English-speaking village residents spoke with troubled expressions of the rise of "individualism" and "personal interest." Again, these anxieties had a familiar ring. But the new aspects of village life I saw and heard about would not allow me to ignore them.

On Wewak's main street, showing Papua New Guinea Motors, Bana Trading Company and the Papua New Guinea Banking Corporation, 1995.

Wewak Market, 1995. The market lies at one end of Wewak's main street, which cuts across the neck of Wewak Point.

A Kragur woman preparing fish for a meal, 1995.

Launching a boat from Kragur's beach on a relatively calm day, 1995.

A meeting for curing illness, 1981. The men are trying to discover and settle the grievance that has incited ancestral ghosts to make the patient sick.

Celebrating Easter, 1981. The people of Kragur and nearby villages gathered at Bou Village for the celebration, which included this flower-bedecked cross.

Children on a verandah, 1981.

Father and child, 1998.
Notice the clay fire platform in
the foreground.

Using one of Kragur's new water taps, 1998. The taps and the water tanks feeding them, paid for by a grant from the World Health Organization, save Kragur women many trips to the stream.

Displaying a carved wooden plate in a typical Kragur house, 1998. Notice the infant napping in a string bag in the background.

A bigman displaying his *kaikrauap*, male and female figures used in magical procedures, 1998. The female figure of this pair is named Shinawar, the male, Kaunup.

A household altar to the Virgin Mary, 1998. The orange fruits marching across the front of the table are inedible but make good ornaments.

Preparing the altar for charismatic worship, 1998. The altar was hastily dismantled that evening after stone throwing broke up the worship service.

The author's outhouse, 1998.
Inside, a floor of logs over a pit.

The author on Mission Hill, overlooking Wewak Point and Kairiru Island, 1998.

CHAPTER 9

The Key to the Village, Structure, and Strife

WHEN YOU'RE DEALING WITH STRUCTURE,
YOU HAVE TO TAKE IT EASY, BE DISCREET.
YOU DON'T WANT TO MAKE ANYONE ANGRY.
(*TAIM YU WOK LONG DISPELA STRAKSA,*
YU MAS I GO ISI ISI, HAIT LIKLIK.
NOGUD KROS I KAMAP.)
—A Kragur villager, 1998

Since I have known Kragur, most of the houses, long and rectangular, have been ranged parallel to the sea. While some form rows, the terrain always cuts the rows short. One of my accomplishments in 1975–1976 was learning my way around the jumbled terraces and fragmentary rows. When I came back for the first time in 1981, there had been some changes. New houses blocked what once had been familiar paths, and I had to hunt for the houses of some old friends. By 1998, even more had changed. As I made my way around, I often had to ask directions, and I sometimes found myself at a dead end, facing a rocky drop-off or the blank back wall of an unfamiliar dwelling.

To an outsider, Kragur might look like a shapeless hodgepodge of houses and people. But it has a complex if unobtrusive order. It would have been much harder for me to get my bearings in 1998 if I had not already understood something of this subtle social framework. It also would be hard to talk about change in Kragur without providing a fuller picture than I have so far of the social institutions that make it a village.

Institutions of relatively recent vintage, such as the Local Government Council and the Catholic Church, play important roles in Kragur society, but the oldest institutions in the village are still the most fundamental. Kinship and links to the ancestors involve villagers in a complicated web of loyalties, responsibilities, and interests and give Kragur its characteristic order. It is an order that allows for considerable jostling for power and resources and is subject to considerable internal stress. But many of its basic features have endured through European colonization, religious conversion, wartime occupation, and the coming of independence. Changing times, however, pose new challenges.

Central to Kragur's social arrangements are the social groups known in the Kairiru language as *koyeng*. In 1998, some Kragur villagers had begun using the Tok Pisin word *klen* interchangeably with *koyeng*. *Klen* is the Tok Pisin equivalent of the English word "clan." English-speaking Papua New Guineans also use clan freely, and references to clans are frequent in the rare articles about Papua New Guinea that appear in American newspapers and in travel literature about the country.

However, what Papua New Guineans, foreign travelers, journalists, and even anthropologists call "clans" differ immensely in their particulars and can exhibit bewildering complexities. Clans, *klen,* or *koyeng* in Kragur, are relatively straightforward compared with similar institutions in some other Papua New Guinea societies, but they still have their nuances. For one thing, even though some villagers themselves were speaking easily of clans and *klen* in 1998, the meaning of the common English word "clan" covers only part of the meaning of *koyeng*. In ordinary English usage, a clan is a group of people descended from a common ancestor who, by virtue of their common descent, recognize themselves as a distinct group. When Kragur people speak of *koyeng*, they frequently mean such descent groups; but they also use the term to refer to residential areas in the village and those who live in them.

Even strict adherence to a narrow definition of *koyeng* (as groups defined by descent from common ancestors) would not eliminate all uncertainty from the system, because Kragur people often disagree on the details of their descent from distant ancestors. To complicate things still further, some of what villagers know about their distant ancestors they keep secret. Uncertainty, contention, and secrecy surround *koyeng* precisely because they are so important.

Koyeng in Time: Descent Groups

I once heard an important leader passionately exhort an assembly of villagers that in their efforts to start businesses and earn money they should work together because Kragur was "one family." This was not mere hyperbole, for shared ancestors and generations of marriages within the village have created a complicated thicket of kinship ties. Descent groups are vital landmarks among the tangled branches of kinship in Kragur. Each individual has his or her own distinctive set of kinship relations, made up of what is given at birth and created through marriage and procreation, and these networks grow and die with the individual. Descent groups, however, endure. They existed before individual members were born and remain after they die.

Descent groups in Kragur are exogamous. That is, people must marry outside the groups into which they were born. They are also patrilineal: their members, both male and female, are the descendants through males of shared male ancestors. More concretely, people are members of the descent groups of their fathers', grandfathers', and more ancient male forebears. Hence, a man's daughters are members of his descent group, but his daughter's children, both male and female, will be members of their own father's descent group. A patrilineal descent group's line ends with daughters but continues through sons.

The boundaries defined by descent through men, however, do not make kinship ties through women irrelevant. People keep close track of all their kin, and there are many important kinship relations not based on common patrilineal descent. Men have continuing obligations to the natal families of their wives and often develop close relationships with their in-laws. A married woman has strong ties in two descent groups. She retains an allegiance to her natal descent group, but she becomes strongly identified with her husband's, particularly after she has contributed children to its ranks.

Nevertheless, a descent group has common interests as well as common ancestors. In Kragur, although the living members of descent groups do not use or administer land collectively, men sometimes speak of the land of its members as a commonly held resource, passed down to present generations from common male ancestors. Other important resources, too, tend to be passed from generation to generation within descent groups. Rights to particular kinds of magic are highly important among these, and even individuals who have no personal rights to important magic speak with pride of the magic other members of their descent groups control.

There are significant gaps and gray areas in my record of Kragur lines of descent. It is likely, however, that no matter how often I were to return to Kragur I could never produce a comprehensive version of descent-group genealogies in which no villager could find flaws. No one has formal responsibility for keeping a descent group's genealogical history. Members of some descent groups can trace the line of male descent back for dozens of generations. In fact, some trace their male ancestors back to, by their account, the first human beings, although these are not necessarily the longest genealogies. But disagreement about the accuracy of a genealogy tends to increase as it reaches back into time, and even members of the same descent group sometimes disagree, especially as they extend their genealogies far into the past. In addition, many villagers prefer that the names of their most distant ancestors not be bandied about in public.

All the descendants of a known male ancestor do not necessarily form a single, named descent group. (I use the same spellings for *koyeng* names in this book that I did in *Hard Times*. They differ from some current village spellings, although village spelling is not standardized.) The descendants of the ancestor Kwan, for example, form two of the current named descent groups. The descendants of Kwan by his first wife, Raisek, make up Koyeng Shewaratin, and those of Kwan by his second wife, Waungi, make up Koyeng Nalwun. Similarly, the descendants of Siliau constitute four named groups. Three of these are defined by descent from different grandsons of Siliau, and one comprises the descendants of one of Siliau's great grandsons, Boyek.

Kragur people do not lose track of the ancestral connections that link the named descent groups. The genealogies they recount stretch far back before the founding of Kragur and show how many of the current named groups are related. They also show how the ancestors moved from place to place over the generations until they eventually reached Kragur. Many descendants of the distant ancestors settled elsewhere on Kairiru, so knowledgeable villagers are keenly aware of their connections to local descent groups in other Kairiru villages. When Kragur villagers use the term *koyeng* to speak of groups based on common descent, they usually mean the named groups within the village, but they sometimes use *koyeng* to refer to the far-flung descendants of a more distant ancestor.

Local descent groups are one of the anchors of the social order in Kragur, but they have some flexibility. They not only absorb women as wives, they can also absorb men and their offspring. For example, one branch of a fairly populous descent group springs from a male immigrant from the northwest end of Kairiru who came to Kragur as a youth to escape raids by hostile groups on his natal village. He first came to stay with a female relative who had married to Kragur, but a Kragur man without sons of his own adopted him, grafting him and his offspring-to-come onto his own line of descent.

A man can also be grafted to his wife's descent group, coming to live and work on its land and allowing his children to continue his wife's descent line, not his own. A man who does this is said to "hang up his knife" with his wife's family. Among other reasons, this may happen if a woman's father has no sons and wishes to continue his line of descent through his daughter's children, or if he has more land to work than his own sons can manage.

Koyeng in Time and Space

Although there are no signposts to label them or fences to mark their boundaries, Kairiru Island is blanketed with named places. One part of the mountainside above Kragur is known as Arai. In 1998, Moraf made a map of it for me. His map (Map 3) shows this small piece of the island alone divided into three named major subdivisions and twenty-seven smaller ones. From walking on the mountain with villagers I know that these divisions themselves are peppered with specific named sites. Like the forest above the village and the beach below it, the ground the village itself occupies is also peppered with named places. The most significant of these are the principal residential areas. Villagers' mental maps of Kragur's geography are immensely more complex than mine, but anyone living in Kragur for long would be living in a

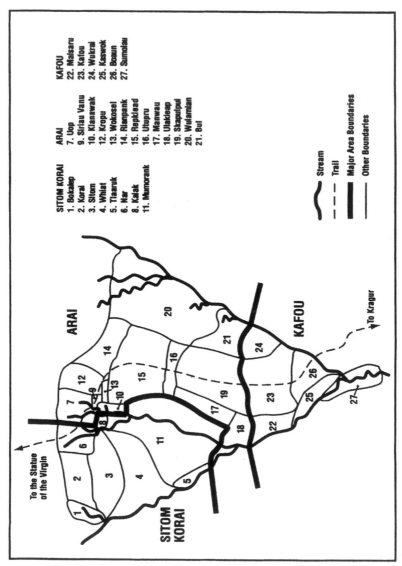

Map 3: Named places on the mountainside above Kragur. The three principal areas—Arai, Sitom Korai, and Kafou—are sometimes referred to collectively as Arai. (Map by S. Umari and D. Buric)

SITOM KORAI
1. Bokalep
2. Korai
3. Sitom
4. Whiat
5. Tlaaruk
6. Nar
8. Kalak
11. Mumorank

ARAI
7. Uop
9. Striau Vanu
10. Klanawak
12. Kropu
13. Wokosel
14. Rianpank
15. Repidead
16. Utupru
17. Manwau
18. Ulakleap
19. Skapulpul
20. Wuiamian
21. Bul

KAFOU
22. Maisaru
23. Katou
24. Wukrai
25. Kaswok
26. Boaun
27. Sumolau

~~~ Stream
--- Trail
▬▬ Major Area Boundaries
—— Other Boundaries

twilight world if he or she did not at least recognize the main residential areas. "They live up in Vanu Iviau," people might say; or "He's gone down to Kragur Nau. I don't know when he'll be back"; or "She's gone to visit her mother in Bomasek."

Some residential areas are firmly associated with particular descent groups and bear their names, even though all adult male descent-group members do not necessarily live there and households headed by men of other descent groups often do. Other areas are not as firmly associated with single descent lines. Nevertheless, villagers sometimes speak of all the areas and the people who live there as *koyeng*. Although people of several different descent groups are buried in the cemetery at the eastern end of the village, one wit liked to call it *koyeng bilong ol shawaung*— that is, *koyeng* of the spirits of the dead.

I was very lucky in 1998 to find that in the course of carrying out his census Muneram had made a map of the village showing the locations of all current households. Map 4 is based on Muneram's map. Muneram had only his original map, drawn and lettered with a ballpoint pen, but he walked over the mountain to St. Xavier's one rainy day, with the map carefully wrapped in plastic, to make me a copy on the school's photocopy machine. Unfortunately, copiers everywhere having much in common, it was out of order. A couple of days later, he accompanied a party going by boat to Wewak. There he was able to make two copies of the map for me at one of the businesses in the center of town.

Knowledgeable men from two descent groups went over it with me and told me in which named area each house stood. The result (Map 5) shows the locations of houses and residential areas as they were in 1998. (It does not show the precise borders of residential areas, but outlines the clusters of houses that stand within each named area.)

In 1975–1976, even without mapping the village, I could see that descent groups did not mesh perfectly with residential areas, and Muneram's map showed the same thing. The location of the households of the male descendants of the ancestor Boyek, also shown in Map 5, provides a simple illustration. These households make up the descent group called Brangiau, but they are not all located in the residential area called Brangiau. Households headed by descendants of Boyek started building houses in the area called Plos within the last fifteen years or so. As of 1998, no other descent groups had built there, and villagers clearly regard this cluster of houses as a kind of annex of the Brangiau area. The single household of a different descent group located in Brangiau, however, and the Brangiau household located in the Nalwun area, spoil the symmetry. Such lone outliers, however, are often easy to explain. Kinship ties through women often permit residence away from natal descent-group ground, and the reason for taking advantage of the opportunity may be as simple as the availability of a suitable level piece of land.

The situation, however, is not always so clear. Trying to clarify the larger issue

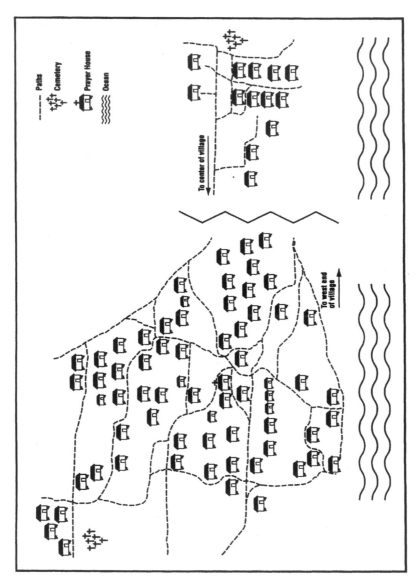

Map 4: Kragur Village. A few houses, distant from the main concentrations of dwellings, are not shown. (Map by S. Waibai and D. Buric)

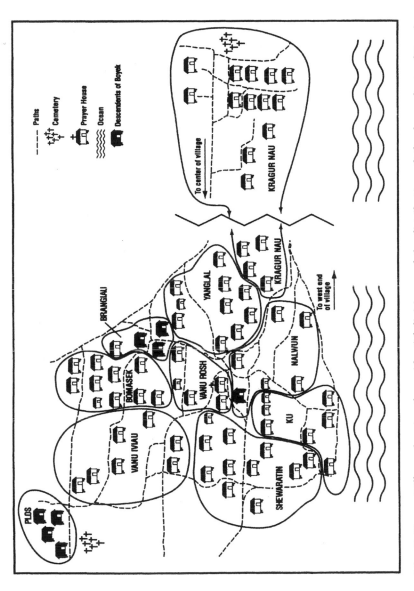

Map 5: Kragur Village, showing the residential divisions and the distribution of the descendents of Boyek. Plos (*upper left*) is a named area but not a *koyeng*. (Map by S. Waibai and D. Buric)

of what a *koyeng* was, one villager told me that in Kragur there were "nine groups and seven *koyeng*." He apparently meant that there were seven major descent lines, each of which also had a residential area bearing its name, and two residential areas that were not identified with single descent groups. The two or three other villagers present nodded in agreement. However, when I got down to specific cases in later discussions, not everyone agreed on what qualified as a *koyeng* and what did not. When I asked if I should understand the name of one particular residential area as the name of a descent group or simply as the name of an inhabited piece of ground, two of my closest collaborators gave me quite different answers. One lived in the area in question himself, as his father had, but he regarded its name as simply "the name of a piece of ground." He continued, "we [who live there] are of all different *koyeng*." My other collaborator, speaking with me on another occasion, implied that the name was primarily the name of a plot of ground, but "people have made a *koyeng* there."

A panel of selected elders might paint a sharper-edged picture of *koyeng* than that which emerges from my conversations with villagers of varied age, status, and claims to expertise. But fuzzy definitions of *koyeng* are definitely part of daily life in Kragur, and part of its culture. Most villagers appear to take it in stride, but some do worry about it. In 1998, a prominent middle-aged man told me he was concerned that people were losing track of the strict meaning of *koyeng*. He worried that children raised on the ground of descent lines other than their own might confuse residence with what he regarded as true *koyeng* membership. He wondered aloud, in English, if it might not be time to raise this issue in public. "They have to know the truth!" he said. I think, however, that villagers do not necessarily subscribe to the same truths in these matters, especially in the heat of a dispute where rights to use land or other resources are at stake.

Magicians and Leaders

If villagers sometimes are a little vague regarding the relationship of descent to the meaning of *koyeng*, they are very clear about the importance of descent to traditional authority. Myriad resources, tangible and intangible, are hereditary in Kragur, passed down primarily within descent groups. Such resources include rights to use certain technologies (including such objects as specific kinds of canoes and fishing nets), rights to perform particular songs and dances, rights to visit particular trading partners on the old sea-trade routes, and rights to do so in canoes bearing particular names and decorations. Those who hold primary rights to certain technologies or songs and dances, for example, often allow others to use them; but using them without permission is a serious offense.

The most important hereditary rights are those to use particular kinds of magic, and the authority of traditional leaders or bigmen rests in large part on their control over important magic. The bigman with primary rights to the magic for growing taro, for example, bears responsibility for supervising production of this highly important crop. A great deal that goes on in the village bears on the productivity of taro gardens. Too much unresolved anger and disharmony can weaken the taro magic; or simply neglecting to clear ground, plant, and weed with sufficient energy can render futile a bigman's magical efforts. So, responsibility for magical husbandry of taro brings with it the right and the responsibility to play a prominent role in many spheres of village life. More than one person may have the right to use taro-growing magic in their own gardens, but it is generally recognized that there is only one "boss" of the taro who bears responsibility for the village at large.

Such magical rights and positions of leadership remain within descent groups, but they are not necessarily passed down from father to son. When a bigman dies, a kinsman of the same generation may assume his place. When the position must finally pass to a younger generation, the successor is chosen on the basis of his capacity for leadership as well as his relationship to his predecessor. I am told that prominent men on occasion have passed on important magical rights to their daughters, but such "big women" exercised their influence behind the scenes. Particular descent groups can claim rights to more kinds and more important kinds of magic than others, so their prominent men have more potent claims to leadership. Most descent groups, however, have members who can claim magical authority of some kind.

There is magic for virtually every kind of activity in Kragur and for increasing the productivity of virtually every kind of food crop. As with taro, those with primary rights for particular kinds of magic also have the corollary rights and responsibilities to supervise related matters. The more important the crop or activity, of course, the broader and stronger the related authority. The most influential bigmen are not only proprietors of important magic, they are skilled orators, effective organizers, and clever politicians. But there is no substitute for hereditary rights to use vital magic.

In recent decades, new leadership opportunities have come to Kragur, and some villagers worry that the authority of the bigmen is eroding, a topic I shall return to in Chapter 12. All of this, however, is taking place against the background of generations of belief in the importance of the bigmen's magical knowledge to the health and prosperity of the village and a strong tradition of hereditary authority. The energetic young person who plunges ahead with a new endeavor without the blessing of the bigmen can find that she or he has stepped on sensitive toes. In 1998, I heard one middle-aged man, son of a prominent garden magician, roundly criticize a younger man for, in his view, aspiring to a position of leadership to which his ancestry did not entitle him. The younger man was not dabbling in garden magic, but he had tried to start various small business enterprises and organize village events that some took as bids for political influence. "Does he want to become a leader?" his critic asked angrily. "If your ancestor didn't have the right to some-thing, you don't either. [This man's] father didn't do anything. He was just a worker for *my* father!"

Politics and Secrecy

Despite the great importance of descent, there is no single authoritative version of Kragur descent-group genealogies. Not only are differing versions of the facts abroad, much information is kept secret for political and magical reasons. Although the secrecy surrounding some genealogical knowledge makes systematizing it impos-sible, it also helps give that knowledge its political clout.

In 1998, I spent many hours with adult men and a few adult women of several *koyeng* refining my pictures of their main lines of patrilineal descent. This had not been high on my original list of things to do during this short stay in Kragur. I had brought with me, however, copies of the descent-group genealogies I compiled in 1975–1976 to refresh my memory of who was who in the village, and pursuing other questions often led me back to genealogy.

Just as they were now referring to *koyeng* as *klen*, some villagers now had a new Tok Pisin term for descent-group genealogies: *straksa*. I assume that educated Kragur people introduced this new word, having adapted it from the English word "struc-ture." I knew these genealogies could be a highly charged topic, so when Bash cau-tioned me to "take it easy, be discreet" when dealing with *straksa* I took him quite seriously. But despite the sensitivity of many genealogical questions, I did not have to coax anyone to talk with me. In fact, Kragur villagers who have any knowledge of genealogy like to talk about it. The discussions we had were not, however, casual occasions. Sometimes two or three men met first to clarify their own understanding of important details before meeting with me. A few men also borrowed pens from me so they could organize what they knew on paper before we talked, something vil-lagers had not done in the 1970s. Occasionally, rather than recording oral histories, I found myself comparing notes. My collaborators were greatly interested in the genealogical information I had recorded in the 1970s, but they gave it weight only if I had gleaned it from an elder of that period whom they regarded as an expert.

Many things villagers told me they divulged in hushed tones. Much of what they knew was not for the ears of members of other descent groups or anyone too young to appreciate its worth. As I sat on the floor of my room one wet and moon-less night, discussing genealogical points with two knowledgeable men and scrib-bling in my notebook in a pool of lantern light, one of them periodically peered out the door into the darkness to check for eavesdroppers. At one point a young man passing by saw the open door and the glow of our lamp. He paused to ask for a light for his cigarette and sat down on the steps to enjoy his smoke, sheltered from the warm drizzle by the overhanging thatch. Our conversation shifted to trivial matters until he left. As he finally sauntered off into the night, my companions grumbled about the young man's bad manners: "Bloody kid!"

I learned a number of things in such conversations about the deeper reaches of *koyeng* genealogies that I had not known before. A few men also told me things about these deeper reaches that I was instructed to keep to myself. They told me not only to tell no one in Kragur, but also not to put what I had been told in a published book. They had no objections to my recording what they told me in my own notebook, however, and sometimes even asked me to read back what I had written to make sure it was accurate. Sometimes they recounted their closely guarded knowledge first and then told me that what I had heard must be kept secret. Of course, I assured them that I would do so and explained that I wanted to hear the details primarily so that I could understand the general principles, the *fasin* (fashion or principle) of the thing, as one would say in Tok Pisin.

I was as discreet as I knew how to be, but it was no secret that I was pursuing genealogical inquiries and, in a place as small and tightly packed as Kragur, it could be no secret with whom I was meeting. Knowing this, in the middle of conversations about the genealogies of their own groups, men sometimes asked casually what the elders of other descent groups had told me. Much of what I was free to share, of course, they probably knew already. For the rest, I had to remind them that I had given others the same assurance of secrecy that I had given them. This, of course, they knew.

Such intrigue, within limits, gives field research extra excitement, but Kragur people handle genealogical knowledge with such care and secrecy for very serious reasons. Rights to leadership, of course, may be at stake. Keeping track of the genealogical connections that link one to land is also of extreme importance. As one Kairiru islander once phrased it for me in Tok Pisin, it is the "key to the village" (Tok Pisin, "*ki bilong ples*"): the key to livelihood and status in village society.

When claims to land have to be justified, simply reeling off a long line of ancestors and asserting that one of these in the distant past first cleared a plot of forest for gardens is not enough. Several elements, however, can lend credibility to such an account. Over and above simply naming a line of predecessors, a full treatment of one's forebears should include an account of where they lived and their movements from one locale to another. (In the Kragur genealogies I am familiar with, events like drought, flood, and warfare explained the movements of the ancestors from one place of settlement to another, until they reached Kragur.) In addition, it helps to be able to ground an account of descent-group history by pointing out features in the contemporary landscape (an immense stone, a deep ravine, a mountain height, the place where a stream empties into the sea) that figure in stories of ancestral wanderings and other events. It also lends credibility if one can account not only for the main male descent line but also the collateral lines (that is, the siblings of one's direct male ancestors and their progeny).

Any and all of these elements could conceivably be invented for the occasion, but the more complex the account the harder it is to fabricate. The harder it is, too, not to stray into territory of which others may have knowledge. Undoubtedly, the oratorical skill with which one presents one's historical evidence also counts heavily. The most skilled orators in Kragur yield nothing in energy and eloquence to advocates and public speakers anywhere.

Yet if all such knowledge may come out in public eventually, why is much of it cloaked in secrecy? As I understand it, the point is to hold as much as one can in reserve, not revealing it until it may be necessary to make or dispute a claim. Once items of ancestral lore have been made public, it may be hard to prevent others from incorporating them into their own accounts. Nevertheless, in the heat of dispute, the parties often must breach their secrecy. In 1998, Ukapi told me of how he and other men from Kragur had used their knowledge to help kin in another Kairiru village win a land dispute. "When it's time to talk," he said, "it's different. We talk a lot!"

There is another important reason for keeping parts of *koyeng* history secret that I have not yet discussed. Villagers use the names of particular distant ancestors in magical spells. Many believe the names themselves have power and that revealing them would make this power available to others. Those who know the names also refrain from saying them aloud, even in private, because saying them too often weakens them. As Moraf put it, "If you say them for no reason they lose their strength" *(Yu kolim nating nating ol i nogat strong).*

The genealogical knowledge of descent-group leaders is a source of group pride. Yet even within descent groups there is rivalry, and leaders do not necessarily share all they know with their fellow leaders. Here, too, some apparently prefer to hold something in reserve with which, I assume, they hope to dazzle other descent-group elders on the proper occasion. Some also seem to take pleasure in letting it be known that they have such secrets. Villagers are sure that some deceased men took great knowledge with them to the grave, but no one can ever know for certain.

Old Structure and New Resources

In 1998, people told me things about their ancestors they had not told me before, and did so with little or no prompting. I was a person of greater stature now and more worthy of the confidence of elders. But some villagers also may have had political reasons for wanting their descent group stories on record. They sometimes call these accounts of lines of descent and historical events *stori* (stories) in Tok Pisin. One young man warned me not to believe all the *stori* I was told, reminding me that "we fight with stories" and implying that some might embroider on their genealogies in order to put an illegitimate claim on record.

I saw no evidence that anyone was engaging in such chicanery, but the young man who had warned me may have been thinking that Kragur people might soon have something new to fight about. Gold had been discovered on Kairiru; not only on Kairiru, people said, but on land to which Kragur people had ancestral claims. According to villagers, a foreign mining firm first carried out explorations in 1987 and 1988, returning in 1994 and 1996, and there was a rumor that it might return again later in 1998. For several years, colleagues working in Papua New Guinea had sent me sketchy news of gold on Kairiru. There was no doubt that there were gold deposits, but apparently mining had not been deemed commercially feasible. The feasibility of mining there, of course, can change as gold prices fluctuate and other mining prospects fail or flourish.

Many Kragur villagers knew that mining had brought more problems than rewards to other Papua New Guineans. Mining on the island of Bougainville had given rise to years of armed conflict, spurred by anger over environmental destruction and disputes over compensation of the local population. Mining at Ok Tedi, in the Star Mountains, had caused grim ecological problems for people along the Fly River, hundreds of miles downstream from the mine itself. Villagers had also seen something firsthand of what mining could do to the land. Prospectors on Kairiru had dug exploratory trenches high up on the mountainside. Villagers told me that the prospectors had left these standing open and the rain was now eroding them deeper and wider, scarring the land once protected by forest cover. Some also had heard that, in order to mine the gold, it would be necessary literally to take the top off the mountain. In fact, this is essentially what happened at two major mine sites in the country. Mount Fubilan lost its top for the Ok Tedi mine and the Porgera mine decapitated Mount Waruwari.

Mining is a vexing issue in Papua New Guinea. While it has spawned massive environmental and political problems, many rural Papua New Guineans still look to mining, logging, or some other kind of large-scale resource extraction as a possible route to prosperity and "development." In addition, mining and oil production provide the government with a large part (almost 20 percent in 1995) of revenue from sources other than foreign grants and loans. Without this revenue, the government would be even more dependent on external assistance.

Some Kragur people knew less than others about the evils mining could bring, but I think everyone knew that it might bring money their way, maybe a lot. There were good reasons, then, to take a special interest in the disposition of land rights and ancestral claims; and that, I was told, was just what had happened. When the mining exploration started, one man told me, "this talk about structure was a big thing" (dispela tok bilong straksa i bikpela samting), and there had been argument as well as mere talk. Not much argument, really, someone else told me; but there were disagreements about who had rights to particular pieces of land.

Interest in land claims stirred by the discovery of gold may have made my inquiries about descent-group histories easier. It certainly made them more politically charged. The situation also illustrated how fundamental to Kragur life the descent system remained and showed that it was still as much a framework for debate as a source of authoritative answers. It is the system's lack of rigidity that gives people opportunities to establish rights to garden land and reallocate resources as families and descent groups grow or decline and households move from village to village or between village and town. But could a system evolved over many generations to deal with disputes over garden land and marriage arrangements keep passions in check if, as many villagers hoped, substantial amounts of money were at issue? Colin Filer has argued that "mineral resource development [has] a . . . tendency to exaggerate the political fragmentation of local landowning communities" in Papua New Guinea, in large part because of the "inability of the local community to distribute the economic benefits of mining in an equitable manner." Another long-time observer, David Hyndman, finds Filer's views much too glib and offers cases to counter what Stuart Kirsch calls "the stereotype of the greedy . . . landowner." One cannot know in advance, however, how Kragur might respond.

Some, including Filer, suggest that mining's damage to the physical environment alone can be enough to cause community strife. Having seen how strong were the community tensions that arose in Kragur from even a season of poor fishing, it is easy to imagine that major disruption of forests, garden lands, and water supplies could foment conflict within the village as well as anger at outsiders. Environmental damage was certainly on some Kragur villagers' minds in 1998, but some also may have been thinking about getting their genealogical stories straight so they would be ready to assert claims to a new kind of wealth. Whatever its fundamental cause, according to a letter from a Kragur man in Wewak I received a few months before leaving for Papua New Guinea in 1998, simply the possibility of mining had been enough to spark acrimonious debate, even turning "brother against brother," my correspondent claimed (in English).

A Question of Balance

Gold mining would put a new kind of stress on the bonds that hold Kragur villagers together, but tension in the ties that bind is not new to Kragur. Migrants and refugees from other Kairiru villages founded Kragur. These earliest settlers came to Kragur's steep cliffs to distance themselves from a bitter dispute in the village where they had been living. Those who followed them had their own motives for leaving their homes, but they were all kin of some kind to the founders, for one did not settle among strangers. Now, as in the past, ties of marriage and common descent provide people with kin all over the island, and even farther afield, to whom they can turn if they need to find a new community in which to live. The fact that households or larger fragments can pack up and move probably has helped many Kairiru villages maintain internal peace. That is, villages have stayed together by splitting apart.

Some social tensions are the price of living in a small, compact community. No human community is free of internal strife, but living and working at close quarters presents special problems, and life in Kragur is lived at very close quarters. The forest is deep and the ocean vistas are broad, but the village itself is tightly packed and its social fabric densely woven. One moves among the same familiar faces each day and in every sphere of life. Given the physical closeness and lack of anonymity of village life, there is virtually no privacy. It is hard to keep one's activities confidential, and almost equally hard to stay aloof from the lives of others and remain ignorant of when they eat, when they bathe, whom they visit, their illnesses, and their domestic squabbles. A certain amount of curiosity about one's neighbors is not thought un-seemly: "Where are you going?" is a common greeting. But even the incurious cannot avoid being privy to their neighbors' comings and goings. "Oh, Smith," one of my neighbors said to me shortly before I left the village in 1998, "We'll miss seeing you walking to the outhouse every morning."

Such a public way of living can be wearing for one not accustomed to it, and villagers themselves sometimes complain of the closeness and lack of privacy of village life. But life in such a tight social world can contribute to more than mere aggravation. Interdependence with one's neighbors means their actions can harm as well as help you. And, knowing them intimately, one knows their weaknesses as well as their strengths. As Stanley Diamond has argued, such a social milieu can produce not only "sophistication and subtlety" about people, but also "dangerous sensitivity" to their actions and imputed motives. This lack of autonomy and "dan-gerous sensitivity" to others is the dark side of life in many small communities throughout the world. "*Pueblo chico, infierno grande,*" as my Spanish tutor, an urban Argentinian, used to put it—that is, "Small town, big hell." This is a decidedly one-sided appraisal, but it is not baseless.

The kind of friction among people inherent in small, closely knit communities is especially dangerous if it is coupled with a tendency to assume that human actions and intentions are the causes of natural as well as social phenomena. The very intensity of personal life in a small community may well incline people to explain things in such a "personalistic" way, to borrow a term from the work of Ted Schwartz. The common Kragur belief that ghosts of the dead, acting out the anger of their living descendants, cause much illness is a vivid example of this tendency.

Many villagers also explain more mundane events in personalistic ways. One afternoon in 1998, the rain of the previous night had persisted all day, accompanied by blustery winds. Moraf looked out at the rain with disapproval from Benau's verandah, where we sat that afternoon with Benau and Kaunup, and remarked that this was not ordinary rain and wind: people in a nearby village who were angry and grief-stricken over a young man's recent death had caused it. Kaunup laughed, and I asked him if he disagreed with Moraf. "The clouds come and it rains," he replied dismissively. Benau, however, took strong exception to this impersonal interpreta-tion of the weather. "No!" he declared, "I agree with Moraf!"

Skepticism like Kaunup's regarding common beliefs is not new in Kragur. Nevertheless, belief in the human causes of events was still prevalent in 1998. In particular, belief in the power of the dead to act in response to the emotions of the living, giving malignant form to social tensions, was much in evidence. I still heard a phrase with which I had become very familiar in the 1970s: "The ground has ears." Always spoken in sober tones, these words are heavy with warning and apprehension. The dead are in the ground, ever present. They know what the living are doing, thinking, and feeling, and they can be harsh with those who carelessly make others angry. Misfortune is inevitable in life and provides Kragur people with all too many opportunities to wonder if someone is nursing hidden anger that stirs up dangerous ghosts (or, perhaps, someone is intentionally using malign magic to cause harm). This in itself can tax relations with others and nurture suspicion and mistrust.

Fuzzy definitions of *koyeng,* competition among and within descent groups, the stresses of life in the cramped world of a village, fear of the dead, and suspicion of the living—all this sounds like a very volatile mixture. Indeed, it can be; yet Kragur, and villages like it, persist. Although kinship networks extending beyond the village allow people simply to leave when conflict escalates, few do so. Making a new start in another village, even among kin, has a price. Newcomers often do not enjoy the same status as more established residents, and the status of a newcomer—in Tok Pisin, *man bilong kam*—can linger for generations. Although descent-group loyalties can cause rifts within the community, the web of crosscutting kinship ties created by marriages among descent groups creates countervailing loyalties and interests.

There is also a rough balance in other matters. While fear that a neighbor's anger may make one sick can nurture mistrust and suspicion, the belief that human conflict causes illness also inspires village-wide efforts to root out and settle disputes or appease anger when people are afflicted by prolonged illness. All else aside, the village is home. The ancestors in the ground may be quick to anger, but some of them are one's own ancestors. And the ground itself and the surrounding seas provide a kind of material security it is hard to duplicate, for life in urban areas in troubled economic times can be uncertain.

With one or two exceptions, Kragur villagers do not wax sociological, speaking of things like "crosscutting ties" and "integrating mechanisms," but they are very self-conscious about community cohesion and aware that they cannot take it for granted. There is even magic to hold the village together, called in Tok Pisin the magic to *pasim ples* (secure the village) or *strongim ples* (strengthen the village). Villagers' descriptions of this magic reveal a great deal about their notions of ideal village life, for they link material prosperity with social harmony, and they speak not only of gross cohesion but also of the quality of relations among people. The magic can be used either to destroy prosperity and unity or to secure them. Used maliciously, the result, as one man described it to me in 1998, is: "Everything drifts now. The children, the pigs, the dogs, they fly away. The village falls apart, people are hungry, people fight." But, if the magic is used for good, as another villager explained, "You can't be hungry, people can't run away, people who are far away must return, no one can break up the village."

In 1998, I was told that the ritual to strengthen the village had last been performed in 1992, "in a small way." Prior to that, it had been performed in 1987, when it was accompanied by the harvest of a large taro garden, planted the previous year, apparently especially for the event. During my stay in 1998, some of the younger men, I was told, urged the appropriate elders to perform the magic. The elders apparently had demurred for the time being. Obviously, the kinds of concerns that moved the younger men to make this request were not new that year. But, since the magic had last been performed in full dress, much had been going on to keep alive and even aggravate villagers' anxiety about the state of village solidarity. Gold entered into it, but so did the changing face of Catholicism, the continuing struggle for and about money, and the complex effects of Western education, the topics of the coming chapters.

Parish Bureaucracy and the Holy Spirit

"CHURCH DEVELOPMENT MUST THRIVE!"
(*CHURCH DIVELOPMEN I MAS KAMAP GUD!*)
—A Kragur Catholic activist, 1998

It is not surprising that in 1998 some Kragur people turned to magic when they became concerned about the strength and the quality of the ties that held them together. As we have seen, in the indigenous Kragur view of the world, the realm of
the supernatural is intimately involved with the daily life of living human beings
and its moral order. Magic for increasing the productivity of gardening or fishing is
fully effective only if the village is free of conflict, and ghosts afflict those who fail to
keep their relationships with other villagers amicable.

Prior to around 1930, the men's cult or *tambaran* cult, a major institution for
relating to the supernatural realm, also played an important role in binding Kragur
people together. Major ceremonies would have required elaborate preparations,
lasting many months and involving the entire community. Although the focus of
activity was ensuring the physical growth of boys and conferring on them adult status,
people probably believed that the ceremonies helped safeguard the health and prosperity of the entire community by securing the goodwill of the *tambaran* spirits.

In addition, the men's cult ceremonies in Kragur involved a now nearly defunct
feature of social organization that added another dimension to the ties forged by
descent and marriage. This was what anthropologists call a moiety system, a division of the community into two groups with reciprocal responsibilities. In Kragur,
these groups were called Seksik and Lupelap. Descent groups of long residence in
the village formed the core of each moiety. More recently arrived descent groups
were divided between the two moieties to maintain a rough balance of numbers. The
moieties were exogamous. That is, people had to marry not only outside their descent
groups but also outside their moieties, so there was a continuing exchange of marriage partners between the moieties. Each division also initiated the male children
of the other into the men's cult.

120

Early missionaries campaigned vigorously against the men's cult, magic, and all indigenous religious practices. The Catholic Church softened its position on such matters considerably in the 1960s. Even in 1998, however, some villagers still resented suppression of the men's cult, pointing out that by the time of the Church's change of heart, they had already lost the secret and sacred *tambaran* knowledge. "We could build a *tambaran* cult house," said one man in 1976, "but who would do the work inside?"

The village-wide men's cult house in Kragur, called Munburi, remained standing long after it lost its purpose. Allied bombing of the occupying Japanese forces during the war finally burned it to the ground. Villagers still speak of themselves as either Seksik or Lupelap and occasionally organize themselves along moiety lines for contemporary purposes, but the sacred function of these social divisions is gone.

Despite such lingering bitterness, Catholicism itself became a force for community cohesion. In 1998, as in the 1970s, many villagers still proudly regarded Kragur as an especially devout community. New generations repeated with confidence and satisfaction the story of how God had acknowledged Kragur's moral stature by revealing Itself to Masos before the first missionaries arrived.

My fourth day in the village in 1998 was a Sunday. It was also one of the occasional Sundays on which Father Clement, usually known as Father Clem, came to the north side of the island to give Mass and serve Holy Communion. On this day, Kragur appeared as unified and eager in its Catholicism as ever. The shaded coastal path, usually as quiet as a track through the deep forest, was busy with knots of villagers in their best clothes making their way to Bou. Reaching the primary school, they left the shade to climb the steep, grassy hill to the weathered church. Inside, where the high ceiling let the heat rise beneath the corrugated metal roof, Kragur men and women of all ages listened attentively to Father Clem's homily and joined in the singing, led by a chorus of schoolchildren and adolescents with guitars at the front of the church. Adolescents, robust young men, youthful mothers comforting tiny infants, shrunken old women, and grizzled old men all stood in the long line to take Holy Communion, many with their heads bowed and their hands clasped in prayer.

Despite such scenes of devotion, Kragur was not quite the same, single fervent congregation it once had been. Catholicism was still a very prominent part of village life, but it had some new faces—one more relaxed, one more bureaucratic, and one more exuberant than anything I had ever seen in Kragur. And although villagers still had in common their allegiance to Catholicism and the church still bore the message of unity, Catholicism could not help contributing to social unrest.

After the Revolution

My account of Catholicism in the 1970s was the result of over a year of observation and many, many lengthy discussions with villagers. I had only a brief look at Kragur's religious life in 1998, so when I say that there was something less intense about the village's Catholicism in 1998, I am going out on a limb. In 1998, of course, I could build on what I already knew about religious life in Kragur and did not have to spend weeks and months gaining people's confidence. And, though my stay in the village was brief, I paid close attention to religious events.

Many villagers have asked me about my own religious beliefs. I always say that I was raised a Christian, although not a Catholic, but that I now doubted the existence of a supreme being. Still, some villagers did not quite understand that my avid interest in religious events in 1998 was not evidence of my faith. When I mentioned casually one day that in America I had not been to church for years, Bash laughed and exclaimed, "So why do you pretend to be a religious person when you come to Kragur?" I explained that I was not pretending, my interest in religious matters was part of trying to learn about life in Kragur, and he seemed to find that answer satisfactory. Like Bash, most Kragur villagers take their religion very seriously. I sometimes amused one friend by calling myself a heathen (in Tok Pisin, a *heten man*), as early missionaries called those who had not converted to Catholicism. But I finally made this joke once too often. Moraf looked at me with concern and said: "No, no! You're a *good* man. You're not a heathen!"

Kragur people seemed no less serious about Catholicism in 1998 than they had been in the past, but I could not help feeling that the mood had changed. People still made the sign of the cross before beginning a meal and placed fresh flowers on household altars. But without the nightly gatherings before the Virgin's statue in the center of the village, members of the Legion of Mary shouting for people to leave their houses and come to pray or leading villagers assembled for council work in the rosary, things were not quite the same. In 1998, daily Catholic observance appeared to be a less collective endeavor than it once had been.

One other change was more apparent. Ibor, the most vigorous local proponent of Catholicism for decades, had retired from public life. Ibor's father had been an early recruit to Catholicism when, in the 1920s, it was still relatively new to Kragur. Ibor himself trained as a lay religious teacher or catechist after World War II and devoted much of his adult life to proselytizing for Catholicism. He served as a catechist in the Papua New Guinea Highlands and on Wogeo Island before settling down to lead Catholic life in Kragur in the 1950s. For Ibor, Catholicism was the key to weathering the rapid changes that ensued in Papua New Guinea following the war. He was the scion of a prestigious line of descent with a legitimate claim to a position of leadership, but his success in placing Catholicism at the center of village life had rested as much on his acumen in practical matters, his eloquent preaching, and his fierce conviction.

Other villagers also played important leadership roles in Kragur Catholicism in the 1970s, but Ibor commanded the kind of respect accorded only the most powerful of the traditional bigmen, and he brought his vision of what Catholicism required into all spheres of life. At times, other villagers chafed at his nearly constant efforts to lead Kragur along the path to righteousness, but his passion and authority tended to discourage public challenges.

Ibor could also be very good company. He enjoyed a joke, was a good storyteller, and was quick with a thoughtful answer to any question. I often sought him out to help me with my research and he always obliged. It was sad, then, in 1998 to find him considerably changed. Pain in his legs made it hard for him to walk and his vision was failing, although I often saw him minding his small grandchildren, looking happy and alert. But when I visited him I found he was no longer the voluble and opinionated man he once had been. He shook my hand firmly and smiled and nodded attentively when I spoke, but he said little in reply. This, others told me, was now his usual manner.

Under Ibor's leadership, although Kragur Catholicism had not been rigidly uniform, it had been guided by a single strong vision. But the atmosphere of communal enthusiasm and collective devotion I found in 1975–1976 was not just the creation of strong leadership. Catholicism was still a revolutionary doctrine for villagers of Ibor's generation. They had been alive to witness the mass baptisms that made villagers into official Catholics in the 1930s and had experienced the crusading zeal of an earlier, less tolerant brand of missionary. Ibor was not the only one still gripped by the excitement of discovery and conversion. In contrast, the majority of villagers in 1998 had been born into a world in which Catholicism was already an established and taken-for-granted institution.

In addition, by 1998 independence was more a mundane disappointment than a frightening mystery. At the time of independence, when I first visited Kragur, villagers' devotion to the Virgin had seemed in direct proportion to their anxiety about their fate in the new nation of Papua New Guinea. For many, I think the shrine erected to Maria high on the mountain had been a talisman against this great unknown.

Ibor's own crusading fervor, the comparative freshness of Catholicism, and the anxieties aroused by independence all helped mold Kragur into a single ardent congregation in the 1970s. All that having changed by 1998, I saw a Catholicism that was perhaps more relaxed. The attitude toward some indigenous religious practices definitely seemed more open.

In his prime, Ibor had encouraged all villagers to learn the rosary well so they could pray on their own or call on the aid of the Virgin in emergencies. But the best prayer, he taught, was communal prayer and, like indigenous magic, communal prayer was most effective if people were unified in thought as well as in action, harboring no doubts and untroubled by anger. Most villagers would have agreed with Ibor on this, but he went a bit further than many others in some of his views. His Catholicism kept an ample place for the beneficial use of indigenous magic, but it gave the Virgin Mary precedence. Many kinds of indigenous subsistence magic make use of carved wooden male and female figures, called *kaikrauap*. These are specially decorated, and during the performance of the magic they serve as the repositories of the spiritual or supernatural powers that the magic activates. Ibor preached that statues of the Virgin had now taken the place of the *kaikrauap.* "Before," he told me, "when they wanted fish or whatever, they decorated these wooden figures"; now, "we honor only Maria."

Indeed, whenever people spoke to me of *kaikrauap* in 1975–1976 they did so in the past tense. I went away with the impression that these religious artifacts, like the *tambaran* cult, had passed from the scene. Twenty-two years later, however, it looked like villagers had merely put them aside temporarily to suit the ardent Catholic spirit of the times. In 1998, in a conversation about genealogy and hereditary rights to magic, a middle-aged man of the Shewaratin descent group mentioned that the Shewaratins had rights to a particular male and female pair of *kaikrauap,* named Kaunup and Shinawar, which had been passed down through many generations from the ancestor Taunur. Taunur himself had acquired the *kaikrauap* from a *masalai* or spirit being. They were in the care of the oldest and most knowledgeable Shewaratin man, Mapos.

A few days later we visited Mapos and he gladly brought out Kaunup and Shinawar for me to see. Kaunup, the male, was about 76 centimeters (2.5 feet) high, bedecked with a cassowary feather headdress and a bark-cloth loincloth. Shinawar, the female, was a bit shorter and wore a colorful fiber skirt. I photographed them standing side by side, and then Mapos asked me to photograph him holding the two figures so that he could give copies of the picture to his sons. These particular figures did not go all the way back to Taunur. They were, however, the present bearers of the hereditary names and had been used in magical rituals. Mapos said they had been carved in 1978, although someone else told me that he thought they had been around since the early 1970s. It is likely that the senior men of Shewaratin and other descent groups had at least a few *kaikrauap* tucked away in the rafters and corners of their houses in 1976, even as the Virgin's statue took center stage.

Some time after the photography session with Mapos' *kaikrauap,* I got a better look at another aspect of indigenous religion that villagers had been more reticent about in the 1970s. Chatting with Moraf and Benau one day, I mentioned how pleased I had been finally to see a *kaikrauap* with some magical credentials. Moraf's father had given me handsome carvings in the style of *kaikrauap,* but I had never before seen figures actually used in magical ritual. This launched Moraf and Benau on a description of just how *kaikrauap* were used in magic and what they had to do with Wankau. In 1975–1976, no one had spoken to me about Wankau at any length, despite my prodding, and I ended up with only vague ideas about this entity. On this day in 1998, however, talk of Wankau flowed freely.

The essence of what Moraf and Benau told me was as follows. To fill the *kaikrauap* with magical power, the magicians treat them (or "wash them," as Moraf and Benau put it) with special vines and other plant material. This I knew, but I had never heard an explanation of what this anointing actually did. Everything, the two men told me, has a kind of spirit. (They used both the Tok Pisin term *masalai* and the Kairiru word *shawaung*.) Anointing the *kaikrauap* fills it with a mass of spirits. Wankau, they said, is the overarching name for the spirits of all things as well as the name of the mythic hero of whom villagers often had spoken in the past. Anointing the *kaikrauap* fills it with Wankau: "You wash the *kaikrauap* and it becomes like God. It's Wankau now." Filled with spirit or Wankau, the *kaikrauap* is ready to help the magician. (Many villagers have told me that the spirits of the dead also aid the magician. I am not sure exactly how the spirits of the dead are related to Wankau. On one occasion Mapos did tell me that when people die their spirits go to the place of Wankau. Whether he meant a distinct location or the dimension of all spirits, however, I do not know. Recall that in the 1970s many Kragur people assumed that the spirits of the dead existed at close quarters with the living.)

I could not be sure, of course, that other villagers necessarily understood Wankau in this way. Moraf and Benau's explanation of magic did seem to make sense of what a number of villagers had asserted without explanation in 1975–1976: Wankau was somehow like God. But I had to remember that some villagers who surely knew of Wankau still had not seen what it had to do with God. Mowush, for one, had been adamant that the ancestors had had no God, only the ghosts of their own dead kin. As with much culture in Kragur or anywhere, there was no correct answer here, only a range of opinions on a common question.

Mapos' affection for his *kaikrauap* was no slur on Catholicism. It does not show in the picture I took, but just to Mapos' right was his altar to the Virgin, a small table displaying bouquets of ornamental leaves and not one but three small statues of Maria. Three pictures of the Virgin and two of Jesus adorned the wall above the table.

Parish Bureaucracy

Kragur Catholicism in 1998 seemed much more comfortable with indigenous religious practices than it once had been. In a rather different vein, it was also becoming more bureaucratized. In the 1970s, although Ibor dominated Catholic life, others also held formal positions of leadership. There was an official Church Leader, the Legion of Mary had its own officers, and someone was in charge of leading the schoolchildren in prayer each evening. All these aspects of local organization were part of the larger organization of St. Martin's parish, which included Kairiru and Mushu Islands, and the diocese, with its seat in Wewak. Since then, however, it looked like the parish had been seized by an organizational frenzy.

In 1998, Kragur people were dropping the names of so many Catholic committees, groups, and officers that I could not keep them straight. One local activist finally loaned me his copy of the "Parish Plan" for 1998. This helped clarify things, although it did not simplify them, for the plan included an organizational diagram worthy of a major corporation. The parish is divided into three areas: A (Mushu Island), B (the south coast of Kairiru), and C (the north coast of Kairiru). Within each area, each village has a Community Steering Team, and the Community Steering Teams send representatives to the Area Steering Team. Each Area Steering Team sends representatives to the Parish Steering Team, headed by the Parish Priest. Also, the Parish Team of Pastoral Animators, the Parish Pastoral Committee, and the Area Pastoral Committees connect horizontally to the Parish Steering Team and vertically to the Parish Priest.

The plan is written in Tok Pisin and renders the names of these committees in the kind of phonetic spelling that makes any English word look and sound like Tok Pisin. So, Community Steering Team is *Komuniti Stia Tim*; Area Steering Team is *Eria Stia Tim*; and Parish Steering Team is *Peris Stia Tim*. Many villagers, however, referred to these entities simply by their initials (KST, EST, and PST), making the more deeply involved Catholic activists sound a lot like government functionaries or corporate middle managers. This organizational scheme is very recent. The 1998 plan says that it was the product of a parish *Ivaluesen na Plening* (Evaluation and Planning) meeting held in December 1996. (Although *Ivaluesen na Plening* sounds like Tok Pisin, one has to wonder just what it conveys to speakers of Tok Pisin who do not also speak English.)

In Kragur, there is also a Catholic Women's group, a youth group (dormant in 1998), and the Legion of Mary. The latter has a village leader, but it is part of a Legion Presidium (which, I believe, is represented on the Area Pastoral Team), of which there are two in Area C to accommodate the Legion's large membership. There is also the KST. According to one of the more active members of the Legion, the KST includes its chair, the Church Leader, the Communion Leader, the Sacrament Teacher, the leader of the Sunday young people's chorus, the chair of the women's group, a youth representative, both councillors, the village representative to the primary school in Bou, and the traditional bigmen.

Tongues of Fire

If one face of Kragur Catholicism in 1998 was a bit stuffy, another was quite the opposite. The singing, clapping, shouting, and speaking in tongues of the Wednesday evening charismatic worship services outdid in obvious energy and enthusiasm any kind of religious activity I had ever seen in Kragur.

Charismatic Catholicism is a species of Christian Pentecostalism, which first took shape in the United States at the beginning of the twentieth century. According to some observers, Pentecostalism is perhaps the fastest-growing religious movement in the world. Catholic Pentecostalism, or charismatic Catholicism, got its start in the United States in the late 1960s and early 1970s, taking inspiration from the larger Christian Pentecostal movement. The same reforms of the Second Vatican Council (often simply called Vatican II) that eased Catholic mission objections to indigenous religious practices in Papua New Guinea also helped give rise to Catholic Pentecostal worship in America. The Vatican II reforms called for a more tolerant, ecumenical attitude. Many Catholics reacted against reforms that, in their eyes, took the mystery out of worship, such as the vernacular mass. A few, however, took advantage of the ecumenical mood to find both revitalization and new mystery in the example of Protestants who were themselves revitalizing their own Pentecostal tradition.

Pentecostalism takes its name and its emphasis from the biblical description of events that befell Christ's followers on the first Jewish Feast of Pentecost after Christ's resurrection. Accompanied by the sound of rushing wind and the sight of tongues of flame, Christ's followers were filled with the Holy Spirit and began speaking in unknown languages; that is, they spoke in tongues. Elsewhere in the Bible, Saint Paul speaks of prophecy, the ability to work miracles, and speaking in tongues as among the gifts or charisms the Holy Spirit bestowed upon early Christians. Hence the term "charismatic." Charismatic or Pentecostal Christianity emphasizes a direct experience of God. Speaking in tongues represents to believers a form of direct communication with the supernatural. Along with other gifts and the altered state of consciousness they often entail, it is a sign of "baptism in the Spirit."

The charismatic worship I saw in Kragur in 1998 was new to me but not to Kragur or Papua New Guinea. One villager reported that he had seen people at charismatic worship in the town of Rabaul in East New Britain Province when he worked there in 1971. They had, he said, behaved as though they were drunk. Another villager, an active participant in Kragur charismatic worship, told me that some Catholics in the East Sepik Province had taken up charismatic worship as early as 1973. Brother Pawil said that some Kragur migrants living in Port Moresby also were involved in a charismatic worship group, which sometimes met at the Islander.

Some villagers regarded charismatic Catholicism as something truly American. "It's a new kind of prayer," said one enthusiast. "It comes straight from America." The fact that the bishop appointed an American priest, Father Eddie Bauer, to oversee the growing interest in charismatic worship may have strengthened its American image. In some ways, the development of charismatic Catholicism in the East Sepik followed the same pattern as it did in the United States. The Church channeled spontaneous interest in charismatic worship by offering "Life in the Spirit" seminars teaching people a standard form of worship and an interpretation of their ecstatic experiences that stayed within orthodox boundaries. Several of the younger men who were active in charismatic worship in Kragur had attended such seminars in the 1980s in Wewak and on Kairiru. One of them proudly showed me a handbook that he had received as part of his training: *A Key to Charismatic Renewal in the Catholic Church*, published by Abbey Press in the State of Indiana, U.S.A.

I heard a lot about this new form of worship during my first few days in Kragur, so when the first evening service rolled around I made sure I was there. The charismatic prayer meeting took place in the open space in front of the small prayer house that stands in the residential area called Vanu Rosh. The prayer house is a small structure with a dirt floor, narrow bamboo benches down each side, and walls open from about waist level up to let the breeze in. Here, those who are too old or ill to walk to church at Bou on Sundays gather for their own small service. Bamboo benches shaded by large trees mark off two sides of the open space in front of the prayer house, and a tumbled, overgrown rock wall makes up a third side. I passed by earlier in the day and saw Kauref setting up the altar for the evening service near the center of the meeting space. He was decorating a small table with the usual ornamental leaves and creating an arch of palm fronds, colorful leaves, and sprays of bougainvillea over the table.

When I arrived at about eight o'clock in the evening, a crowd had already gathered. Not wanting to be too conspicuous, I sat down on a flat stone at the edge of the crumbling rock wall on one side of the clear space, to the rear of the altar. When Moraf arrived, however, he saw how uncomfortable I was and sent his oldest son to retrieve a battered chair for me from somewhere. I carried the chair down to the floor of the meeting area and took a place at one end of the bamboo bench, facing the altar. Sitting at the outer edge of the circle of light cast by a kerosene pressure lamp, I could see just well enough to take notes, if I was not particular about legibility.

Schoolchildren and adolescents with guitars and tambourines were crowded close beside the altar, playing and singing, mostly in Tok Pisin but also in English.

HE'S TOUCHING ME NOW,
LORD, TOUCH ME AGAIN!

Soon, at a break in the singing, Kauref initiated what were apparently the main proceedings. He briefly announced the names of people who would be offering prayers during the service and then the singing started again. Many of those sitting and standing around the edges of the clear space joined with the young people's chorus. Kauref offered a Bible reading from Saint Paul. Periodically, individuals stood to pray, and prayer alternated with singing without perceptible pauses. *"Pre strong!"* (Pray strong!), Kauref urged. People raised their prayers in excited and passionate voices, some praying loudly through the songs.

Mi nogat powa! Mi nogat nem! Yu antap tumas!
(I have no power! I'm nobody! You [God] are above everything!)

Husat i mama bilong mi? Maria i mama bilong mi!
(Who is my mother? Maria is my mother!)

Looking around at the crowd, I saw that, in addition to the chorus, many other adolescents and men and women in their twenties and thirties were present. I saw a few men and women with wrinkled skin and graying hair, but they were in the minority. I could see none of the most prominent men, but although the circle of lamplight was intense near its center, it was dim at its edges and many villagers sat in the outer darkness.

From the time the praying began, a lean middle-aged woman paced vigorously back and forth, waving one hand aloft, urging the singers on, greeting each person who came forward to pray and praying loudly herself. I took special note of her because I had never before seen a woman take center stage like this in a public meeting in Kragur. Among other things, I had never seen a woman pace back and forth in front of a village assembly as she was doing. This was a style of behavior usually reserved for orating bigmen.

Soon after settling me comfortably, Moraf himself plunged into the activity. I knew he was an enthusiastic supporter of charismatic worship, but I had not seen him in action. He stood, shirtless and perspiring, somewhat to the right of the pacing woman, not far from the singers. His eyes closed, he swayed slightly to the rhythm of the music, twisting his head in what seemed a rather unnatural way. He, too, held one hand aloft, but not in the style of an orator. Rather, the stiff hand jerked and twisted this way and that, not quite in sync with the motions of his head. He was turned away from me much of the time, so although I could tell that he was speaking I could not clearly make out his words. In what I could hear, I made out snatches of Kairiru, Tok Pisin, and English. Some of his utterances, however, contained nothing familiar to me. Later on, Moraf told me that he had been speaking in tongues that night.

Several days later, Biaunat, another active charismatic worshipper, told me that my presence had inhibited some of the villagers at the service that night. They knew, he said, that charismatic worship came from America, and they thought this was behind my interest in observing them at prayer. If Biaunat was correct, some villagers thought that I, as an American, was checking to see if they were doing it right. I had forgotten how many people now in the village had never met me and knew little about me. I had slipped easily back into my role as ubiquitous observer, but many younger villagers were not accustomed to seeing me and my notebook at every public event. Whatever the case, the prayer meeting had not looked particularly inhibited to me.

Neither of the charismatic prayer meetings I attended ended on an inhibited note. They did not even end peacefully. At the first, things began to fall apart after about an hour and a half. The singing and praying were proceeding apace when a woman sitting on the sidelines started to complain loudly about something. Kap, sitting beside me, leaned over and told me that she was saying something about people stealing from her gardens. One of those leading the prayers shouted back that this was not the time to take up such matters. At this point, a muscular young man who had been singing and praying loudly, ripped off his shirt, shouted that he was a sinner, and threw the guitar he was holding to the ground.

Other people began shouting, Kauref was making calming motions with his hands and imploring, "Please! Please!" and two or three men hurried forward to grab the altar and take it out of harm's way. Then a stone the size of a fist came hurtling out of the darkness just above the meeting place. It thudded on the bare earth without striking anyone, but those who had not already started to drift away began to scatter. I was standing by my chair, still trying to understand what was going on. I then saw Bash coming toward me through the milling bodies. He grabbed the chair and said, "Let's go!" He had been sitting in his house, he said, when he heard the commotion break out and decided to come see if I was all right and get me out of there in case a real fight broke out.

Bash suggested that I stay clear of future charismatic prayer meetings. When charismatic prayer night came around again the following week, I was considering his advice. I ate that evening with Moraf and his family. We talked for a while after the meal, and then, feeling unusually sleepy, I went back to my house, shut the door, and lay down to rest. I went to sleep, but I woke up again about 9:00 P.M. I was feeling alert, so I decided to walk down and see how the prayer meeting was getting on. I could hear the sounds of praying and singing, but otherwise the village was very quiet. The night was also very dark, so I needed my flashlight to find my way. Passing one house, three bony dogs, who had always been quite friendly in the daytime, dashed out from underneath, barking frantically and worrying at my heels, but they left me alone as soon as I crossed the invisible boundary of their territory. When I reached the meeting place, I came upon a scene like the one that had ended the previous week's meeting.

Apparently, praying and singing had only just degenerated into another shouting match. Three or four people were standing just inside the door of the small prayer house, and I joined them there to watch unobtrusively. Kauref was again making futile appeals for calm and someone was hustling the altar table away. An arch of palm fronds and ornamental leaves was left standing, but suddenly an adolescent boy came charging from the darkness above the meeting place shouting, "I'm crazy! I'm crazy!" (in Tok Pisin, *"Mi longlong! Mi longlong!"*), stomping about fiercely and pelting the remaining decorations with stones as he did so.

When a large stone flew through the door of the prayer house, I decided to take my leave. Affecting an unhurried gait, I stepped out of the house, turned away from the meeting place, and began to stroll away, as many others were doing. I did not think I was in any real danger and did not want to miss anything interesting. Bash, however, had been in earnest when he suggested that I stay away from the prayer meetings. I knew he would be annoyed that I had ignored him and would feel he was an inadequate host if I were to sustain even a scratch or a bruise. Sure enough, while I was still alongside the prayer house I saw Bash coming toward me. I accompanied him to his house, where two other men joined us on the verandah to listen to the prayer meeting's noisy ending from a distance. They smoked and shook their heads in disapproval as we listened to the shouts and what sounded like a guitar being smashed. I learned the next day that a guitar had indeed lost its life that night.

Disruptive Spirits

I did not have another chance to risk injury for the sake of anthropology or to worry my friends by attending a charismatic prayer meeting. At the Bou church service the following Sunday, it was announced that the bishop wanted people to forego charismatic worship for Lent. Some villagers undoubtedly found this a sacrifice, but others did not miss it. Apparently the two shouting and stone-throwing episodes I observed had not been the first incidents at charismatic prayer meetings, and some villagers had little good to say about charismatic worship. Sitting on his verandah after my second rescue, Bash was disgusted. "You look at this," he said, gesturing toward the prayer house. "The kids are controlling the village!" Benau, too, was angry: "It won't be long before I get rid of all this!"

Villagers who were uneasy with charismatic worship had a variety of concerns. Some found it puzzling but were reluctant to condemn it outright. "Prayer is a good thing," one man told me, "but I don't understand this kind." Some also found it potentially dangerous. When worship turns to violence, said Bash, "They're toying with God!" *(Ol i pilai long God!).* "God will turn his back on them!" *(God i givim baksait!),* said Benau.

Many charismatic worshippers, of course, were seeking just the opposite. Charismatic prayer, Moraf told me, brought people closer to the "bigman above," that is, closer to God. For some, the experience had been dramatic. "Before," said Biaunat, "I thought there was no God, but now I realize I was wrong." The possibility of some kind of direct experience of God is a fundamental part of charismatic or Pentecostal Christianity. This aspect of charismatic worship also reminded me of Kragur in the 1970s, when many villagers would have appreciated some concrete assurance that God was real. Some hoped I could help them, but were disappointed to hear that I had not seen God either.

Even so, trafficking with the supernatural is not without its risks. The day after the second violent prayer service, Koreyet, a woman of about my own age, hailed me from the door of her house as I passed by to ask me what had happened and to offer her views. The charismatic worshippers, she thought, had strayed onto dangerous ground and had literally "raised the Devil" (Tok Pisin, *Ol i kirapim Satan i kam insait!*). The charismatic leaders themselves believed that it was possible to raise evil spirits as well as the Holy Spirit. They told me that Eddie Bauer knew how to tell if a good or evil spirit was possessing a worshipper. None of the charismatics thought they had crossed into Satan's territory; but Koreyet was not the only one who thought they were playing with fire.

Passing through Wewak on my way home, I chatted with a number of church personnel and found some worried that the growing popularity of charismatic worship might divide Catholics. Brother Pawil, for one, feared that people might begin to see the charismatic movement as a new church and not just a particular form of worship, although this had not happened in Kragur. Even the most avid promoters of charismatic worship were involved in other church activities, and the charismatic leaders had their own places in the thicket of parish and village committees. Even so, such worship did raise issues of community unity and harmony. The charismatic leaders decried the incidents at prayer meetings as vehemently as anyone, but these incidents left a social mess behind them. Bigmen, councillors, and church leaders had to meet with the parties involved to sort out the grievances, levy modest council fines, and, they hoped, lay anger to rest. Beyond this, many villagers saw charismatic worship as widening other social rifts.

When Koreyet called out to me and spoke of her fear that the charismatics were raising the Devil, she also told me that she had been worried when she heard that a stone had been thrown in my direction. She thought I should not have been there in the first place. "You shouldn't go with all those young people!" she scolded. People of all ages attended the charismatic prayer meetings I went to, but the young did predominate and many villagers saw it as a practice primarily for the young. Not only was it for the young, they were managing it badly. "These kids are getting above themselves!" complained Paypai. "They say they're getting 'new life' [through charismatic worship], but they have no respect!"

Kauref, perhaps the oldest of the leaders of charismatic activities, knew that many older villagers disapproved of charismatic worship; but, he said, they did not understand it. He himself had joined in and he understood. "A lot of young people like it because it's changed their lives. . . . They pray . . . and they feel the presence of God." Despite his reservations, Brother Pawil, too, found good in charismatic worship. The mainstream style of Catholic worship, derived from German missionaries, was very rigid, he said; whereas charismatic worship allowed people to express themselves, and Papua New Guineans were good at that. Nevertheless, in 1998 many of the older women and men, including the weighty bigmen, were steering clear of the singing, strumming, and testifying.

Age aside, women tended to find charismatic worship more appealing than men. They liked the "freedom," said Kauref, using the English word. Although the principal charismatic leaders in Kragur were men, there seemed to be no barriers to anyone plunging enthusiastically into the praying and singing or stepping forward to offer an individual prayer or testimony. Women as well as men, I was told, could speak in tongues, and some could interpret such speech.

Pentecostal worship has made new space in religious life for both women and the young in other parts of the world as well. Pentecostal theology, writes Joel Robbins, "tends to downplay the importance of all identities except that of believer." And the worship itself, as Harvey Cox points out, focuses on "breaking out of the constraints and limitations of everyday life," including the social constraints, and communion with the Holy Spirit is typically open to all. In many parts of the world, women in particular have seized the opportunities this affords, and they are often found in the forefront of the Pentecostal movement.

Kauref approved of this equality in worship, but it did not please everyone. The pacing, gesticulating woman I saw at the first prayer meeting had looked every inch a leader of the proceedings. She turned out to be someone I knew, but, many years older now, I did not immediately recognize her. When, the next day, I asked Paypai who the female "leader" was, he practically spat out the words "She's no leader!" Kragur people take offense at any pretensions to leadership they see as unjustified, but my guess is that Paypai found the idea of a woman as a prominent public leader especially galling.

According to Brother Pawil, some Kragur women's enthusiasm for charismatic worship had angered their husbands. In addition to weekly evening services, there were also occasional prayer gatherings that brought together worshippers from several villages. These were church-sanctioned events in which women participated equally with men. They also took women away from home and their endless chores for entire days at a time. Pawil's sympathies were clearly with the women. "Women have been controlled by men for a long time," he told me (in English). "This offers a new freedom from male-dominated society. The long hours of prayer [and the women's absences from home] are a way of indirectly telling men *they* can go wash clothes and so on."

Catholicism and "The Mystery of Unity"

Even as some parish innovations were shaking things up a bit in Kragur, the church was paying a great deal of attention to community cohesion. In recent years, villagers told me, the parish had sponsored "retreats" (some used the English word) for villagers as part of its "New Image of the Parish" program. There had been as many as five in Kragur. Brother Pawil had led some of them. In each, villagers had divided into several groups, by sex and age, and talked about the things they liked about

Kragur, the things they did not like, and the kinds of changes they expected or would like to see. Then everyone gathered together to discuss the results of the small group discussions. It sounded like a corporate team-building exercise, except the "team" here was a village, and harmony among genders, generations, and kinship groups, not marketing and engineering divisions, was the goal.

Pawil thought that one of the retreats had helped to patch up a long-standing rift between certain *koyeng*. Of course, encouraging people to speak their minds about village problems could also create friction. For instance, at one retreat a group of young people reported from their small group discussion that village leaders did not have enough *save* (that is, knowledge) to do their job.

The "Parish Plan" also illustrated the church's concern with social solidarity. According to the plan, the meeting that produced the plan began by identifying the problems of the parish. Prominent among these was failure to *bung wantaim*. To *bung wantaim* is to rally together, to unite. A slogan of independence that appeared on multitudes of T-shirts and posters, it is a phrase heard all over Papua New Guinea. The parish leadership (probably Father Clem), however, had given the term a special meaning by incorporating it into a kind of parish slogan included in the plan: *"Sios i Misteri Bilong Bung Wantaim"*—that is, "The Church Is the Mystery of Unity." This is a familiar Christian idea, although it might have had special resonance for some villagers (if they could comprehend the term *misteri*, merely borrowed from English rather than translated). Part of the "mystery" of much indigenous magic is the power of the supernatural, power that often depends on the community's unity of purpose, displayed in ritual gatherings.

The other side of too little *bung wantaim* was too much *mi pasin*, which the Parish Plan listed among the parish's problems. *Mi pasin* translates literally as "me fashion." It means thinking only of oneself or, more loosely, being too individualistic. At Bou one Sunday, I heard Father Clem tear into the problem of *mi pasin*, in Tok Pisin, with fierce energy: "If you want to be important, watch out! The purpose of man is not to become important, but to help others! [If you follow] their talk about me, these efforts to surpass others, we will go wrong! [Jesus taught us] to unite, to work together to create something."

As Complex as Ever

Kragur Catholicism was not quite what it had been in the 1970s, but its role in 1998 was at least as complex. Even as the church promoted community unity and decried individualism, Catholicism nevertheless helped keep social ferment bubbling. Villagers were still united in their pride in being good Catholics; but there were more ways to take part in Catholicism than there once had been, and more opportunities to disagree on what was the best way. There was no public opposition, for example, between the Legion of Mary and charismatic worship, and some people took part in both kinds of activities. But a Legion leader sat down with me one day and listed the reasons why, in his view, the Legion's practices were superior to the charismatic approach. One of the detractors of charismatic worship also charged that its participants were seeking personal recognition, not community good, through displaying conspicuous passion in worship. (Avid charismatic worshippers, of course, denied such motives.)

The new parish organization was intended to provide more opportunities for active participation and to weave the different facets of Catholicism into a single entity. But when women and young people took more prominent places—whether in the church bureaucracy or in ecstatic worship—it tended to annoy men and older villagers. The church, however, could not ignore the fact that women and the young were wearying of their subordinate roles.

Catholicism also still figured in the troubling issue of money. According to Father Clem, money was a prime cause of selfish individualism. "A person who cares too much about this thing called money can't care about others because he is thinking only of himself!" he declared one Sunday at Bou. Kragur villagers were there in strength that day, listening attentively to this warning; but Father Clem could not tell them exactly *how* to make their peace with money.

Money

MORAF: THAT AMERICAN WOMAN SINGS A SONG CALLED
"MONEY CHANGES EVERYTHING." IT'S TRUE.
(*DISPELA MERI BILONG AMERICA EM I WOKIM SINGSING*
"*MONEY CHANGES EVERYTHING.*" *EM I TRU.*)

SMITH: CYNDI LAUPER?

MORAF: THAT'S RIGHT. CYNDI LAUPER. THAT'S A PROPHETIC SONG.
(*EM I STRET. CYNDI LAUPER. EM I WANPELA PROFASI SINGSING.*)

In 1975–1976, villagers' intense interest in money sometimes could seem to be at odds with their devotion to the Virgin. "Some people don't think about God's work," Brawaung once complained. "They just think about business." But some of the Virgin's most avid devotees were also keenly interested in money. They were less interested in business, however, than in what they regarded as money's deeper mysteries. I am quite sure that some villagers worshipped the Virgin at least in part because they thought it might be a more effective way to penetrate the secret of European wealth than the more mundane activity of business. Adam and Eve could obtain everything they wanted without effort, Ibor told me, until they lost God's grace by disobeying His laws. "If we had grace," he said, "we could get anything just by thinking about it."

There was a fine line and sometimes no line at all between ordinary Catholicism and cargo religion in Kragur in the 1970s. I think all kinds of religious activity in that decade owed some of their intensity and urgency to anxieties about independence. And both villagers' Catholicism and the cargo lore circulating made access to money and other kinds of European wealth a religious issue.

In 1975–1976, I also made my own small contribution to interest in supernatural paths to money simply by living in Kragur. Cargo religion lore typically holds that the spirit world is the ultimate source, not only of familiar, indigenous kinds of wealth, but also the novel and extravagant wealth of the Europeans. It often suggests that Europeans either know how to commune with the dead to acquire money or are spirits of the dead themselves. While this may seem exceedingly strange to many Europeans, Steven Leavitt argues that this way of construing the problem of European wealth and Melanesian poverty puts it in familiar terms for Melanesians: it becomes a problem of moral relations with ancestors and personal relations with spirits.

Many anthropologists report that rural Papua New Guineans with whom they lived insisted that the anthropologists were the spirits of deceased relatives, even though the anthropologists denied it vigorously. In my case, one man told me he knew that I was his long-dead brother. A few other villagers simply came to see me late at night to tell me stories they had heard about magical ways of getting money from the dead or to ask outright if I knew of such magical techniques, called *bembe* in Tok Pisin. I always claimed complete ignorance. I know, however, that some did not believe me.

One man asked me several times to come with him by night to the village cemetery and show him how to petition the dead to send money from the spirit world. I declined the invitation. Nevertheless, my simple presence in the village in the crucial year after independence and the possibility that, as a European, I might have spiritual connections raised at least a few villagers' hopes for a supernatural route to European wealth.

Such hopes, only barely beneath the surface of daily life in Kragur in the 1970s, were more deeply hidden in 1998. They were not, however, entirely absent. One afternoon I went to a nearby village with a Kragur man of my own age. As darkness fell, we were returning along the coastal trail, bounded by forest on the landward side and separated from the ocean by stands of coconut palms. Conversation was difficult because we had to walk single file and—the moon not yet having risen—I was preoccupied with lighting my way along the undulating rocky path with my flashlight. My companion, however, took advantage of the privacy of the trail to tell me a story I had heard several times before, twenty-two years ago.

The story was about a Kragur man who once by chance saw a European Catholic priest carrying out a secret ritual in which he summoned the spirits of dead Papua New Guineans and obtained money from them. Since I knew the story, it did not matter that much of it was lost in the sound of the waves on the beach on one hand and the night noises of the forest on the other. When he finished, my companion asked if this report of the priest's powers could be true. As usual, I answered that I knew nothing of such things myself, nor did any of my American friends. He did not pursue the subject, but I doubt that his curiosity or his hopes were satisfied. They had already endured for decades.

I think younger generations know less and care less about such things, but it is hard to be sure. Shortly before I left, I spent part of one long, hot afternoon sitting on a verandah with several young men, the oldest of whom had been infants in

1976. While we enjoyed the pleasant buzz brought on by the combination of betel nut, high heat, and dense humidity, we talked about what Kragur had been like in those days. When I told them that some of their fathers, having no shoes, had played basketball against other village teams on the concrete floor at St. Xavier's in socks alone, they found it extremely funny. They also laughed when I mentioned how much interest there had been in *bembe* in the 1970s.

Brother Pawil, however, worried that some of the charismatic worshippers might expect more than an experience of God's presence. They might, he said, think that "God's blessing," when it came, would be material as well as spiritual. There is a strong millenarian streak in Pentecostalism in general, and I heard one charismatic enthusiast talk eagerly of the day when God's laws would replace the laws of men. At least on the surface, however, in 1998 most villagers seemed resigned to pursuing money through commerce with mere living mortals, despite its very modest returns.

Scratching for Kina

One moneymaking activity was conspicuously absent in Kragur in 1998: copra production. Villagers told me that no one had produced any copra in Kragur since the late 1980s. The palms were not producing well, some said, and no one was planting new ones. Copra prices had fallen off in the late 1980s, which may have discouraged production. But even though prices rebounded in the late 1990s, it looked like villagers had decided that keeping up their small plantations in the market's off years was not worth the effort.

Producing copra had been the chief source of cash income in the 1970s. It had also been a major occasion for community cooperation as villagers pooled their efforts to harvest and process everyone's mature coconuts. No similar endeavor had arisen to take its place. There was, however, plenty of petty trading. The small-change transactions in betel nut and betel pepper went on daily. Every Sunday after services at the Bou church, many of the worshippers gathered under a large tree just a few steep yards down the hill from the church for a small but bustling market, where villagers sold garden produce, betel nut, and betel pepper to each other and to the Bou schoolteachers. One or two Kragur families whose houses were located along the trail from Kragur to Bou also set out betel and other produce for sale to the knots of people returning from church.

There were two functioning trade stores in the village and at least two men who, they said, had trade stores that were temporarily out of business for lack of capital. The two going concerns, like the trade stores of the 1970s and 1980s, appeared to do most of their business in rice and canned mackerel. They also stocked some new items, such as Ramen noodles, a luxury item I sometimes found topping my morning plate of rice. Both stores operated out of their proprietors' houses and posted their price lists. One also had posted a sign announcing that all sales were for cash and the store gave no credit, something I had never seen in Kragur in years past.

Having given up on copra, many villagers had turned to small-scale market gardening. St. Xavier's and St. John's bought island garden produce to feed their students and staff. Someone at St. John's, I was told, also bought produce to resell in Wewak. Islanders, too, sometimes took produce to Wewak to sell in the market. A few Kragur villagers had also become regular suppliers of produce to the hospital, the army base, and other larger customers in Wewak. To please their mainland customers, some of the market gardeners were cultivating a variety of what they called European vegetables, including cabbages, carrots, corn, and capsicum peppers.

There had been some market gardening in Kragur in the 1970s, but in 1998 more villagers were involved on a more regular basis. A few were going at it in a very businesslike way. Bokim, who had his own small boat, bought garden produce and cocoa beans from his fellow villagers for resale in Wewak. Another man and his family had earned a reputation for the skill and industry they brought to their market gardening efforts. Waiwun told me himself how he tried to adjust his planting to take advantage of changes in the demand and prices for different crops in Wewak. Waiwun and Bokim both kept careful records of income and expenditures. Their records showed, for example, how much they spent on petrol, motor oil, and food on their marketing trips to Wewak and that they deducted these from their sales receipts. Bokim had completed a course in basic accounting at Divine Word Institute in Madang. Waiwun said that he had learned how to keep books in grade six of primary school. He added, with justifiable pride, that many people with more schooling than he had did not understand business as well.

None of the business ventures I was able to examine in the 1970s and 1980s had kept such careful records, balancing income against expenditures. I am not sure that Bokim was taking account of depreciation on his boat and motor, and neither Bokim nor Waiwun counted the value of their time and labor against their incomes. This latter, however, made sense. With few or no other opportunities in the cash economy in Kragur, devoting their time to market gardening did not cost Bokim or Waiwun money. A wise business person in Kragur, of course, would make sure that business ventures did not interfere with producing enough food for his or her own family to eat. The more enthusiastic market gardeners, however, seemed to eat as well as anyone, and better than some.

Careful accounting was a great improvement over what I had seen in business efforts in the 1970s. Nevertheless, some obstacles to the success of village business were all too familiar. Transportation remained a fundamental problem. The old St. Xavier's boat, the *Tau-K,* had long since gone to its rusty reward by 1998, depriving all Kairiru islanders of an important source of regular and inexpensive passage to the mainland. St. Xavier's staff and students still made regular trips, but now they used only small boats with little room for extra passengers or cargo. More villagers owned small boats than in the past, but some charged as much as 10 kina per passenger one way and an extra fee for cargo. (These boats had to cover their own costs, which were not small. Bokim recorded a cost of 46 kina for fuel and oil for one of his boat's round trips to Wewak.)

With taro selling at from 1 to 2 kina a kilo, the cost of passage to Wewak could take a big bite out of the profits of a lone trader. Some villagers sold betel and other produce in Kragur to finance their marketing trips to Wewak. Waiwun and his family had at one time been reduced to carrying produce on foot over the mountain to St. John's. This job had fallen to Waiwun's wife, Raisek. There is plenty of heavy lifting for everyone in Kragur, but carrying bulging string bags on one's back is usually considered women's work.

What were Kragur people getting from such efforts? Precious little, they told me. In 1997, they had earned very little by produce marketing because there had been almost no food to spare. Even in good years, however, the receipts from market gardening were very modest. One man told me that in a normal year a family might earn 60 kina, although his family sometimes made only 30 kina. One of the more active gardening families had cleared about 150 kina in a recent year, according to their records, but I think few families did this well.

How far did 30 kina or even 150 kina go in Kragur? "Today we get a lot of money," Bash told me, "but it isn't the same as it used to be. The old people, before, they got money and it was worth a lot. [Now] there's a lot of money, but everything is really expensive." Bash was certainly right about the changing value of money. In 1998, as a result of currency devaluations required by the World Bank and declining prices for Papua New Guinea's major exports, the value of the kina against the Australian dollar was about half what it had been in 1994. Most manufactured goods sold in Papua New Guinea are imported, more than half coming from Australia, so the kina's steep decline had resulted in double-digit inflation. Prices of rice and canned mackerel, which are among the country's chief food imports, also had soared. Villagers told me they felt this especially during the drought, when many used what money they had to try to make up for the loss of garden produce.

For many years, the cost of sending children to school has put more financial pressure on Kragur people than the cost of rice and canned fish. In 1998, it cost 30 kina a year to send a child to Bou school and 600 to 700 kina a year to attend one of the high schools in the Wewak area. Some traditional activities also required more money than before. Even in the 1970s, the feasts and gifts of food that are part of funerary observances in Kragur often included a lot of rice, canned fish, and beer. In those days, however, rice and canned fish did not have the style of taro and fish or game from Kragur's own waters and forests. In contrast, in 1998 some villagers told me that there was now more prestige in providing rice at such events. ("If you don't have rice, you don't have a name.")

Some villagers also confided to me that in recent years they had had to borrow hundreds of kina from other Kragur people to finance proper funeral rites for family members, and these debts weighed on them heavily. When locally produced foods were the main items in feasts and exchanges associated with death, marriage, or other events, villagers had to depend on contributions from their kin to amass the quantities needed. In turn, they were obligated to provide food when their kin had to mount their own events. But money debts were obligations of a different kind. Money is harder to come by in Kragur than garden produce, and lenders apparently wanted their money back as soon as possible.

The cost of high school fees or funerals dwarfed villagers' earnings from market gardening. It looked like the use of money in the village had grown faster than people's earnings. Some occasionally got a big payday from selling a pig or a substantial quantity of betel. Many, however, would have found it impossible to meet their financial needs without help from their migrant relatives.

The money situation in Kragur in 1998 looked little better than it had in the 1970s. Discouragement, however, had not accumulated from generation to generation, and some young adults in 1998 were full of hopes and ideas for moneymaking ventures. One especially entrepreneurial young family man pinned his hopes on gradually expanding his market gardening efforts, including finding ways to sell produce in Port Moresby or even export produce outside Papua New Guinea. A number of villagers were interested in the tourist business. A few years before, browsing in a Washington, D.C., bookstore, I had picked up a travel guide for Papua New Guinea, a volume billed as "A Travel Survival Kit." Naturally, I turned to the section on the East Sepik Province and then the section on Wewak. Skimming down the page, I saw mention of Kairiru Island and the advice to see the proprietor of the Bana Store in Wewak (a general store on the main street) for a place to stay on Kairiru. This meant Kragur, of course, because Bana's proprietor was Kragur born and bred and his father and sister were named as contacts on the island.

Reading this gave me a sharp shrinking-world sensation. Also, while going and coming from Papua New Guinea on Air Niugini in 1995, I saw that the airline's magazine, *Paradise*, contained stories promoting the islands off Wewak as tourist spots. One was titled simply "East Sepik Islands" and the other, more evocatively, "Sun and Sea Shells." "Visits to all the outlying islands along the Wewak coast can be organized through Windjammer Hotel on Wewak Beach," one of the *Paradise* articles advised. Islands other than Kairiru got most of the attention, and all of the photos of gleaming beaches and blue waters. But Kairiru was at least mentioned.

Despite such publicity, in 1998 it looked like you could still spend a lot of time on the north coast of Kairiru without running into any tourists. Bash and others told me that occasional tourists did make the trip, ferried over from Wewak for the day. People on some of the Wewak islands had built guest houses—local-style structures reserved for visitors—hoping to lure tourists to stay longer. Some Kragur people were thinking of doing the same. They were keenly interested in hearing about my tourist excursion on the Sepik River, what kinds of financial arrangements the *Melanesian Discoverer* made with the river villages, and what the tourists did in the villages. They were also interested in the wood-carving trade that was a central part of the tourism business on the river. Occasional collectors of artifacts visited Kairiru—trawling for the remaining carved bowls, drums, and *kaikrauap*—but no regular boatloads of affluent Europeans eager for souvenirs.

I was able to tell Bash, Bokim, and others that the owner of the *Melanesian Discoverer* paid a basic fee to every village it visited, with higher payments to villages that offered particularly good performances of "traditional" song and dance or some other kind of spectacle. In one village on the river, for example, tourists could have their faces painted with designs associated with male initiation rituals.

Prospects for striking it big in tourism in Papua New Guinea were limited in 1998. The country was attracting about the same number of tourists it had in the 1970s. Many observers attributed this stagnation in part to the country's well-publicized crime problem. Nonetheless, I answered Kragur people's questions as best I could. Some were very basic. One man asked me just who these tourists were: did the governments of their countries pay them to travel around like this? Another spoke of building a guest house with a concrete floor and a metal roof. I advised against this. Tourists, I said, wanted thatched houses and bamboo floors. They also wanted clean, new outhouses. In short, most tourists wanted a village experience with somewhat more elaborate hygiene.

You also had to keep tourists busy, I advised, so they did not get bored and become a nuisance. I suggested that offering craft lessons, deep-sea fishing from canoes, nature walks in the bush, and similar activities could not only relieve tourists of a little more of their pocket money but also relieve the pressure on villagers to sing and dance for the tourists' entertainment.

One young man sought my advice on another business matter soon after I arrived. On my first Monday in Kragur, I went to the morning assembly for council work. The main issue that day was organizing labor to start building a medical aid post and a residence for a paramedical worker on the west side of the village. These would be timber and thatch structures. The local government in Wewak had agreed to send a paramedical worker (usually called an Aid Post Orderly) to live in Kragur if the village would provide a house and the aid post itself. When discussion of the day's work on this project ended, Manup stepped forward and announced that he and others were collecting money to apply for a government grant to buy a diesel work boat for Kragur to help ease the chronic problem of transportation to the mainland. They needed 100 kina to register as a nonprofit village organization before they could apply. Although they asked for only 1 or 2 kina from each family, Manup and his colleagues failed to arouse much interest.

Later that day, Kalem came to see me bearing the grant application and asking me to read it. It was in English and Kalem spoke English well, but the application instructions were in the English of development agency bureaucrats and spoke of such things as "civil society" and "testing the viability of environmentally sound complementary, more economical means of service delivery." Kalem was not certain that a Kragur group would be eligible for the program. Reading the application, I soon realized that the grant program, called the Targeted Community Development Fund (TCDF), was the descendant of the World Bank-funded NGO support program I had helped design in 1995. But it did not look quite as grassroots friendly as the program originally envisioned.

A World Bank staffer later told me that applications were available in Tok Pisin (although I never got to see how the Tok Pisin application rendered the English version's dense bureaucratic verbiage). But the program finally put in place was clearly for established organizations with records of accomplishment and some mastery of dealings with banks, tax regulations, financial statements, and "group officers' resumes." No group in Kragur was ready to meet such requirements. The TCDF was for "community based" organizations, but many communities in Papua New Guinea, like Kragur, have plenty of *straksa* but not much of what governments or international agencies recognize as organization.

In 1998, Kragur people in towns also were trying to help the village get a better grip on the cash economy. Well-educated migrants had set under way two new efforts to create opportunities for villagers to earn money. Several Kragur migrants and other urban islanders in Wewak were deeply involved in a project called the Bismarck Fishing Corporation, named after the Bismarck Sea, on which Papua New Guinea's north coast faces. They envisioned a purchasing, storage, and marketing system through which people from the offshore islands, fishing part-time and using existing fishing methods, could supply fresh fish for Wewak. They had formed a board of directors, including legal counsel, in 1997, and were seeking financial support from provincial political leaders and perhaps a foreign partner. Also, one of the migrants in Wewak was trying to interest Kragur villagers in growing vanilla. Vanilla beans, he argued, offered high market value per unit of weight and so were a good crop in an area where transportation was costly. He was working with a government extension agent whose experiments with vanilla growing in the East Sepik indicated that villagers could grow high-quality vanilla on their lands. One Kragur villager had begun planting a vanilla plot that, it was hoped, would demonstrate to the others the crop's possibilities.

Each of these ventures had its strengths and weaknesses, but neither promised easy money in the near future. The Bismarck Fishing Corporation was at only an embryonic stage. Anyone who started planting vanilla would have to tend it for several years before it produced a salable harvest. Purchasing the vanilla planting stock also took more money than most villagers could easily acquire, although the crop's advocate was looking into ways of lowering the cost.

Working Together

It was hard not to be impressed by the obstacles to business in Kragur: the familiar problems of transportation, lack of capital and business expertise, and the shaky condition of Papua New Guinea's national economy. Even a skilled entrepreneur could hope for only a narrow profit margin. A few villagers nevertheless remained optimistic. One of Kragur's most energetic entrepreneurs had little sympathy for those who dwelt on the barriers to making money. "People think money is something only for the whites. There are plenty of ways to make money but people just don't understand." He himself understood better than most how to squeeze a few kina from difficult circumstances and how to build on meager beginnings.

Still, if all the complexities and difficulties of earning money in Kragur had been of the kind one can learn about in business school, things would have been relatively simple. In 1998, just as in the past, the technical problem of acquiring money was wound up tightly with a larger issue: how did money fit with village values and social relationships? A big part of this was the question of how to reconcile money with Kragur's Good Way. The fact that business brings wealth has led numbers of villagers over the years to suspect that at its heart there might be some moral and religious truth, some special kind of social harmony. If this were so, there could be no conflict between the pursuit of money and the Good Way. But while some villagers have hoped that business would bring both moral and material fulfillment, others have worried that too vigorous pursuit of money could lead them away from righteousness and fray the ties that bound them together.

In the 1970s, belief that the Europeans' remarkable wealth was evidence of moral superiority, in the form of remarkable social harmony, helped to account for much of the confusion about the good way to deal with money. In 1998, I still encountered romantic distortions of what life is like in the world of the whites. But Kragur villagers did not regularly bend my ear with pronouncements on how wonderfully and spontaneously cooperative and harmonious whites were, as they had in the 1970s. Perhaps greater knowledge of the wider world had fostered a more realistic view of white or European society, or maybe villagers were now more concerned with how a few other Papua New Guineans were becoming so rich. The short time I spent in Kragur in 1998 did not allow me to settle the issue, although I would like to think that the romantic view of the basis of European wealth is losing its hold, allowing villagers to think more clearly about money.

Yet in 1998 moral questions about money and business were still very much alive. Villagers were casually buying and selling betel nut on Kragur's paths and verandahs, behavior that would have caused great consternation in the 1970s. But if many villagers felt that the Good Way could accommodate this small-scale intravillage trade in local produce (as opposed to trade-store goods), others were still uneasy. Kari, a middle-aged army veteran, told me: "Before, everything like betel nut and betel pepper was 'easy go, easy come.' [He interjected the latter phrase in English.] Now everything is money, money, money. But we want Kragur's Good Way to stay."

The propriety of buying and selling among themselves was one issue. Another was the propriety of turning away from collective business ventures. In 1975–1976, many villagers thought that the good way to engage in business was to do so collectively. This not only pooled resources, it also displayed the same kind of unity and harmony that enlisted the support of supernatural forces for growing taro and catching fish. On the darker side, it reflected widespread village suspicion of those who appeared to put their welfare too blatantly before that of the group.

Copra production was the center of business activity in Kragur for decades, and it was a collective endeavor. Each of the two main social divisions, Lupelap and Seksik, held its own account at the Copra Marketing Board, and households tended their own stands of coconuts, but the entire village often pooled its labor for copra processing. For decades, some villagers also have struck out on their own, operating trade stores, raising pigs for sale, or carrying sago to the market in Wewak. This has always, however, had its dangers. To succeed too conspicuously on one's own could arouse envy and anger and this could stir ancestral ghosts to bring illness and misfortune. Many trade stores have gone under because their owners decided it was better to dispose of their stock on credit and be thought generous than to count their kina closely and become objects of envy.

Yet with the demise of copra, enthusiasm for collective business efforts also appeared to have declined. One can find advantages in this. It is true that it is hard for one person or a nuclear family or even two or three families to marshal the money, labor, or land for business on any but a very small scale. But households, not the assembled village, carry out most routine subsistence production in Kragur, so organizing in smaller groups may be a more familiar way to pursue sustained endeavors. In addition, smaller endeavors make it easier to explore a greater variety of market possibilities.

Collective business endeavors in a community like Kragur also have their special problems. People bring every social rift as well as every social tie into the business organization. When a venture fails (which new businesses often do, even in thoroughly commercial societies), there is fertile ground for heated accusations of incompetence and malfeasance. Rifts widen, suspicions fester. Some inevitably see the failure as part of a larger problem of village disunity, casting doubt on Kragur's moral stature as well as its business skills. This does not mean that collective business ventures are impossible, only that they have their distinctive difficulties.

Those who strike out on their own must still tread carefully. And, in 1998, some Kragur people still questioned both the business wisdom of solo or small-group enterprises and feared their social consequences. Brother Pawil saw a decline of interest in collective business efforts as part of a larger trend about which he was "very sad." People were becoming "more individualistic," he said, especially with regard to business. This was bad for business, he thought, as well as for community unity. "They [i.e., villagers] have this idea about business: 'I want to be an individual' . . . [but] there's no way they can do anything productive individualistically." Some entrepreneurial villagers did indeed sound like individualists. Speaking of his business plans, one ambitious young man told me: "I have confidence in myself. I don't have confidence in the community."

Satap's Analysis

Whatever the pragmatic reasons for drifting away from collective business ventures, concern that business ambition was fueling destructive individualism remained. One worried villager had thought about this a good deal and spoke to me at length of his views on the damage that the pursuit of money was doing to village life. Satap came to see me one evening just a few days before I left Kragur. Satap is a very literate former seminary student. His concern with the quality of village social ties probably was rooted in part in Christian ideals of brotherhood and community, but he also spoke with feeling of what he saw as the indigenous customs and traditions that sustained Kragur. His views called to mind Father Clem's warning that thinking too much about money fostered selfish individualism. Satap's analysis, however, was more sociological than religious.

His considerable formal education showed in the neatly written list of points he wished to cover that he brought with him. Although we spoke primarily in Tok Pisin, Satap found it easier to make many of his points if he used such English terms as "reciprocity," "individualism," and "relationships." Yet for the most part he did not speak in abstractions. His analysis may have drawn on Western sociological ideas, but his eyes were on the concrete details of the village's daily life.

"Western influence," he said (using the English phrase), in the form of business and the desire for money, was weakening social relationships in Kragur. Money was taking over. It was in 1982, he told me, that Kragur had last mounted a feast honoring a dead man of renown in a traditional way. The "clans," he said, had competed in amassing taro to feast on and distribute. The bigmen had counted 8,700 taro displayed in heaps for the event, using the Kairiru language counting system that enumerates taro and similar objects by fours. But since then, rice and canned fish had been displacing taro in such events. Not only that, people now preferred to sell their tobacco and pigs for money rather than husband them for use in funeral feasts or other ceremonial exchanges. Interest in the cash value of taro, pigs, and tobacco, said Satap, had started to dry up the flow of "reciprocity"—that is, reciprocal giving —that had always marked daily life in Kragur: "Each one just wants to make his own life easier."

Just a few days after I arrived in Kragur, Moraf had told me that the two major divisions of the village, Seksik and Lupelap, were not internally united the way they used to be. Instead, more and more, individual *koyeng* were going it alone. Now, late in my stay, Satap said he thought that things had gone much further. "Clans," he said, were becoming clans in name only. They were no longer a "binding force," as he put it in English. Instead, groups of two or three brothers and perhaps their children banded together to pursue money. This was in part, he allowed, because clans did not work well in business, but it had its consequences. One was that people were paying less attention to the intricate web of kinship relationships that has long organized much of social life. For example, young children were going around calling their elders by their names, not by the proper form of kinship address. More serious, young people were not confining their sexual escapades to those with whom they could properly marry. "They go play cowboy in the bush!" (*Ol i cowboy pilai long bus!*), as Moraf—who joined Satap and me that evening—put it.

Villagers were also beginning to accept the Western view that time is money, Satap lamented. You could see, he said, that a few people, like Bokim, hated to "waste" even an hour. Bokim in particular was keen on "saving" time. Satap and Moraf said he had even conducted a class for Kragur women to show them how they could use their time more efficiently. The time-management class, they said, had done little or nothing to change the pace and pattern of village life. To my eyes, the pace of life in Kragur looked as unforced as in the 1970s, and people went about their tasks or assembled for council work in the same leisurely manner. But Satap and Moraf told me that the opportunity to work as laborers for mining prospectors in the late 1980s and mid-1990s had, at least temporarily, made Kragur people more time-conscious. For 4 kina and three meals a day, Satap said, men and women alike had been willing to arrive at the work site high on the mountain punctually at 8:30 A.M. every day.

This does not at first sound terribly destructive of social relationships, but Satap reasoned that, as Kragur people have become more avid for money and have begun to equate it with time, they have begun to neglect their social ties: "They're busy for themselves, they have no time for others." In America, he said, if people do not see someone for a while, they do not worry. Americans take it for granted that others are constantly busy with their own affairs, he explained; but in Kragur, if someone fails to visit for long, the relationship sours.

Satap's observations—and Pawil's similar observations on business and individualism—should have been the beginning of my research, not the end. In anthropological research, what people say is vitally important, but one cannot assume that it describes what people actually do. But if what Satap said was close to the mark, then villagers were in a difficult situation. They were beginning to act as though time were money, but they were still judging others' behavior by older standards. I would have liked to investigate the effect of money on Kragur with greater care. Did others see the same things Satap did? Was behavior really changing as fast as he feared? I did not have detailed data on how clan members behaved toward each other in the 1970s, and in any case there was no time to collect data for comparison in 1998.

Villagers clearly had not lost interest in their genealogical ties and their rights as descent-group members. Yet much of what Satap said was plausible. During our long conversation Moraf often nodded in agreement and added his own examples. I had seen with my own eyes some ways in which money was a more obvious part of daily village life. I also heard other villagers enunciate new ways of thinking about how, in a world of money, their ties to other villagers were changing.

In 1998, the best way to provide for one's security in old age in Kragur was still to have many children and hope that at least some of them would either stay in the village and see to your needs when you became infirm or, if they left the village, send enough money home to keep you in fish and rice. Children, however, are not always reliable, especially when they are far away, living the city life. Waiwun told me one day that his wife, Raisek, had been worrying about what would become of them if their children moved away and forgot them. How would they live when they grew old? Their market gardens, he told her, were also their children. Like other parents in Kragur, they worked and sweated to feed, clothe, and school their offspring. But, Waiwun counseled, to be secure they also had to nurture their business.

The general kinds of changes of which Satap spoke are common when societies with noncommercial, kinship-based economies like those of rural Papua New Guinea become involved with societies and economies in which money and commerce rule. As people become more dependent on money, they often become less dependent on traditional social groups and collective activities. Their attentions draw back to closer circles of kin.

Why does this happen? The Europeans who brought money to Papua New Guinea used it according to rules very different from those governing gift or sociopolitical exchange in the indigenous economy. Migrant workers saw this, but back in the village, people sometimes chose to ignore those rules and treat money as if it were another form of indigenous wealth, like pigs or taro. The European example, however, can be hard to ignore, because the colonial and postcolonial eras brought new needs and wants—like paying taxes or school fees or buying better tools—that encouraged people to withhold money from the networks of social obligation that govern the distribution of taro, tobacco, pigs, or fish. The physical form of money lends itself to this; compared to food, it is easy to hide and hoard. If there are opportunities to acquire money regularly without relying on kin, through wage labor or small-scale trade, people can also become less dependent on their kin for some of the necessities of life. They can, if they wish, shake loose from some of their traditional social obligations.

While money often tends to pull people apart in a place like Kragur, it also gives them an opportunity to move apart that they never had before. When they do so they are not just responding to the lure of money; they are also reacting to a chronic tension in indigenous society. This is what Bruce Knauft calls the "tension between giving and keeping," and it was probably a feature of many Melanesian societies long before the Europeans came.

Of course, doing more keeping than giving can be a very rough road. However strong the temptation to keep, doing so may grind against deep-seated feelings that the connections formed by giving are part of one's fundamental identity. Loosening kinship ties in Kragur is also a risky business, thanks in part to the watchful ghosts. In 1998, villagers had not yet reached an easy accommodation between Kragur's old ways and the new ways of money. Many still thought it was the ways of money and not those of the village that should bend. "A man who has money," said Kap, "he wears shoes, socks, long pants; people respect him. But this isn't the town, this is the village!" And, he implied, it should have its own standards. Some, however, saw those standards eroding, and Kap's own protest reflected fear of that very thing.

New Knowledge, New Problems

"I TELL THE YOUNG MEN, THE PAST IS PAST. YOU HAVE TO
CHANGE YOUR IDEAS, YOU HAVE TO THINK ABOUT BUSINESS. I SAY TO THEM,
FORGET ABOUT ME, I'M THROUGH. THE WAYS OF OUR FATHERS AND
GRANDPARENTS ARE FINISHED. YOU FOLLOW THE WAYS OF SCHOOL."
*(MI TOKIM OL YANGPELA MAN, TAIM BIPO EM I OLOSEM TAIM BIPO.
YU MAS SENSIM TING, OLOGETA SAMTING BILONG BISNIS YU MAS TINGIM.
MI TOKIM OL, MI MASKI, MI LUS. FASIN BILONG PAPA TUMBUNA I PINIS.
YUPELA I BIHAINIM FASIN BILONG SKUL TASOL.)*
—A Kragur villager, 1976

"GOOD KNOWLEDGE GROWS AND GROWS.
BAD KNOWLEDGE GROWS ALONG WITH IT."
(GUDPELA SAVE I GRO I GRO. SAVE NOGUD I GRO WANTAIM.)
—A Kragur villager, 1998

As we have seen, although the place of money in Kragur in 1998 was still controversial and villagers were still cash poor, money was definitely more firmly established in everyday life than it had been in the 1970s. Education, too, had long been important in Kragur, but by 1998 the general level of formal education had far outstripped that of the 1970s. The difficulties of integrating the growing numbers of formally schooled villagers into community life rivaled those of coming to terms with money.

Traditional authority in Kragur rests on descent and command of esoteric knowledge of magic and the complex history that supports rights to use magic on behalf of the entire village. The importance of knowledge as a resource in Melanesian society in general is such that Lamont Lindstrom calls it an "information society," although traditional Melanesian information societies were "grounded in talk" rather than in literacy or electronic information technology. Western schools brought another kind of esoteric knowledge to Kragur, and Kragur people seized on it eagerly. They understood that knowledge is power and that they would need a new kind of knowledge in the new era they were entering. They have been unusually successful in acquiring this new knowledge, but they see mixed results. This new knowledge, they fear, tends to undermine traditional authority and foment disharmony among Kragur people, putting younger villagers at odds with traditional leaders and, some charged, at odds with each other.

Take Me to Your Leader

I expected to find that leadership and authority were in flux in 1998. This was nothing new in itself, although I was curious about where things were headed and how far they had gone. But Papua New Guinea is, as another tourism promotion slogan once put it, the "Land of the Unexpected," and almost immediately on arriving in Kragur I encountered an apparent resurgence of traditional authority. Villagers were referring to one of the bigmen as "chief," although I had never known Kragur to have a chief. I finally concluded that it was quite likely that Kragur now had one at least in part because Kragur people were worried that traditional leaders were losing their grip.

Like clans, a chief is what many Westerners might expect to find in a place like Kragur. However, as with the word "clan" but even more so, the familiar term can mask considerable unfamiliar complexity. On my first or second day in Kragur I began hearing people refer to Mowush as "Chief Mowush." I found this odd both because they were using the English word "chief" and because they were bestowing it on one man, singling him out from among the other bigmen. It had been apparent in the 1970s that some bigmen carried more weight than others. But if villagers regarded any single bigman as Kragur's paramount leader, it escaped my attention. A few villagers did tell me that the leaders of their own descent groups were the principal leaders of the entire village, but they could not all have been correct. I took their competing claims as confirmation that leadership in Kragur was diffuse and hierarchy less than rigid.

In 1998, it disconcerted me to hear a young man in his twenties casually refer to what he called in English the "chiefly system" of the past, when "one man spoke" and people obeyed. I am all too aware of the gaping holes in my knowledge of Kragur, but it unsettled me to think that I might have failed to notice something as obvious, one would assume, as a chief. Of course, whether or not Kragur had a chief depends on what one means by "chief," and Kragur people are free to define "chief" in any way they like. However, two of the principal characteristics of a chief as anthropologists usually use the term are that he or she holds a position of paramount, centralized authority and the authority is hereditary. Leadership has a large hereditary component in Kragur, but the term "chief" implies a degree of concentration of authority in the hands of a single leader that I had not seen there.

In 1975–1976, I had tried to locate a single preeminent leader, if there was one.

Far from finding a single leader, many villagers told me that one of the things that made white people different from themselves was that whites had strong central leaders. What they had seen of white society, of course, was the comparatively hierarchical and disciplined organization of mines and plantations, the Catholic mission, and the colonial government; but these institutions had made a powerful impression. For example, when I bluntly asked Urakil if perhaps in the past Kragur had had a single leader, he said, "No, [but] the whites are different."

Nonetheless, in 1998 some villagers also told me that it was usual to designate a single bigman, selected from one of two very prominent descent groups, as the weightiest of the bigmen. They also named a string of bigmen going back to 1976 who had preceded Mowush as first among the bigmen, although they had not called these men chiefs. Some men with their own claims to status and authority questioned Mowush's credentials as chief. There were other bigmen, they said, with greater magical knowledge. "Chief, nothing!" sneered one of his critics. Some, however, were ill at ease simply with the idea of a chief. One of the townsmen told me that he had never heard of Kragur having a paramount bigman. Some villagers also cautioned that it would be wrong to put too much emphasis on one man or one descent group. The bigmen should work together, they said: a canoe needs both a hull and an outrigger.

I was not the only one who found the title itself puzzling. When I asked Kauref why people called Mowush "chief," he replied: "Is it Australian? English? Tok Pisin? It's not clear. When you mix English, Tok Pisin, and our own language it confuses people." Others took even stronger exception to the term. "Chief is English," said Samoff, a retired elementary school teacher. "[It means] one man who is the boss of a department, [like the] chief minister or chief justice." "It's the way the whites talk," said Paypai. "They call their boss 'chief.'"

I am still not completely sure how to understand Kragur's chief. My experience in Kragur argues that real magical power needs no gilding and the glory of the title would be negligible if others questioned it. I never asked Mowush himself how he came to be called chief, and almost no one I did ask knew or cared to say who had first proposed that Kragur designate a chief. One townsman did say he thought that one of the other urban professional men had originated the idea and had suggested who should bear the title.

There is definitely a strong hereditary principle in Kragur leadership and at least a rough hierarchy among the bigmen. Although it is not the general rule, hereditary leadership and hierarchy run deep in the cultures of some of the people of Papua New Guinea. Richard Scaglion argues that the idea of chiefly authority has "deep historical roots" among Austronesian-speaking peoples in Papua New Guinea and is more common there than among speakers of the languages of the other major language group, the Papuan (or sometimes simply "non-Austronesian") languages. The Kairiru language is Austronesian, and this may be evidence of a historical precedent for paramount leaders among Kairiru-speaking people. Yet if there is such a precedent, not all Kragur people feel its strength equally.

Among the strongest advocates of the idea that Kragur had always had a chief were members of the two prominent descent groups that allegedly always supplied Kragur's chiefs. I do not think, however, that making Mowush chief was only an episode in a contest for power. I am willing to bet that among the motives of those who wanted a chief for Kragur was the hope that this would help strengthen the role of traditional authority. And perhaps some Kragur people thought that the village needed more centralized leadership to foster greater unity or to enable the village to deal more effectively with European-style centralized institutions like the government or a mining company. Local groups elsewhere in Papua New Guinea have found that creating a chief, whether from whole cloth or from cultural precedent, is useful in the modern political arena. In the Pacific Islands in general, chiefs have often become important symbols of local or national culture and identity, strengthening them against the influence of Western culture and institutions.

Those Were the Days

Whatever people's intentions, in 1998 the institution of chieftainship in Kragur was not steady on its feet. Mowush's supporters clearly had not brought all the bigmen and all the *koyeng* into the fold. Most villagers, however, were less concerned about who was senior among the bigmen and what to call him than about the effectiveness of the bigmen in general. I only had to sit down on someone's verandah, offer betel nut, and open my notebook to hear complaints that today's bigmen, while still powerful, were not as powerful as their forebears. Many also complained that other villagers (but never the complainant her- or himself), especially young people, were losing respect for the bigmen.

Nostalgia for the powerful magicians and wise leaders of the past may well be a constant in Kragur, predating even the colonial era. I certainly heard plenty of it in the 1970s. Most of the current bigmen, villagers told me then, had been absent for years as migrant laborers when they might have been at home acquiring in full the knowledge and wisdom of their elders. I heard similar laments in 1998, except that now the same bigmen whose knowledge people had questioned in the 1970s were regarded as the wise elders of the past. The belief that the rank and file used to pay more attention to the bigmen also may be a constant. In any event, the complaints I heard on this score in 1998 were quite like those I had heard in the past: before, when the bigmen tabooed certain activities for magical reasons, people obeyed, but not now; before, no one contradicted bigmen when they spoke in public, but not now. I found myself thinking, however, that there might be more to this refrain than the usual rosy nostalgia.

Or perhaps I was prey to a similar nostalgia. When villagers told me how young men drunk on homemade alcohol had beaten people and fought among themselves with bush knives, I found it hard to imagine this happening in Kragur. True, village leaders eventually put a stop to it and destroyed most of the distilling equipment, but there had been several incidents before they managed to do so. In my imagination I pictured some of the bigmen I had known in 1975–1976, old and shriveled as they were, leaning on their walking sticks, facing down and dispersing the drunks and then shaming them in a public meeting in the days following.

These bigmen could be impressive in their wrath or they could put dire unspoken threats into a quiet word. People heeded them out of fear, as well as respect, because they believed the bigmen could use their magical knowledge to harm as well as to help, and they believed that, if angered, the bigmen would not scruple to do so. As Bash put it, "When a leader talked, everyone was afraid. If the leader wanted to wreck everything, he could wreck everything; there would be no food. If he wished a man to die, he died." To stop a fight or a disturbance, said Moraf, a leader had only to point at the miscreants and fix them with his gaze (in Tok Pisin, *opim ai, poinim han*—that is, stare and point).

Were the young people not afraid of the bigmen anymore, I asked. Many villagers had asked themselves the same question. Some thought that people in general did not fear sorcery as much as they used to, perhaps because they felt that Catholicism protected them. Sorcery was not what it used to be either, said others. The Catholic missionaries, they said, had actively suppressed sorcery, not understanding that it could be used for good as well as evil. As a result, knowledge of sorcery was scarce (in Tok Pisin, *save nogud i sot*). Some even wondered if the young no longer believed in the power of the bigmen to magically bring abundance or take it away. Or perhaps the bigmen themselves were too hestitant. Said one member of a prominent descent line, not yet a bigman himself, "The bigmen have just disappeared. At prayer meetings, at village meetings, the young people do all the talking. A lot of little rats are running the village!"

It was too true that most of the bigmen of the 1970s, the bigmen who figured prominently in the events described in *Hard Times on Kairiru Island*, were dead. Kanau, Mangoi, Mer, Moke, Munuo, Tarakam, and Taunur (to use their *Hard Times* pseudonyms) were all dead. Ibor had retired from public life and Lapim lay in his house, crippled by disease. Some of the hearty middle-aged men with claims to bigman status did seem unsure of what to do about the more belligerent little rats. The night of the guitar-smashing ruckus at the charismatic prayer meeting, Benau sat on Bash's verandah and threatened to put an end to charismatic worship. Sakun looked at him wryly. "Don't let me stop you," he said. Sakun was calling Benau's bluff, but he too preferred to stay on the verandah.

It would have been difficult to gauge just how deeply village youths believed in magic or feared sorcery, and no one could know how the bigmen of the 1970s would have coped with a group of truculent, muscular young men soaked in 80-percent alcohol. But young people as well as old expressed concern about the bigmen. Satap, only in his twenties, thought that the young people had lost respect for the "clan leaders," as he put it in English. And Yabok, only sixteen, told me that the young had no respect. They were prone to *bikhet*, he said, using a Tok Pisin word that translates literally as to "bighead" and means to flout authority or to be blatantly uncooperative.

Satap and Yabok were too young to be indulging in nostalgia, although not too young to repeat the conventional wisdom. What I could see in Kragur in 1998, however, suggested that the current bigmen faced growing challenges to their preeminence. Many villagers agreed that one of Kragur's most cherished accomplishments, success in schooling, bore much of the blame. Like so much else I heard in Kragur in 1998, complaints about the very mixed blessings of Western education were not new. But I had never heard villagers voice them with such vehemence, perhaps because schooling was more deeply entrenched in the village than ever before.

A Well-Educated Village

Kragur people started their own primary school after World War II, and in the dozen years preceding my arrival in 1975 they had sent a higher percentage of young people to St. Xavier's High School than any other Kairuru village. Several villagers who began their schooling in the 1950s went on to attend teachers' colleges, university, and seminaries, and became teachers, public servants, and members of Catholic orders. Kragur people were proud of all these accomplishments, but some were disappointed with the returns on their investment in the education of their children.

Many regarded the money paid for school fees very much as an investment. They hoped that their children would succeed in school, get good salaried jobs, and regularly send money back to Kragur. (Partly because of such hopes, villagers favored educating sons over daughters. The latter, they feared, would eventually marry and forgo any chance of paid employment.) But openings in the province's high schools were limited. Many students failed to qualify and left school after completing grade six, with little chance of finding lucrative employment.

Many adults in the 1970s were not sure what use a grade-six education was in village life. Literacy in English was of some value if government documents had to be deciphered or there were letters to faraway kin to read or write. Basic numeracy was useful for dealing with the little money that did pass through their hands. But most regarded a grade-six education as no more useful in the village than it was in the urban job market. In any event, most grade-six graduates in the village in those days were only in their teens or twenties, so they were not taken very seriously in public forums.

Nevertheless, Kragur people still pinned many of their hopes for the future on schooling. Taunur was an old man in 1976, one of the last to remember the men's cult and one of the biggest of the bigmen, proud of his status and of his magical knowledge. But he sometimes spoke as though the days of his kind of knowledge were over. "I tell the young men," he said, "the past is past. You have to change your ideas, you have to think about business. I say to them, forget about me, I'm through. The ways of your fathers and grandparents are through. You follow the ways of school."

Despite their ambivalence about the immediate results of education, Kragur villagers' general instinct that it is a good bet economically is valid. A study conducted for the World Bank in Papua New Guinea in the latter half of the 1990s found that the higher the level of schooling of the household head, the less likely it was that household members lived in poverty. The specific findings are striking. For example, 51 percent of those in households where the head had no schooling were poor. Where household heads had completed only grade six, just 30 percent were in poverty. ("Poverty" was defined in terms of levels of consumption of food, housing, and other goods and services.)

Kragur people could not cite such facts and figures, but they have reached the same general conclusion and continue to send many of their sons and daughters to school. By 1998, the roster of Kragur people who had obtained not only high school but tertiary education included, not only more public servants, nurses, members of Catholic orders, and teachers, but also business people, a university professor, a geologist, two physicians, and a lawyer. The general level of schooling among resident villagers also had increased. According to Muneram's census, about 46 percent of resident villagers fifteen years old and older had at least a grade-six education. I am sure this is a larger share of villagers than in 1975–1976, although I do not know exactly what the number was in that year. Kragur's performance is demonstrably better than the average in Papua New Guinea. In 1998, some 60 percent of all Kragur people fifteen years old and older, resident in the village or nonresident, had at least grade-six educations, compared to 42 percent for all Papua New Guineans.

In addition, in 1975–1976 there were no men in the village who had progressed past grade six and only two women, both of whom had finished grade ten at Yarapos High School, a Catholic high school for women on the mainland. By 1998, about twenty men and women who had completed either grade ten or higher in high school, as well as two men in their twenties with seminary educations, were living and raising families in Kragur.

Villagers call the doctors, lawyers, public servants, and other professionals who live in urban areas, and also the better-educated resident villagers, *saveman* (pronounced sa-vey-man, with a long *a* in man). This Tok Pisin word probably comes from the Portuguese verb *saber*, to know, and means the learned or educated men. One can also say *savemeri*, educated women, but the history of schooling in Kragur has been such that there are fewer occasions for that. Among the *saveman* and *save-meri* in Kragur in 1998 there were new generations who had returned to live in the village after years of work away from home, and they were different from the returned migrants of the 1970s. In the 1970s, returned migrants had usually spent their years away working on coconut or cacao plantations, in gold or copper mines, or in other manual labor. In 1998, a former police detective and retired school-teachers and army personnel had brought their families home to live. Some of the professionals and public servants still pursuing their careers were building houses of permanent materials in Kragur in anticipation of their own retirement.

Benau was exaggerating, but his description of Kragur in 1998 did capture something of the changing face of village literacy: "The village is filled with educated people and retirees. Only a few are left who can't read and write" (*Ples i pulap long ol saveman, ol retired man. Wan wan man i no save ritrait i stap yet*).

The Evils of Education

Despite their pride in Kragur's educational success, many villagers had concluded that the "ways of school" Taunur lauded were not all good ways. Some looked at the more outrageous behavior of the young and concluded that they had somehow perverted their schooling. When I asked Moraf if he knew who had inked "Satan Boys" on the house timber and what it might mean, he did not know, but he did find it annoying and saw a perversion of education at work: "I get angry at some of these young kids. We get them a good education and they turn it around and do crazy things with it."

Puzzling over why one or two boys had disrupted the prayer meeting by pitching stones into the crowd from the darkness beyond the circle of lamplight, Kauref, a retired policeman, sounded like Moraf. He used the same Tok Pisin verb, *tanim*, meaning, among other things, to turn around or transform something. "You go to school," he said, as though addressing the culprits, "and you get good knowledge, but you turn it around." But there was also a feeling abroad in the village that what young people learned in school had an inherent dark side. As Biaunat put it, "Good knowledge grows and grows. Bad knowledge grows along with it."

Disrespect, discord, and individualism were the dark side of what children learned in school, according to some villagers. Young people with only a little education, they said, not only opposed and contradicted the bigmen in meetings, they rudely criticized other villagers in public. Why did they do this? Because, I was told, they thought they knew a lot more than they really did. And, suggested Benau, perhaps because they had learned a way of behaving that might be appropriate elsewhere but did not fit in the village: "They contradict and oppose [the bigmen]. Later, they apologize, but only much later. This is something the whites do, it's like they do in parliament." (There have, in fact, been very few whites, naturalized citizens of Papua New Guinea, in parliament, but Benau apparently regarded the institution itself as essentially a foreign one.)

Education also, some claimed, encouraged an unwelcome individualism. Education, said Biaunat, had led people to think only of their own endeavors. "When *you* ring the [village] bell," he says, "you come. But when someone else rings it, you don't come. Education is ruining the village." Mansu, a former councillor, born before World War II, saw the same thing: "All these educated kids, they think they can do something on their own." Why and how education did this to people Biaunat and Mansu and most others who echoed their views did not say. Benau, however, did hypothesize that people were learning European ways in school: "They pursue 'self-reliance,' [they] help just their [immediate] families. They won't help their brothers and sisters. Maybe this is the European way? The married couples don't think about their mothers, fathers, brothers. They help them only once in a while."

In 1998, I did not have the opportunity to observe very much of how young people acted in public meetings. I did see that younger villagers, women as well as men, had more opportunities than in the past to occupy at least minor formal leadership positions. The colonial period had created opportunities for villagers to become councillors, deputy councillors (Tok Pisin, *komiti*), or leaders in Catholic religious life. By 1998, a host of new leadership posts had been added. There was the variety of new Catholic leadership posts plus an additional councillor, with his additional *komiti*. And each of the two council divisions, or wards, now had a Village Development Committee, and each of these included a women's representative and a youth representative.

None of this demonstrates that the comparatively young leaders of these groups were combative and rude. But the new institutions did place more and younger villagers in formal public positions. In some cases these new leadership positions allowed them to take active roles in institutions larger than the village. They traveled to meetings in other villages, at St. John's or even in Wewak, representing Kragur, taking notes, and bringing back announcements and reports. While this might not impress a grizzled bigman, it might embolden the new leaders to speak up more often and more loudly in village affairs. And those who do speak up may have school knowledge, but not the hereditary right to leadership that accompanies closely guarded traditional knowledge.

It is also conceivable that schooling could incline young people to feel less tightly bound by obligations to wide circles of kin and the community as a whole. In schools they have learned to compete as individuals for grades and for the opportunity to advance to high school or beyond. The history of education policy in Papua New Guinea from the colonial era through the present is one of debate about the aims of schooling: Should it focus on preparing students for jobs in the modern money economy and for life in the world beyond the village or should it try to prepare them for richer lives in the village? Should it emphasize training for an educated elite or should it stress raising the common level of education of the broad populace? Policy and practice have swayed between these poles, but training for a world of individual striving in a competitive economy has remained a pronounced part of schooling. Unfortunately, the kind of striving for individual achievement that fits in well in school, in urban areas, and in the money economy is not a good fit with village life.

Nevertheless, getting as much schooling as possible is still the educational policy of most Kragur people. From Monday through Friday, my morning meal with Moraf's family was accompanied by efforts to get his two middle children off to primary school in Bou on time, prodding them to go to the stream to bathe, making sure they were wearing clean clothes, and giving them packets of food to stow in their book bags. From where I usually sat I could look out a wide window and see other barefoot children hurrying back from the stream or already on their way along the path to Bou.

Writing and arithmetic are now integral parts of village life. Even some of the younger bigmen, men in their fifties, pulled dog-eared notebooks from among the betel nuts and tobacco leaves in their baskets when they sat down to discuss their descent-group histories with me. Even so, villagers could not shake their concern that, for all its virtues, schooling was hard to reconcile with the old ways. "We're half like the ancestors and half like the whites," said Kap. "When you mix things like this, there's trouble." The die, however, has been cast. To some extent this does drive the generations apart and set villagers at odds with each other. "The old, the young, there's a big gully between them," said Satap. "They have different kinds of experience. Education is good, but so is wisdom." Kari saw a similar problem. The bigmen and the educated young men, he said, have an especially difficult time understanding each other. They are, he said in English, on "different wave lengths."

CHAPTER
13

Worlds Apart

"How often have they come with bullshit and lies?"
(*Haumas taim ol i kam bulsit, giamin?*)

—A Kragur villager, commenting on the projects
of the educated migrants, 1998

"[The] attitude toward change is not a positive one."

—A well-educated Kragur migrant, commenting
(in English) on village attitudes, 1998

Satap, young and well-educated himself, saw the widening gap between older villagers and the more schooled young as a "real obstacle to development." The tensions over attitudes and authority could indeed make it harder for villagers to unite behind a single goal; but those divided by age and schooling are also likely to disagree on what that goal should be. Many of the best-educated sons and daughters of Kragur, of course, have taken up town life. The gap between villagers and these urban Kragurs is probably even wider than any division to be found within the village, and relationships across this gap are troubled.

Many villagers look to the successful urbanites for leadership in the Westernized world of money, business, and bureaucracy. Villagers have often been disappointed with the urbanites' performance as their guides in that unfamiliar world. But what really drives a wedge between urban Kragurs and villagers is the extent to which urbanites have come to feel at home in that world. The moral standards of life in the world of money, business, and bureaucracy clash with those of the village, and urban Kragurs cannot lead villagers in that world or even toward it without questioning village moral assumptions.

A History of Disappointment

Throughout Papua New Guinea, migrants from village to town occupy a delicate position. Ties to villages and village lands provide them with a kind of security that their lives as wage and salary earners cannot, but to maintain those ties they have to balance the expectations of their village kin—particularly their financial expectations —with the temptations and demands of town life. The money townsfolk provide their village kin also can have complicated effects. It meets important needs; but some observers argue that it can discourage villagers from pooling community resources to develop local moneymaking endeavors. The money migrants send also enriches the gift exchanges that mark major life events and maintain important social bonds in the village. But though this can give new vitality to old social forms, enlarging the role of money in such exchanges also adds to villagers' financial worries.

Kragur villagers and Kragur migrants need each other, but their relationship is tense as well as complicated. In 1998, a number of villagers felt that the best-educated and most successful migrants had failed Kragur. Their major complaint was not that these urban *saveman* had not sent enough money back to the village, but that they had not used their knowledge to help villagers find ways to earn more money themselves. Some villagers were still smarting from the failure of village development efforts that urban *saveman* had initiated in the 1970s. These—a village development fund and the Village Development Youth Club—had been languishing when I visited Kragur in 1981, and by the mid-1980s they were defunct. The two ventures accumulated bank accounts by soliciting contributions from resident villagers and migrants. I contributed to the development fund myself when it was initiated in 1976. The youth club also raised money by selling garden produce in town. But according to resident villagers in 1998, when these enterprises sputtered to a halt there was no money left to distribute to the contributors.

There was talk in 1998 of other failed *saveman* business ventures, but I did not investigate them. I think some villagers also felt, if not betrayed, then at least let down when their local candidate, one of Kragur's well-educated urban professionals, lost his second bid for a seat in parliament. They knew an election campaign was not a sure thing, but some had placed high hopes, labor, and even their scarce money into the campaign and, in their view, had received nothing in return.

Many who had pitched in when the *saveman* asked for their help were more than disappointed, they were bitter. Some accused the leaders of both business and political enterprises of dishonesty as well as just poor management. They also criticized the educated urban migrants for not cooperating among themselves and for confusing people by promoting different, competing proposals for improving the village. (Indeed, I have heard some urban *saveman* disparage the projects of other *saveman* in rather strong terms.) And villagers criticized the attitude of the *saveman*. Many of them, they said, were arrogant and high-handed. "The men come from town," said Bash, "and they say 'You do this and this and this.' Then they go away." And, said Kap, "they don't respect the bigmen." Unfortunately, some of the *saveman* also simply fail to make themselves understood. Kari has more education than most villagers, having attended an agricultural college, and he laughed when he described one of the *saveman* littering his Tok Pisin with English words like "compromise." "The old people don't know what 'compromise' means," he chuckled.

Above all, villagers were angry that the urban *saveman* had repeatedly asked for their support but had been unable to bring many of their plans for village improvement to fruition. "A lot of men get a lot of education," one man told me. "They give people hope, but their work fails. Next time people will tell them 'You're bullshit men!' " Kalof, a man in his late twenties, married and with three small children, was willing to give the leaders of the fishing venture a chance. But it was, he said, their last. Everything else the *saveman* had tried, he said, had failed, and he told them that if this, too, came to grief, it was time they left villagers to do things in their own way.

Some villagers took pains to point out that not all the educated urban migrants deserved·such criticism. And, while moved by the stories of repeated disappointment, I had to recognize that villagers expected rather a lot from the *saveman*. No matter how well-coordinated their efforts or how respectful they were of the bigmen, the migrant *saveman* would not have found it easy to create successful business endeavors in Kragur, a marginally accessible community in a country with chronic, severe economic problems and no coherent national development plan. Furthermore, many older villagers in 1998 still equated the knowledge of the whites, acquired in school, with knowledge of that most characteristic of the whites' institutions, business. Yet most of the *saveman*, accomplished as they were in their own fields, had no business training or experience.

I talked at length with the migrants promoting both the fishing and the vanilla projects. They had given these endeavors much thought and were investing a good deal of time and effort in them. They were quite aware that there were still problems to be solved and obstacles to overcome. I am not sure, however, if they knew how ready many resident villagers were to distrust all proposals brought by the *saveman* from town. True, the urban *saveman* were more conversant with the ways of the larger world than most resident villagers, but many villagers saw them as out of touch with the realities of village life. Longtime urban residents, especially those who have never raised a family in the village, may well forget how demanding daily village life can be.

But the *saveman* also have insight into village life. When we spoke in 1998, one highly educated professional from Kragur impressed me with his understanding of many of the obstacles to certain kinds of village business endeavors. For example, he had analyzed the costs of running one of the small boats a few villagers owned, and he understood better than most villagers how nearly impossible it was for such a craft to pay for itself by hauling passengers and cargo.

This same man was also, he said, rather embarrassed by the deference with which many villagers treated him and other educated migrants. They treat us, he said, like "*mastas*," using the old colonial Tok Pisin word for whites. I have witnessed such deference, but it does not obviate the suspicion with which many also regard the leadership offered by the educated migrants. "How often have they come with bullshit and lies?" one young husband and father said to me. "I believe in the bigmen of the past!"

Worlds Apart

The world beyond the village in which Kragur's educated migrants live has changed a great deal since the 1970s. When I first went to Papua New Guinea in 1973, white people and indigenous Papua New Guineans generally moved in different spheres. Members of the educated indigenous elite worked and mingled socially with white government functionaries and business people, but this indigenous elite was very small. (At independence in 1975, only about a thousand Papua New Guineans out of a population of between 2.5 and 3 million—less than one-tenth of 1 percent—had graduated from the University of Papua New Guinea or other tertiary educational institutions.) For the most part, in 1973 the world of government offices, hotels, restaurants, banks, and businesses was a white world, albeit one supported by a great deal of Papua New Guinean menial labor. Colonial attitudes also were abundantly evident. Many long-term white residents of the country spoke casually of "natives" and often expected the "natives" to behave with proper subservience. But things were changing.

When I went out to the oil-company camp looking for a site for my fieldwork, the first villagers I met insisted on taking me to see the Catholic priest then staying nearby, a white-haired German who had been in Papua New Guinea for decades. I was eager to be on my way to villages farther from the oil exploration site, but the priest offered me a welcome meal of sandwiches and cold fruit juice and said that he would help me find a guide. To do so, he went to a window and called out to two young boys who were passing by. There was a white man here who would pay them to take him to Kupiwat, he told them. The boys replied that they had to ask their teacher's permission first because they had school that afternoon. The priest came back to the table shaking his head. "That never would have happened ten years ago," he said. "Ten years ago, if you asked someone to do something they just did it."

Things have changed even more since then. Papua New Guineans run the government, teach at the university, and staff the air-conditioned offices of the hotels, banks, and airlines that serve tourists and visiting consultants. The bars at the Islander and the Windjammer are crowded with Papua New Guineans, and Papua New Guineans fill the business class as well as the coach seats on Air Niugini flights to and from Port Moresby. But Papua New Guinea has not completely dismantled the barrier that separated whites from "natives" in the colonial era. To a great extent the educated elite has taken over the privileged sphere whites once dominated and has acquired attitudes toward the poor rural masses much like those with which colonial whites once regarded "natives" in general. (The educated elite is much larger than it once was, but it is still a very small part of the population. In the early 1990s, just over 2 percent of Papua New Guineans had received a university education.)

In the mid-1990s, Deborah Gewertz and Frederick Errington interviewed dozens of Wewak's more affluent Papua New Guinean residents, including "lawyers, doctors, nurses, bankers, clergy, teachers, managers, entrepreneurs, shopkeepers, army personnel [and] civil servants," both male and female. They also mingled with them at Rotary Club events, the Yacht Club, and the Wewak Resort and Country Club where these business and professional people went to socialize and network. Gewertz and Errington found that this elite group had attitudes about success and poverty that would be right at home in country clubs or other gatherings of the affluent in Australia or the United States. They generally maintained that success in the modern world of education, commerce, or professions was the fruit of hard work, discipline, and planning, while poverty reflected laziness and a lack of planning, discipline, and perseverance. In short, success was available to all those Papua New Guineans who possessed the appropriate virtues.

These successful Papua New Guineans indeed had planned and worked hard, but a couple of things were missing from their view of poverty. First, access to education in Papua New Guinea is severely limited—by its expense, by the scarcity of places in secondary and tertiary institutions, and by geography. In some parts of the country students must live away from home even to attend primary school. Those who succeed in school have worked hard, but they have also been lucky.

Second, in order to take part in the life of the urban elite, Papua New Guineans generally have to weaken their ties to their village kin. In villagers' eyes, attending the university, working for the government, or habitually wearing shoes and socks should not dissolve the bonds of kinship. But the wearers of shoes and socks (the *susokman,* as they are called in Tok Pisin) find that it is difficult to live up to village definitions of their kinship obligations and simultaneously provide for the basics of urban life—housing, food, business clothing—and take part in urban elite social life, including the professional networking that goes on in restaurants, in clubs, and on the golf course. Gewertz and Errington argue that villagers tend to define success as meeting a wide variety of kinship obligations; but for the urban elite, success means providing an affluent life for one's immediate family, and that usually means putting strict limits on generosity to more distant kin.

Village kin may see this as lack of generosity, but they are judging by the moral ideals of village society. In terms of those ideals, material wealth is for creating and maintaining social bonds, and wealth gained at the expense of social ties is tainted. But what looks like antisocial greed to the village is necessity and prudence to the urban elite. If they fall on hard times because they have given unstintingly to their village kin, their urban peers will not praise their generosity; they will criticize their moral weakness. To join the elite, then, Papua New Guineans have had to work hard; but they have also needed good luck, and they have had to enter a different world of morality.

The moral world inside the village, of course, is changing. Some villagers themselves probably live by the village moral ideal only as much as they have to. The opportunity to accumulate material goods and consume without fear of what kin and neighbors might think is certainly one of the possible attractions of urban life. Of course, Papua New Guineans may also have other reasons to leave the village and to keep their distance. One of the Kragur townsmen, for example, told me that he did not visit the village much anymore because he could no longer stand the outhouses. Social life in the village, too, can be oppressive. There is not only virtually no privacy, but the dense network of kinship ties that provides security and familiarity also imposes a dense network of obligations. Meeting these obligations can be all-consuming, and failing to meet them to others' satisfaction can make one the target of gossip, festering grievances, and, if one is a believer, angry ghosts and even sorcery. To quote myself, "Life in societies where everyone knows everyone else and is bound to everyone else in a multitude of social relationships creates friction, and this friction can generate unpleasant heat as well as soothing warmth."

Kragur people who know both the village and life in a more impersonal setting notice the difference. Kaunup has lived all his life in East New Britain Province, where his father—born and raised in Kragur—manages a plantation. The family lives in an area where, more than in most parts of Papua New Guinea, people make their livings through growing cash crops and engaging in other forms of business. Kaunup told me that he preferred the way of life there, not only because he thought it was easier to make a living, but also because the houses were farther apart, you were not expected to go to meetings all the time, and you could live the way you wanted to without feeling constrained by community pressure. "People can follow their own ways" *(Ol i ken bihainim we bilong ol yet),* he said, and this was good. It is not too much to say that life away from the village offers not only a new variety of experience, but also new opportunities for inventing and reinventing one's self. Such a life has its own drawbacks, but the autonomy one enjoys is one of its attractions.

Village life does have its own kind of autonomy, however. Villagers may be enveloped in a web of kinship obligations, but they are not nakedly dependent for their basic livelihoods on a boss, a distant government department, or a mercurial national economy. And fellow villagers can see each other as whole people, not just as bosses and employees, buyers and sellers, cogs in a bureaucracy, or inhabitants of different social strata. Yet life in town or in the world of business offers a novel form of autonomy that contrasts attractively with some dimensions of life in the village.

Nonetheless, given plenty of plausible reasons to loosen village ties, do elite Papua

New Guineans also have to label those back in the village as lazy, undisciplined, and improvident? Whatever the combination of motives that brings people to the educated urban elite, once there it must be hard not to find the rural poor at least partly at fault for their own poverty. The essentially Western institutions that create the elite—schools, the business world, and the institutions of government inherited from a Western colonial regime—are awash in notions of individual responsibility, competition, and the social value of individual wealth. And once one has achieved elite status, accepting such values would ease any qualms caused by enjoying privileges unattainable for most Papua New Guineans.

Whatever one may think of the comparative merits of urban elite and village moral standards, the differences divide village people from their kin who have mastered the new knowledge and succeeded in the new world that it dominates. A gap between resident villagers and town-dwelling Kragur people is nothing new. In 1975–1976, villagers sometimes criticized urban migrants for enjoying the high life and forgetting about the hard lot of those back in Kragur. The migrants, some said, just "bloody sit on their asses and work for their bloody fortnightly pay" or "sit drinking tea and enjoying themselves in Moresby." Since then, more Kragurs have joined the ranks of comparatively affluent urbanites. And there are more and more people like Kaunup, the offspring of men and women who left the village years ago, for whom a stay in Kragur is a novelty or a distraction from life in their real homes.

I could not say how closely the attitudes of educated and successful urban Kragurs resemble those of the Wewak elite with whom Gewertz and Errington partied at the Wewak Resort and Country Club. Village and educated urban Kragurs clearly do not always see eye to eye on the latter's financial obligation to their village kin. The Kragurs in towns, one villager told me in 1998, generally come through with money to help out with the expenses of death ceremonies, but they are prone to plead penury on lesser occasions. (The few who have helped their village kin to acquire such costly amenities as boats and motors are exceptional, although helping out with school fees is, I believe, rather common.)

I would be on shaky ground if I presumed to judge urban Kragur people's generosity, especially as I often find myself in a similar position. My friends and nominal kin in Kragur sometimes ask me for help with paying school fees or repairing an outboard motor or financing a funeral feast. In my view, they tend to overestimate my financial capacity. They are many and I am one. I have to save for retirement, the 1992 Toyota is not going to last forever, the roof on my house is fifty years old, and the mortgage company still owns most of my home. If money runs short, my nominal kin in Kragur can only send sago. From their perspective, however, I am still very privileged and probably do not feel the obligations of even nominal kinship as sharply as I should.

Some of the Kragur townsmen who want villagers to become more financially independent do not speak of how village requests for money strain their own financial resources. Instead, they reason that for their own good villagers have to learn new ways of thinking about money. To do well in the contemporary world, they argue, villagers must recognize the monetary value of things like betel and garden produce and adopt the virtues of thrift and self-reliance. As Mwairap put it in 1998, it was good if villagers learned that nothing is free. And another townsman was concerned that if the urban Kragurs were too generous it would keep villagers from facing contemporary realities: "I think it's injurious to give them money," he told me in his excellent English. Still another told me that he knew villagers sometimes asked me for financial help, but I should give them ideas, not money.

I have met only a small number of the Kragur people who live outside the village, and those I know best are those who have stayed closest to home and remain most involved in village affairs. Despite their continuing involvement with the village, these men (the urban Kragurs I know best are all men) often cannot help but see Kragur from the vantage point of the town. From this point of view, the village is not just different; it is backward.

It was not surprising that when Taram looked at Kragur in 1998 he found that "[the] attitude toward change is not a positive one." For men with college or university educations it also must be hard to avoid adopting a paternalistic tone. Suggesting that we arrange to talk when he came to the village in 1998, one of Kragur's university graduates said he thought it would be better to meet privately, because "we [that is, he and I] are on a different level of understanding" than villagers in general. It was true that we both had much more formal education and wider experience of the world beyond the village, but this can dull as well as enhance one's appreciation of the views and concerns of those rooted in the village.

Some Kragur people who have moved away and stayed away may not care very much about the village anymore. I know, however, that others are deeply concerned with life in Kragur, although many may tend to see it from the perspective of their own urban lives. They live in a world in which striking out on one's own or accumulating more material wealth than your neighbors or kin is not only acceptable but laudable. They may well have more in common with other relatively affluent urban Papua New Guineans, whatever village or language group or province they come from, than with their own village kin. The danger is that too much time spent with the urban elite can breed the attitudes Gewertz and Errington describe, including the conviction that villagers are not just poorer, but have themselves to blame for it. But this assumption neglects the great inequality of opportunity in Papua New Guinea and the country's rather feeble commitment to erasing the legacy of colonial privilege.

Something to Hold on To

"WHENEVER I'M AWAY, I CAN'T STOP THINKING ABOUT THIS PLACE."
—A Kragur villager, returned to settle in Kragur
after many years working in Papua New Guinea's towns (in English), 1998

I went back to Kragur in 1998 to see how it had changed and, I hoped, to catch up on the constant discussion about how it *should* change that was so much a part of village life in the 1970s. In those days, villagers argued and speculated about how to improve the material circumstances of their lives and what it meant to be good people and to live together in harmony. At issue for many was not just making Kragur a better place, but keeping the village from decay and dissolution. The most disheartened villagers warned me that if I came back in a few years only a handful of old people would be left. Who would want to stay in a village that was poor and full of conflict and the illness and misfortune that disharmony spawned? And how could such a place survive in the new era of national independence?

Fears of its imminent demise proved unfounded, and in 1998 I no longer heard predictions that Kragur would disappear. But villagers were still concerned about the village's future, and not without reason. A variety of trends and influences were keeping Kragur in a state of social agitation. While a mainstay of village life, Catholicism still managed to stir things up. Charismatic worship in particular gave women, the young, and the mildly rebellious opportunities to carve out new zones of freedom from established authority and hierarchy. School learning was becoming significantly more common, and its tensions with older forms of knowledge and power were becoming more pronounced. Assertive women were scandalizing conservative men; youths filled with spirits of various kinds butted heads with their elders; the educated young were annoying almost everyone, including each other; traditional leaders were struggling to define and assert their authority; and the gap between villagers and urban Kragurs was more apparent than ever. Some villagers found themselves divided by support of rival parliamentary candidates. The possibility of mining put an edge on concerns about land rights and juxtaposed the promise of money with the need for careful husbandry of garden land, forests, and streams. The increasing importance of market gardening and other cash-crop production might also put pressure on land resources.

Kragur has had no respite from social upset for generations, and it would be a mistake today, just as it was in the 1970s, to take the most pessimistic villagers' predictions at face value. "First time hard, second time harder," one thirty-something man said to me (in English) in 1998, comparing the challenges his parents had faced to those of his own generation. I am afraid he exaggerates. Yet I, too, felt the imminence of new kinds of challenges. I am not greatly concerned simply that change continues to shake up the old social order; shaking up the old order gives people a chance to build something new. The familiar tensions and the building lines of stress in the social fabric I saw in 1998 were not just the product of destructive outside influences. Women and young people were reacting against restrictions characteristic of indigenous life. People who chose town life were not just seeking urban opportunities; they were also fleeing from the age-old difficulties and limitations of village life.

I *am* concerned, however, about what Kragur people will make of the opportunities to reshape their social world. There is much to be lost as well as gained. For example, bigmen may lead in part through fear, but their authority helps to anchor the system of kinship and hereditary rights that underwrites not just the bigmen's authority itself, but also the rights of the rank and file to essential resources. The tension between giving and keeping may fray nerves, but it is an unavoidable aspect of the system of mutual obligations that ensures villagers' material security. Even fear of vengeful ghosts helps to knit Kragur together. It is a stressful and capricious way of enforcing social norms, but it also motivates powerful outpourings of collective energy when villagers gather to call off the ghosts that are making someone ill or thwarting gardening or fishing efforts.

I am concerned that losses could rival gains in large part because of the direction that life is taking in Papua New Guinea in general. National society in Papua New Guinea is no longer the society of colonial Europeans; it is a Papua New Guinean society. Yet it is more and more a society in which people's worth is measured in money and extreme social and economic inequalities are tolerated. This is the larger society within which Kragur must exist, and it provides a dangerous model.

Money Again

Taram was right in 1998 when he said that people in Kragur were still arguing about things they argued about in the 1970s. A lot of debate and speculation about the nature of the good life and how to achieve it in the 1970s had to do with money, and in 1998 it still did. There was also evidence that, while Kragur still enjoyed few of the advantages of money, its dangers were closer at hand. Whether they observed without comment that Kragur now followed "the ways of the town," analyzed with consternation the effects of money on reciprocity, or stated with approval that customary gift giving was "withering away," numbers of Kragur people thought that things were truly changing. What I could see myself—the acceptance of open commerce in betel and garden produce within the village, the trade store sign brazenly denying credit, the efficient yet impersonal accounting of a few young entrepreneurs, the growing, often burdensome importance of money in village sociopolitical exchange—lent support to Kragur people's own observations. True, even many of those eager for better ways to earn money still regarded business as, in Mansu's words, something on the *waitman sait* (that is, the whiteman's side) of life. But beyond Kragur, Papua New Guineans themselves were taking over the *waitman sait* and creating a postcolonial society in which "Money makes you a man."

Money is a two-edged sword in contemporary Papua New Guinea. Where the country's citizens have higher cash incomes they are also healthier and enjoy easier access to education. For better or worse, more money also means a louder voice in the political arena. And poverty as well as the search for riches can damage community harmony. Although romantic views of the harmony of white societies may be waning, many Kragur people continue to suspect that being poor is evidence of their inability to get along together and this suspicion can be self-fulfilling. Limited opportunity to earn money feeds the discontent of young villagers, and limited access to the things that money can buy, including better health and education, increases everyone's discontent. But there is no doubt that becoming more deeply involved in the commercial economy can encourage people to try to reduce their obligations to wider social networks.

In 1998, the growing significance of money in Kragur tended to influence political loyalties, undermine traditional authority, exacerbate the tensions between giving and keeping, and aggravate the differences between old and young, villagers and town dwellers. The potential ecological damage done by gold mining could put village cohesion to the test, but so would the dramatically deeper immersion in a world in which land and labor are items of commerce that mining would bring. Figuring out how to acquire more money loomed large among many villagers' concerns in 1998, but many were equally concerned about what the growing interest in money was doing to villagers' relations with each other.

Cooling Ideology

Encountering money and the capitalist economy does not necessarily throw the moral world of a community like Kragur into disarray. What happens, to use the language of Jonathan Parry and Maurice Bloch, depends on people's success in "taming" or "domesticating" the new influences. In the 1970s, some villagers seemed to be attempting to tame the world of money and commerce by promulgating a version of the Good Way that subordinated the pursuit of money to the virtues of harmony and generosity. Some probably hoped that cultivating these virtues would eventually bring them money, too, through supernatural channels. And even in the 1970s, the inescapable question for Kragur was not if it would take part in the world of money and commerce but how it would do so. Still, many villagers appeared to be using the Good Way to try to keep the problems of money at bay.

In 1998, from some perspectives, Kragur looked to me very much the way I had written of it before. But one of the more striking ways in which it differed was that the force of the Good Way as a defense against both the domination of money and the shame of poverty was waning. A sense that, in spite of everything, Kragur is somehow a special place has bolstered village solidarity and morale in the past and is not absent today, but I think that the Good Way is losing strength.

The story of how God marked Kragur by visiting the ancestor Masos before Christian missionaries arrived has been a particularly reliable support for a sense of positive common identity in the colonial and postcolonial world. It clearly has helped to underwrite the Good Way. In 1998, people still told the story with pride, and they were not shy in pointing out what it meant: God chose Kragur instead of other villages and Kragur had needed no help from missionaries or other Europeans to make God's acquaintance. However, the legacy of Masos is not immune from skepticism. Nuor told me in 1998 that, according to his estimation, the Masos incident could have taken place after the first Society of the Divine Word missionaries arrived in the area. Although the missionaries had not yet shown up in Kragur, Nuor speculated that Kragur people might have heard rumors of them and their teachings. But despite creeping doubts, many Kragur people still hold fast to the story of Masos, including some educated townsmen. One university graduate spoke to me (in English) of how important it was to record the story and to repeat it to each new generation: "If we don't, some day our children and grandchildren will think it's just a myth."

Still, I did not hear as much talk of the Good Way in 1998 as I did in the 1970s. Mixed with the many complaints about individualism, disrespect for elders, or neglect of kinship obligations, people sometimes interjected assurances that, in spite of everything, the fundamental way of Kragur remained the same. *"Pasin i wankain"* or *"Pasin i stap pinis"* some would say ("Our ways are the same" or "Our ways remain"). They still were generous and helpful people, the villagers told me, and they could put their differences aside when there was work to be done. One well-educated townsman also suggested that an egalitarian ideal was still alive. He told me that it was still Kragur's way to judge people by their *pasin*—that is, their behavior and character—not by how much schooling they had. But such assurances were less muscular than the declarations of Kragur's dramatic moral superiority and remarkable spirit of harmony and cooperation that had rung in my ears on my first visit there.

Villagers' declarations of Kragur's distinctive virtue in the 1970s drew a good deal of their intensity from a heated atmosphere that could not be sustained. Fears about independence and hopes for mystical redemption, whether via the Virgin or the ancestors, touched virtually every aspect of life then. There is much in the cooling of that atmosphere not to regret, and the very vehemence with which Kragur people declared their virtue suggested the degree of their anxiety and doubt. Changing times, however, also have rendered the Good Way more soft-spoken.

Even in the heated 1970s, affirmations of Kragur's moral worth left many important details vague, and the teachings of Masos did not prepare the village for every moral decision. Kragur people were generous, yes; but what was generosity in a world where wealth was counted in money, not taro? Masos, in accord with God's message, told Kragur people that they should be hospitable to visitors. This clearly meant they should not kill them, but did it also mean they should not charge them room and board?

In 1998, the Good Way remained a reminder of important moral issues and something everyone could take pride in. It appeared, however, to have lost its old bite and to be even less specific about questions of money and generosity. In 1998, with the exception of Father Clem's spirited warnings against the seductions of money, I heard no fervent public speeches about keeping money in its place (behind God, Maria, and perhaps the ancestors) of the kind I had heard in the 1970s. Urban Kragurs spoke approvingly of the good way or good spirit of their birthplace, but what makes a good person in the village is not quite what makes a good person in town. Inside Kragur, movement toward the kinds of differences in monetary fortunes and interests characteristic of town life would belie claims that Kragur was a place of unusual harmony and solidarity. The more affluent might still find it plausible, but I think others would see it as an empty slogan, especially those who still thought of social harmony as both the source and the result of *shared* prosperity.

As circumstances allow, Kragur people undoubtedly will turn more and more to commerce for their livelihoods. They will satisfy more of their material needs through buying and selling, and money will play an increasing role in their social lives. They will rely for their material security more on their abilities to earn money and less on their kin. Limited opportunities to rely on commerce on Kairiru's north coast, however, will probably keep the pace of economic change relatively slow. Without truly radical change in the system of land and resource rights, Kragur cannot turn into a Melanesian version of an American suburb, where households can carry on their lives in substantial isolation from each other if they wish. Nor can anyone, through clever business dealings, deprive others of all access to the basic means of producing a livelihood. Catholicism is perhaps less vividly collective than it once was, but I believe it, too, is still a counterweight to the idea that money is the measure of a person's worth. Nonetheless, I think Kragur could drift ever more rapidly toward, not just deeper involvement with money, but greater social fragmentation occasioned by its pursuit.

Unless, that is, Kragur people embark on a more self-conscious effort to tame and domesticate money. Vague hopes and admonitions to preserve the good spirit are unlikely to be enough, any more than allegiance to a vague ideal of equality has been enough in itself to prevent the dramatic inequalities that mark life in the United States.

Not Exactly What They Meant

I believe that many Kragur people still hope greater success in the money economy will strengthen the village. Even though they would probably have to loosen some kinds of traditional restrictions to achieve such success, it could indeed improve life for them all. But if they shed the customs that have long helped to restrain inequality and reinforce mutual obligations and have no thought for finding new ways of moderating excessive self-seeking, the results could be deeply unfortunate. The paired dangers are more dramatic inequality and diminished capacity to endure together the hardships and crises brought by international markets, international bankers, government ineptitude, meteorological events, or ecological pressures.

There has always been inequality in Kragur, but the inequality possible in a market economy is of a different kind than that in an indigenous economy of sociopolitical exchange and kinship obligation. Unrestrained and undirected by strong community and kinship obligations, differences in income and wealth can grow into wide social and economic chasms. Differences of degree can turn into differences of kind; a society in which even the unequal are clearly interdependent can become one in which inequality is a wall between people and poverty a mark of fundamental inferiority. The irony of the development of new forms of inequality in Papua New Guinea is that it is taking place in part because people are trying to break loose from the constraints of older forms of inequality and hierarchy. Achieved under the guise of development, the new inequality illustrates Sandra Wallman's dictum that even successful development is often a double bind that leaves people saying, " 'I got what I wanted, but it's not what I meant.' "

In many so-called developed countries there is great inequality. Those on the bottom of the heap often suffer from severe material deprivation, but material deprivation is only part of the problem. Inequality also limits the possibilities for democratic social, cultural, and political life. And even inequality that stops far short of imposing absolute material deprivation can affect material well-being. There is increasing evidence, for example, that in affluent Western societies the fact of inequality itself—the experience of living on the lower rungs of a steep ladder of status —has a pronounced effect on health. Inequality also, of course, tends to weaken community interest among people, and what may appear to an outsider to be very little inequality can have profound effects in this regard.

Preserving Kragur's most valued resources—its scarce cropland and its ample, unpolluted fresh water—in years to come may require a strong sense of common interest. Gold mining is a potential threat to these resources, but so are population growth and the need to grow more food for local consumption and more crops for sale. In an article published in 1996, Bryant Allen pointed out that Papua New Guinea's population was growing much faster than were opportunities for wage employment. At 2 million in 1966 and 3.9 million in 1990, the population, wrote Allen, was conservatively estimated to reach 5 million by 2005 and 6.6 million by 2015. It was also estimated that "labor force growth will exceed wage employment growth by 40,000 persons per year for the foreseeable future." Most wage employment will continue to be in urban areas. Even so, towns and cities will be able to absorb into their commercial economies only a fraction of the population increase. Villages will face the problem of providing decent lives, food, and cash incomes to rapidly growing numbers of residents and of doing so without degrading the environment. Allen argues that the national government can help most by improving rural life through providing better roads and better education and health services, but a great deal of responsibility remains for lower-level governments, nongovernment organizations, and communities themselves.

In 1998, Brother Pawil was convinced that people in Kragur were becoming more individualistic and that their business ambitions had a lot to do with it. "The community aspect [of life] is not as strong," he told me. There were many plans for community projects, he said, but people did not follow through because of the growing individualism. It was in business in particular, he said, that villagers wanted to act independently. This disturbed Pawil a great deal. I think it clashed with his notion of what a Christian community should be like, but he also thought it would prove economically ineffective.

I do not agree with Pawil entirely that, as he put it, "There is no way [Kragur villagers] can do anything productive individualistically." As I have already said, collective businesses bring their own thorny problems, and there is a case to be made for smaller-group endeavors. There is also a good case for greater individual autonomy. But there are some very important things that Kragur people cannot accomplish as individuals: they cannot effectively tame money; they cannot create a community in which a "good spirit" reigns and people recognize mutual responsibility for their common welfare; and they cannot work together to protect the resources on which they all depend.

Global Forces, Local Yearning

National trends in Papua New Guinea have not been friendly to efforts to build and maintain a strong spirit of collective effort in local communities. The national government has been making a weak showing so far in helping local communities to face the kinds of challenges Bryant Allen delineates. Many of the country's more fortunate and successful citizens are detaching themselves from village roots and learning to value individual striving for affluence. Some anthropologists even argue that efforts by the country's leaders to instill in Papua New Guineans a sense of national identity also tend to encourage the possessive, individual-centered values of the capitalist commodity economy. So far as a coherent vision of collective purpose and direction is concerned, most national leaders are as much at sea as anyone.

National leaders, of course, do not have a free hand. As Stuart Firth notes, Pacific Islands countries in general are under great pressure to adopt policies that conform to the needs of global corporate and financial interests. Principally, this means reducing the role of the state in the economy and opening the national economy to international forces. As Firth also points out, some national leaders may wish to do this anyway, but they find it politically expedient to blame the forces of globalization. Yet pressures from aid donors, international financial institutions, and investors, argues Firth, in fact leave them little latitude. The result is that governments are reduced to "transmitting international forces rather than sheltering people from them." In a country like Papua New Guinea, this makes the position of the elite as well as that of the rural masses insecure.

In the short term, Papua New Guinea could do worse than to adopt some of the policies the World Bank and other international lenders and aid donors are pressing upon the country. No international institution, however, can give Papua New Guinea its own distinctive vision for the future. To push successfully against the limits of global systems and international institutions, a government and a people need their own strong sense of direction. Papua New Guinea has not found this yet. A clear positive direction—one that goes beyond wanting to be free from external control—is a tall order for any country, especially one as new and loosely joined as Papua New Guinea. Unfortunately, a country like Papua New Guinea pays an especially high price for lacking such a direction.

The pressure of forces far beyond their control is all the more reason for Kragur villagers to seek a way of life that will provide security and stability for all. I may be romanticizing what is possible in Kragur. Colin Filer, a decidedly non-romantic observer of events in Papua New Guinea, has suggested that when Papua New Guinean communities fail to cooperate with environmentally destructive mining projects it is in part because they cannot cooperate with each other or even agree on their collective goals.

Kragur, too, is politically fragmented. And—whether to enjoy greater private affluence or a new kind of personal autonomy—some Kragur people would like to distance themselves from the village. Many, however, want Kragur to adapt to changing times; but they also cling to Kragur's village virtues and want it to be a place where people somehow face the future together. Like Kalem, some "can't stop thinking about this place" even when they are far away. Like Moraf, many yearn to *strongim ples* so that "no one can break up the village." It will take more than yearning or magic to accomplish these goals.

A couple of days before I left, Bash was contemplating Papua New Guinea's distinctive character and its uncertain future. "If Papua New Guinea is going to develop," he said, "it's going to have to develop in its own way." He could have said the same of Kragur, and I am sure he had Kragur in mind. Kragur people have to keep talking about what Kragur's own way should be, but they must stay alert because circumstances are pushing them hard toward a destination many would find disappointing.

Epilogue

In Kragur in 1998, I reviewed my notes every day, looking for places in a conversation where I had failed to ask an important question, issues in need of more investigation, or new topics to pursue. For every question I could answer, several new ones arose, and some of what I learned cast into doubt things I thought I already knew. As the day of my departure from Kragur approached, in late March, it was obvious that I was barely going to scratch the surface of my growing list of new and neglected topics before I left. But I had to be satisfied with what I had. It was a stroke of great good luck, I reminded myself, that had brought me to Kragur again at all.

I was not altogether sorry to be going home. Life in Kragur moves at an easy pace, but it has its own kind of intensity, and anthropological fieldwork can be very intense. Especially in a close and crowded village, it begins when you wake up in the morning, or someone wakes you up, and lasts until you close your door to go to sleep at night. Even if you begin to feel at home and occasionally drop the role of observer and investigator, it is hard to shake the feeling that you really ought to be taking notes. It is also almost impossible to avoid being implicated in local rivalries and intrigues, simply by virtue of with whom one associates; and the more people accept you as a kind of honorary villager, the more difficult it is. Being drawn into local political life is often informative, but trying not to step on something too explosive can be taxing. Anything else, however, would not be fieldwork.

During my last few days in the village my schedule was full. Several families invited me for going-away meals and I dined on local delicacies almost every night. Bokim, Kauref, Kwan, and their kin, and Moraf and his family each put on particularly elaborate feasts, complete with speeches and presentations. At Moraf's family gathering, I managed to prostrate myself by chewing too large and potent a betel nut. The combination of the betel's unaccustomed strength and the heat from the fire and the bodies packing the house suddenly turned my muscles to Jello and drained all the blood from my head. I spent a large part of the evening stretched out on the floor, resting my head on the log threshold of an open wall, letting the cooler outside air revive me.

I did not have much to pack. The major task was the delicate one of giving away the equipment and supplies I was not taking home: my lantern, bucket, plates, and cups, the remaining peanut butter, jam, biscuits, and so on. Knowing that this was my custom, several people had already discreetly indicated their interest in particular items, but I had to think first of those who had been especially helpful to me. My spare pens and notebooks were more popular gifts than they would have been in the less literate 1970s. To meet the debt I felt I owed to some parties I got out my wallet. I reserved my favorite hat, my sport sandals, and one of my two pairs of shoes for Moraf, who was to accompany me to Wewak.

I do not like long good-byes. I often prefer to be dropped at the airport and wait for my plane alone, but this is not how things are done in Kragur. On the wet and overcast morning of my departure, a small group gathered to sit with me while we waited for Bokim and Moraf to prepare the boat. We finally made our way to the beach and stood in the drizzle while several young men maneuvered the boat into position on log rollers, ready to launch into the small breakers. The wicker chair was again waiting for me, and after a last round of handshakes and a few embraces I was bundled into place and the young men ran the boat out into deep water. Moraf was at the helm and Bokim served as crew.

Moraf is known as a fine pilot; he also has a flair for the dramatic. He ran straight out to sea, then cut sharply to the left across the mouth of the bay so that he could turn back and cruise past the full length of the main village and I could wave to those standing on the beach and along the top of the cliff. The last figure we passed was old Mapos, standing at the edge of the cliff on Shewaratin ground at the eastern end of the village, dwarfed by the tall palms behind him and the mountain above. We were soon out of sight of Kragur and negotiating the rough waters at Urur Point. After we rounded Urur, the skies cleared and the sea settled into long, steady swells that let us run at a good speed, passing a school of dolphins and, a little later, sailing through a small school of glittering flying fish.

In Wewak, I stayed with Pawil at the Marist house again. I had three days before my flight to Port Moresby. The Kragur townsman promoting vanilla planting had arranged for me to spend most of one day visiting a trial vanilla plantation inland from the town with an agricultural extension officer and a group of village councillors. I wanted to visit Brother Matthew at Wirui. I also had errands to run. Moraf was staying with kin just outside Wewak, but, concerned with my safety, he insisted on accompanying me on my round of shops, the post office, and the bank.

Pawil and Moraf took me to the airport in the Marist Brothers' vehicle. We left early so that Pawil could show me the monument at Cape Wom commemorating the Japanese surrender to the Allies in 1945 and the Japanese War Memorial, erected in 1969 on top of Mission Hill, popular tourist sites I had never visited before. From Mission Hill there is a clear view of Kairiru. Pawil took my picture with Kairiru in the background. I took a picture of Pawil and Moraf posing in two of the battered Japanese helmets that sat on top of the low memorial structure. We arrived at the airport in plenty of time, but the flight arriving from Vanimo in the West Sepik Province, which was to continue on to Port Moresby, was almost two hours late.

Pawil and Moraf settled in to wait with me. At one point Moraf went outside to chew betel nut, but remembering the incident at my farewell dinner, he refused to give me any.

I stayed overnight in Port Moresby. Brother Pat Howley was working with an NGO there and I had arranged to meet him that evening. But his transportation failed him, and taxis in Port Moresby being what they are, especially after dark, we had to cancel our plans. Taram and another professional man from Kragur did join me for breakfast at my hotel.

Port Moresby's new airport had opened since I arrived in the country just a few weeks before. Modern and gleaming, it contrasted sharply with the run-down buildings I had known since 1973. The international terminal admitted no one without a ticket, and it was fully enclosed, carpeted, and air-conditioned. That morning, it was almost empty and almost eerily quiet, except for an instrumental version of "Blue Hawaii" emanating softly from speakers somewhere. There were comfortable upholstered seats, a sparkling new gift shop, and the atmosphere of international travel limbo. This should not be dismissed lightly. I have endured long waits for flights in the old domestic terminal in Port Moresby when it was not only hot and crowded but also without functioning rest rooms. Broken toilets are nothing to sniff at. Still, once inside the new international facility I felt like I had already left Papua New Guinea far behind.

Since 1998, Papua New Guinea's economy has continued along a bumpy road. The World Bank is still part of the scene; rather, under a new prime minister, it has returned to the scene. The bank virtually cut off relations with the Papua New Guinea government in 1998 when the leader of the World Bank mission left the bank to serve as economic advisor to the current prime minister in return for substantial remuneration. This violated bank policy, and both talks and lending ground to a halt.

In 2000, the World Bank issued an assessment of its role in Papua New Guinea thus far. Among other things, it reported that, while the Targeted Community Development Program "got off to a promising start," it had foundered because, according to the assessment, the Papua New Guinea government had not contributed its anticipated share of financial support. In general, the assessment found the results of the bank's efforts disappointing. It laid some blame on the Papua New Guinea government, but it also criticized the bank itself, charging "insufficient appreciation of local conditions and sensitivities" and noting that "inadequate integration of difficult local conditions, cultural norms, village-level perceptions, and political needs constrained the Bank's effectiveness in the 1990s. . . ."

Papua New Guinea's loan negotiations with the World Bank and other international institutions, and debates among the country's leaders are still contentious. The bank's assessment acknowledged the debacle of the Land Mobilization Program and concluded: "In retrospect, the project required a sensitive, cautious approach that fully integrated local perceptions as well as a public education campaign and [an] effort to bring representative NGOs on board." The news from Papua New Guinea, however, still tells of accusations, rumors, and demonstrations stirred by new proposals for revising the country's land laws. Controversy continues over what to do about faltering education, health, police, and other public services. The World Bank's insistence that certain government-owned industries be privatized also has aroused opposition.

In the first few months after returning from Kragur, I performed several tasks I had promised to carry out for Kragur people. I sought out and talked with a major international vanilla buyer on behalf of the infant Kairiru vanilla project and sent information he provided back to my contacts in Wewak. I gathered information on the plans of an international fishing enterprise for a possible endeavor in the East Sepik for one of the leaders of the Bismarck Fishing Corporation. I found the address of the linguist who had worked in Kragur in the late 1970s and sent it to the Kragur people who were still hoping to reestablish contact with him. I wrote to the proprietor of the *Melanesian Discoverer* on behalf of several parties in Kragur who were hoping to find a way to get in on the Sepik tourist trade. I also sent some copies of a Papua New Guinea tourist guidebook to interested Kragur people so they could see what the trade in other locales was offering.

I continue to exchange sporadic letters with several Kragur people. Lately, some of my letters seem to be disappearing along the way, which makes correspondence difficult. Most of the news I receive concerns births and deaths. Lapim, Kwan, Aram, Bokim's and Pawil's mother, Biaunat's father, and Bashi's infant daughter all have died since 1998.

Pawil wrote that a new international joint venture for tuna fishing in East Sepik waters (not the one I investigated for him) will probably make it difficult to proceed with the Bismarck Fishing Corporation's plans. A few months later, the *Post-Courier* reported that construction of a large tuna-processing plant not far down the beach from the Windjammer had begun. The plant, when completed, "is expected to be the biggest of its kind in the Western Pacific," according to the newspaper story.

Pawil also sent me a copy of a small book of Kairiru stories and legends that he had been working on for some time. Published by Wirui Press, a publishing firm in Wewak owned by the Catholic Church, it is called *Kairiru: Island of Legends.*

For years, Kragur villagers have talked about the possibility of installing a small hydroelectric generator in one of the nearby streams. Such devices provide both St. Xavier's and St. John's with electricity. According to a couple of recent letters, Kragur townsmen and a member of parliament arranged to have an engineer investigate the feasibility of installing a generator near Kragur and the engineer found a favorable site. One correspondent, however, thinks that the parliamentary member's support is just part of his election campaign and might not amount to anything in the end. Not all villagers are keen on the idea either. Nonetheless, I cannot help picturing Kragur glowing with fluorescent tubes and pulsing with radios.

I will probably go back to Kragur again, although I do not know when. I may actually have to plan my next trip. If a generator is installed, I will not experience again the pitch-black nights or the disembodied voices floating along the paths. In other ways, too, it probably will not be quite the way I described it before or how I have portrayed it here. The most fundamental changes, however, may not be the most obvious. Whatever happens, I hope I will find Kragur people healthy, prosperous, and still able to boast of their good spirit.

Notes

Introduction

pp. xi–xii   To reach Kairiru's north coast: I draw some of my information on Kairiru's dimensions and topography from Borrell (1989). Brother William Borrell taught for many years at St. Xavier's High School and enlisted islanders in the project of describing and cataloging Kairiru's plants. He completed this volume while a research associate at the University of Melbourne School of Botany in 1980–1989.

p. xvi   The lake itself: See Boyek (2000, pp. 10–13) for an account of the supernatural being Kairiru.

p. xvi   The Kairiru or Tau language: On the distribution of the Kairiru language, see Wivell (1981, p. 1).

pp. xvi–xvii   He divided the region: Terrell (1986, p. 15) discusses the origins of the place-names Polynesia, Micronesia, Malaysia, and Melanesia.

Chapter 1. Nostalgia, Dreams, Progress, and Development

p. 2   The temperature on Kairiru: My information on temperature and rainfall is taken from Borrell (1989).

p. 6   Even people's "traditions": For an overview of literature on tradition as subject to revision, even invention, see Feinberg (1995). See Sahlins (1994, p. 381) for an example of "the invention of tradition" in Europe.

p. 8   "Development": For a variety of anthropological perspectives on development, see Escobar (1995), Gardener and Lewis (1996), Grillo and Rew (1985), and Grillo and Stirrat (1997). See Hobart (1995, p. 1) on worrying too much about the *term* "development."

p. 8   It is also too late: On some of the variety of ways in which people around the world understand development, see Dahl and Rabo (1992) and Wallman (1977).

p. 8   David Gegeo: Gegeo discusses *diflopmen* among the Kwara'ae in Gegeo (1998).

p. 9   People cannot even argue: Sahlins (1994, p. 380) notes the need for cultural agreement in order for people to argue.

p. 10   By 1998: On defining the good society as part of development, see Long (1992, p. 273).

Chapter 2. Finding Kragur

pp. 12–13   As Kluckhohn put it: I have taken the quotation from Kluckhohn from Wolcott (1995, p. 130).

p. 14   The Sepik region in the 1970s: Huber (1988) refers to the Sepik region as a frontier.

p. 14   The town as a whole: The population estimate is taken from the Papua New Guinea Bureau of Statistics, 1976, and is cited in Huber (1988, p. 11).

p. 16   Just a few years later: Information on the percentage of Christians in the population of Papua New Guinea is from Barker (1992, p. 145).

p. 16   It was the seat of the bishop of Wewak: Information on Catholic mission personnel in the East Sepik Province is from Huber (1988, p. 12).

p. 16   Many anthropologists: On anthropological neglect of Christianity in Melanesia, see Barker (1992, p. 145).

p. 17   This allowed me to learn: On the sometimes contradictory effects of Catholicism in Kragur and Kragur people's complicated relationship with the Catholic Mission, see Smith (1990a) and Smith (1988), respectively.

p. 18   Kairiru's freshwater streams: On the Japanese occupation and Kairiru's water supply, see Watanabe (1995, p.70).

p. 18   Brother William Borrell: On the possible artesian source of Kairiru's water, see Borrell (1989, p. ix).

p. 18   One of the stories: For the story of the *masalai* Kairiru, see Boyek (2000, pp. 11–12).

Chapter 3. The Virgin and the Ancestors

p. 25   In common English usage: Many anthropologists reject the practice of applying the church/cult distinction to the *tambaran* institution and Christianity. I was probably introduced to this issue early in my studies with Ted Schwartz. For examples in print, see Schwartz (1973, p. 170) and Scaglion (1983, p. 483).

p. 25   Cult spirits: For a description of the nature of ancestral spirit(s) in one Sepik *tambaran* cult, see Tuzin (1997, pp. 109–110).

pp. 25–26   In 1935: My information on the history of Catholic mission activity on Kairiru and in Kragur comes from Kragur villagers' own accounts and from Brother Patrick Howley, headmaster of St. Xavier's in 1975–1976 and a resident of Kairiru for several years; Emil Brigil, son of the first catechist to visit Kragur and in 1975–1976 head of the Copra Marketing Board in Wewak; and Father Francis Mihalic of the Society of the Divine Word.

pp. 27–28   In one 1907 incident: This raid is recounted in the report of a German colonial official. See Rodatz (1907).

p. 28   Several villagers suggested: On conceptions of God in Kragur in the 1970s, see Smith (1988).

p. 30   Given this view of things: On Kragur perceptions of European order, see Smith (1984) and Smith (1990b).

p. 31   Fellow anthropologists: Regarding anthropologists' reports of pre-mission knowledge of God in the East Sepik, Robert Welsch and Joshua Bell recently told me of a case from one of the other islands offshore from Wewak.

Chapter 4: Food, Money, and the Strangeness of Capitalism

p. 35   The minimum legal wage: Information on the urban minimum wage was obtained from staff at the Wewak Sub-District Office in 1976.

p. 39   The term "gift exchange": The term "gift exchange" goes back at least to the French scholar Marcel Mauss and his famous work *The Gift*, first published in 1925. See Mauss (1967/1925).

p. 39   The term "sociopolitical exchange": On sociopolitical exchange in Melanesia, see Sillitoe (1998, p. 85).

p. 40   But gift giving: On the bonds created by sharing food in Melanesia, see Knauft (1999, p. 47).

p. 40   The opposite of an economy: On the mixing of gifts and commodities in actual societies, see Apadurai (1986, p. 11) and Carrier (1992, pp. 201–204).

p. 40   Andrew Strathern: On Melpa ceremonial giving, see Strathern (1991, p. 220).

pp. 41–43 Ian Hogbin: On Wogeo overseas trade, see Hogbin (1935, p.401).

pp. 43–44 In many Papua New Guinean societies: On rights to a variety of types of land in Papua New Guinea, see Chowning (1977, p. 39).

p. 44   I can write about: On the percentage of land held under indigenous systems, see Larmour (1991, p.1).

p. 44   There are also, of course, national and provincial laws: My characterization of aspects of Papua New Guinea land law neglects many complexities. It is based on Brown and Ploeg (1997), Dubash and Filer (2000), Larmour (1991), McWilliam (1991), and sections of the Papua New Guinea Land Act of 1996. Stuart Kirsch and Glenn Barry directed me to important sources of information. Colin Filer and Kathy Whimp directed me away from some egregious errors. Responsibility for shortcomings is mine alone.

p. 44   Landowners are entitled: On the complexities of compensation for resource development in Papua New Guinea, see Toft (1997).

pp. 45–46 The fact that Kragur people: On conceptions of time and patterns of work in Kragur, see Smith (1982b).

Chapter 5. Money and the Moral Puzzle of Prosperity

p. 48   This tension: On "the heart of cultural contestation" in Melanesia, see Knauft (1996, p.214).

p. 49   Elaborating such contrasts: See Thomas (1991, p.204) on the importance of contrast in shaping tradition.

p. 51   What I observed in 1975–1976: On Christianity and colonial perceptions of harmony, see Nader (1991, pp. 44–59).

p. 51   A 1946 Australian government patrol report: My information on the Lalau incident comes from a Wewak Patrol Report for 1946–1947, which I obtained at the Papua New Guinea National Archive in Port Moresby.

pp. 51–52   Many anthropologists: On the cultural context of cargo cults in Melanesia, see Schwartz (1973). For some classic works on cargo cults, see Burridge (1995 [1960]), Lawrence (1964), Schwartz (1962 and 1973), and Worsley (1968). For some recent discussions of what cargo cults are all about, see Dalton (2000).

p. 52   Christianity also helped: On the importance of Christianity in cargo beliefs in Melanesia, see Schwartz (1973, p. 170). See Ahrens (1997, pp. 19–34) on the millenarian tradition in Christianity and Christian missions.

p. 52   There is an irrational element: Schwartz (1968, p. 51 and 1973, p. 157) discusses the irrational element in cargo cults and the excitement of the cult as its own reward (1973, p. 167). On the universal human proclivity for millenarian or messianic religion, see Schwartz (1973, pp. 168–170) and Burridge (1995 [1960], p. xvii). On visions of America in one cargo religion, see Lindstrom (1990). On Americans' millenarian proclivities, see Cox (1995, p. 21).

p. 53   Years later: See Smith (1995) on corporate teamwork.

p. 54   Over and over again: On Kragur perceptions of European order in work, see Smith (1984).

Chapter 6. To Papua New Guinea for the World Bank

p. 59   Industrial logging: On the complexities of logging in Papua New Guinea, and elsewhere in the Pacific, see Barlow and Winduo (1997).

pp. 60–61   For this brief sketch of Papua New Guinea history I have drawn on Connell (1997), Griffin, Nelson, and Firth (1979), and Zimmer-Tamakoshi (1998).

p. 61   Indigenous political agitation: See Pokawin (1982) on attitudes toward independence.

p. 61   In 1995: Quotations from Julias Chan and Michael Somare are from Wesley-Smith (1996, p. 428). Infant mortality statistics are from Connell (1997, p. 171). Connell (1997, p. 232) also notes the increasing severity of malaria.

p. 61   Average life expectancy: Life expectancy statistics are from the World Bank (1995, p. 5).

pp. 61–62	In 1994: On the condition of the health infrastructure in 1994, see Connell (1997, p. 240). Connell (1997, p. 118) refers to public-service "desk jockeys."
p. 62	In the years: See Connell (1977, pp. 25–28) on the debate over development goals at the time of independence.
p. 62	Some scholars have argued: On international political and economic circumstances and Papua New Guinea's failure to develop, see Amarshi, et al. (1979). For a contrasting view, see Lea (2000).
p. 62	Independent Papua New Guinea: On problems with uneven development of sectors of the Papua New Guinea economy, see Lea (2000) and World Bank (2000, pp. 1–2). See also Australian International Development Assistance Bureau (1989, pp. 17–20).
p. 62	Colonial rule: See Connell (1997, pp. 222–226) on the Australian development pattern in Papua New Guinea.
pp. 62–63	The increasing inequality: On the disadvantages of women in postcolonial Papua New Guinea, see Connell (1997, pp. 266–269), Knauft (1999, pp. 168–180), and Macintyre (1998).
p. 63	Everywhere: On the rising crime rate, see World Bank (1995, p. 3).
p. 63	In July: On protests against the ERP loan conditions, see Wesley-Smith (1996, p. 431).
pp. 63–64	The national coalition of NGOs: For critical views of the World Bank see, for example, Cornia, et al. (1987) and George and Sabelli (1994).
p. 64	True, the currency devaluation: Information on duties on canned fish is from *The National,* November 8, 1995, p. 18.
p. 64	Several years later: For differing views of the role of public-service personnel costs as a factor in inefficient service delivery, see World Bank (2000, p. 9), World Bank (1995, p. 7), and Curtin (2000, p. 24).
p. 64	Loan conditions: On forestry provisions in the ERP loan package, see Dubash and Filer (2000).
pp. 64–65	Probably the most incendiary issue: On the controversy over the LMP, see Dubash and Filer (2000, pp. 39–40). I also draw on Lakau (1997), Turtle (1991), Wesley-Smith (1996), and Tony Power (personal communication).
p. 65	In the East Sepik province: Fingleton (1991, p. 159) and Ward (1991, p. 181) discuss the East Sepik legislation and "some of the subtleties of customary land and resource rights."
p. 66	Many Papua New Guineans: See Jacobsen (1997, pp. 231–232) on lack of articulation between precolonial and electoral and parliamentary political systems.
p. 66	Above all: Foster (1997) provides a variety of perspectives on "nation making" in Papua New Guinea. Gewertz and Errington (1991, pp. 191–192) discuss lack of recognition of the higher power of the state among rural Papua New Guineans.

Wanek (1996) discusses several varieties of antipathy to the state in Papua New Guinea. On the state as the Antichrist, see Robbins (1997, p. 50).

p. 66   Near the end of the 1990s: Connell (1997, p. 3) compares Papua New Guinea's problems with those of other developing countries.

p. 67   Real rural incomes: Comparative information on real incomes is from Connell (1997, p. 190).

Chapter 7. Weekend on Kairiru

p. 75   Deborah Gewertz and Frederick Errington: On Wewak's emerging middle class and its relationship with village kin, see Gewertz and Errington (1999, pp. 29–30).

Chapter 8. Free Ticket to Paradise

p. 82   Forces of nature: On drought and frost conditions at the end of 1997 and Australian aid, see Wesley-Smith (1998, p. 453).

p. 83   It also shut down: See Manning (1997, pp. 5–6)on the effects of the drought on Ok Tedi mine. On the effects of drought and frost on the Papua New Guinea economy, see Yala and Levantis (1998, p. 2).

p. 92   Home brew: On home brew liquor, see *Papua New Guinea Post Courier* (1998). Smith (1982a) describes drinking behavior in Kragur in the 1970s.

Chapter 9. The Key to the Village, Structure, and Strife

p. 115   Two major mine sites: Dan Jorgenson confirmed my recall of the case of Mount Fubilan and informed me of the case of Mount Waruwari.

p. 115   Mining: See Filer (1998, p. 154) on government revenue from mining and oil production.

p. 116   Colin Filer: On the "inability of the local community to distribute the economic benefits of mining in an equitable manner," see Filer (1998, pp. 155–156). For an opposing view, see Hyndman (1994, pp. 172–175). See Kirsch (1997, p. 144) on the "stereotype of the greedy . . . landowner."

p. 116   Mining's damage: Filer (1998, pp. 156–157 and 160) and O'Faircheallaigh (1992) discuss community strife caused by damage done to the environment.

p. 117   On "dangerous sensitivity" to others in a small community, see Diamond (1963, p. 94). On "personalistic" explanation, see Schwartz (1972, p. 33 and 1973, p. 165).

Chapter 10. Parish Bureaucracy and the Holy Spirit

pp. 126–127 Pentecostalism: For background on Pentecostal and charismatic Christianity, see Murphy (1988) and Cox (1995). On charismatic and Pentecostal Christianity in the Pacific Islands, see Robbins, Stewart, and Strathern (2001).

p. 133   Age aside: On leveling identities in Pentecostal worship, see Robbins (2001, p. 9). See Cox (1995, p. 200) on Pentecostal worship and breaking out of every-day constraints. See Cox (1995, pp. 137 and 123–138) on women as leaders in the Pentecostal movement. Strathern and Stewart (2001, pp. 99–201) provide an example of women using Pentecostalism to define their roles in a changing society in the Western Highlands Province of Papua New Guinea.

Chapter 11. Money

p. 137   Many anthropologists report: On anthropologists as dead ancestors, see Leavitt (2000).

p. 138   Copra production: Information on copra prices is from Yala and Levantis (1998, p. 11).

p. 140   In 1998: Information on inflation is from Yala and Levantis (1998, p. 4).

p. 142   Prospects: Observations on crime and tourism are from Yala and Levantis (1998, p. 12).

p. 145   The propriety: On Kragur people's attachment to collective business ventures, see Smith (1990b).

p. 145   Smaller groups: Regarding other advantages of smaller-scale enterprises, see Sillitoe (2000, pp. 151 and 159).

p. 149   If there are opportunities: On money and weakening kinship ties, see Knauft (1999, pp. 157–194).

p. 149   While money often tends to pull people apart: See Knauft (1999, p. 226) on the "tension between giving and keeping"; also Bercovitch (1994) and Weiner (1992). The argument regarding giving, keeping, and identity draws on the work of Marilyn Strathern (1998).

Chapter 12. New Knowledge, New Problems

p. 150   Traditional authority: See Lindstrom (1990, p. 10) on Melanesia as an "informa-tion society."

p. 151   I expected to find: On the changing nature of leadership in Kragur in the 1970s, see Smith (1985).

p. 152   Strong hereditary principle: Scaglion (1996) discusses language and precedents for chieftainship in Papua New Guinea.

p. 153   Local groups: On chiefs and the idea of chiefs in contemporary Papua New Guinea and the Pacific in general, see Errington and Gewertz (1990), Scaglion (1996), and White and Lindstrom (1997).

p. 156   Study conducted for the World Bank: Data on poverty and education in Papua New Guinea are from Gibson and Rozelle (1998, pp. 11 and 63).

p. 156   Kragur's performance: Data on educational attainment in Papua New Guinea are from Gibson and Rozelle (1998, p. 64).

pp. 158–159 Debate about the aims: Crossley (1998) discusses alternative aims for schooling in Papua New Guinea.

Chapter 13. Worlds Apart

p. 161   The money townsfolk provide: See Carrier and Carrier (1989) on the complex effects of remittances from migrants in Manus Province. Gregory (1982) analyzes the relationship of the cash economy to the gift economy in contemporary Papua New Guinea.

p. 163   The world beyond the village: On university graduates at the time of independence, see Wanek (1996, p. 50).

p. 164   The educated elite: Data on numbers of Papua New Guineans with university education are from Gibson and Rozelle (1998, p. 63).

p. 164   In the mid-1990s: On Papua New Guinea's emerging middle class, see Gewertz and Errington (1999).

p. 164   Access to education: On the limited capacity of schools, see Connell (1997, p. 245) and Tautea (1997, p. 182).

p. 165   To quote myself: Smith (1994, p. 61).

Chapter 14. Something to Hold on To

p. 169   I am not greatly concerned: I owe some of these thoughts on the value of shaking up the old order to similar remarks by Bailey (1971, p. 298).

p. 170   Two-edged sword: On the benefits of cash income in contemporary Papua New Guinea, see Allen (1996).

p. 170   Encountering money: On "taming" and "domesticating" money, see Parry and Bloch (1989, p. 18).

p. 173   There has always been inequality: My characterization of the changing nature of inequality in Papua New Guinea owes much to the work of Gewertz and Errington (1991 and 1999), who discuss the contrast in terms of what they call "commensurate" as opposed to "incommensurate" differences. On successful development as a double bind, see Wallman (1977, p. 13).

p. 173   There is increasing evidence: On the effects of inequality in itself on health, see Henwood (2000) and Lardner (1998).

p. 174   Bryant Allen: See Allen (1996) on the dilemma posed by the gap between population growth and wage employment opportunities.

p. 175   To instill in Papua New Guineans: On national identity and individualism, see Foster (1997, p. 177).

p. 175   Stuart Firth: Firth (2000) discusses the Pacific Islands in the global economy.

p. 175   Colin Filer: On political fragmentation and opposition to mining, see Filer (1998, p. 175).

Epilogue

p. 179   See Curtin (2000)on economic conditions in Papua New Guinea in 2000. On the fate of the Targeted Community Development Fund, see World Bank (2000, p. 6). For the World Bank's self-critical assessment, see World Bank (2000, pp. 5 and 11).

pp. 179–180 The bank's assessment: For the World Bank's postmortem on the LMP, see World Bank (2000, p. 7).

p. 180   Pawil wrote: On the big new tuna-processing plant, see *Papua New Guinea Post-Courier Online* (2001).

Glossary of Tok Pisin and Kairiru Terms

Pronunciation:

Consonants in written Tok Pisin are pronounced as they are in English. Vowels are pronounced as follows:

a as in "arm" or "papa"
e as in "bed"; or as the *a* in "plate"
i as in "hit" or "little"; or as in "machine"
o as in "hot"; or as in "old" or "no"
u as in "put"; or as in "tulip"

My transcription of Kairiru-language words can be read the same way.

Terms:

TP = Tok Pisin
K = Kairiru

bembe (TP):	magic for obtaining money from the dead
beten (TP):	prayer
beten korona (TP):	the rosary
bikman (TP):	bigman or traditional leader; sometimes used to refer to any man of importance in a particular sphere
buai (TP):	betel nut
bum (K):	term of address for grandfather or grandchild. This is a reciprocal term of address used between grandparents and grandchildren.
bung wantaim (TP):	to gather together or unite
bus (TP):	the bush or forest outside the village and its gardens; or, from the perspective of town, rural areas in general
divelopmen (TP):	development
haus boi (TP):	a house for men to sleep or gather in; a men's ceremonial house
heten (TP):	heathen
kago (TP):	cargo; European goods and material wealth
kaikrauap (K):	a carved human figure used in indigenous magical procedures

kastom (TP):	leaders whose authority rests on indigenous criteria
kaunsil (TP):	elected village leader in the Local Government Council system
kentin (TP):	a small village store
klen (TP):	clan
komiti (TP):	deputy to the village kaunsil
konan (K):	a long-bodied fish that inhabits the coastal waters of the Sepik region
koyeng (K):	group defined by descent from a common ancestor; residential area, often dominated by the members of a particular descent group
leiny (K):	a particular language, as in leiny Kairiru (Kairiru language)
luk (K):	term of address for a sibling of the opposite sex
mam (K):	term of address for father
masalai (TP):	a powerful, often dangerous spirit or supernatural being
masta (TP):	archaic term of address for whites or Europeans
mi pasin (TP):	selfishness, individualism
moin (K):	woman; female (adjective)
nikanik (K):	story
pasin (TP):	the way or fundamental character of something or someone
passim (TP):	to fasten or strengthen
pekato (TP):	sin
ples (TP):	village; place
ramat (K):	man, sometimes used in the nongendered sense of people
ramat shawaung (K):	ghost of a human being
rop buai (TP):	a large bunch of betel nut, still on the stem
saveman (TP):	educated or wise man; often used to refer to people with extensive Western-style education
savemeri (TP):	educated or wise woman; often used to refer to people with extensive Western-style education
shawaung (K):	spirit of something
singsing (TP):	a traditional song, sometimes accompanied by dance; a performance of traditional song and dance; a magical spell
staus (TP):	outhouse
stori (TP):	story; to tell a story; historical account legitimating claims to hereditary rights to authority or resources
straksa (TP):	lines of descent and genealogical relations
strongim (TP):	to strengthen
susokman (TP):	person who wears shoes and socks; an urban person

taik (K):	term of address for a sibling of the same sex
tambaran (TP):	the tutelary spirits of the indigenous men's cult and the cult's sacred paraphernalia
tapiok (TP):	a food prepared from the root of the cassava plant
tinpis (TP):	tinned or canned fish, usually mackerel
tredstoa (TP):	a small village store
walap (K):	big (adjective)
warap (K):	a feast and distribution of goods given to commemorate a deceased leader and validate his descendant's claim to authority

References Cited

AHRENS, THEODOR
1997   "Millenarianism in Christian Missions: A Few Historical Reminders." In *Millennial Markers*, Pamela J. Stewart and Andrew Strathern, eds., pp. 19–34. Townsville, Australia: Center for Pacific Studies, James Cook University of North Queensland.

ALLEN, BRYANT
1996   "Land Management: Papua New Guinea's Dilemma." *Asia-Pacific Magazine*, no. 1 (April), pp. 36–42.

AMARSHI, AZEEM, KENNETH GOOD, AND REX MORTIMER
1979   *Development and Dependency: The Political Economy of Papua New Guinea.* Oxford: Oxford University Press.

APADURAI, ARJUN
1986   "Introduction: Commodities and the Politics of Value." In *The Social Life of Things*, Arjun Apadurai, ed., pp. 3–63. Cambridge: Cambridge University Press.

AUSTRALIAN INTERNATIONAL DEVELOPMENT ASSISTANCE BUREAU
1989   *Papua New Guinea Economic Situation and Outlook.* Canberra: Australian Government Publishing Service.

BAILEY, F. G.
1971   "The Management of Reputations and the Process of Change." In F. G. Bailey, ed., *Gifts and Poison*, pp. 281–301. New York: Schocken Books.

BARKER, JOHN
1992   "Christianity in Western Melanesian Ethnography." In James G. Carrier, ed., *History and Tradition in Melanesian Anthropology*, pp. 144–173. Berkeley: University of California Press.

BARLOW, KATHLEEN, AND STEVEN WINDUO
1997   *Logging the Southwestern Pacific: Perspectives from Papua New Guinea, Solomon Islands, and Vanuatu.* Special Issue of *The Contemporary Pacific* 9(1).

BERCOVITCH, EYTAN
1994   "The Agent in the Gift: Hidden Exchange in Inner New Guinea." *Cultural Anthropology* 9:498–536.

BORRELL, O. WILLIAM, F.M.S.
1989   *An Annotated Checklist of the Flora of Kairiru Island, New Guinea.* Published by the author, Marcelin College, 160 Bulleen Road, Victoria, Australia.

BOYEK, HERMAN
2000   *Kairiru: Island of Legends.* Wewak, Papua New Guinea: Wirui Press.

BROWN, PAULA, AND ANTON PLOEG
1997   "Introduction: Change and Conflict in Papua New Guinea Land and Resource Rights." *Anthropological Forum* 7(4):507–527.

BURRIDGE, KENELM
1995   *Mambu: A Melanesian Millennium.* Princeton, N.J.: Princeton University Press.
[1960]

CARRIER, JAMES G.
1992   "Occidentalism: The World Turned Upside Down." *American Ethnologist* 19(2):195–212.

CARRIER, JAMES G., AND ACHSAH CARRIER
1989   *Wage, Trade and Exchange in Melanesia: A Manus Society in the Modern State.* Berkeley and Los Angeles: University of California Press.

CHOWNING, ANN
1977   *An Introduction to the Peoples and Cultures of Melanesia.* Menlo Park, Calif.: Cummings Publishing Company.

CONNELL, JOHN
1997   *Papua New Guinea: The Struggle for Development.* London and New York: Routledge.

CORNIA, GIOVANNI, RICHARD JOLLY, AND FRANCES STEWART
1987   *Adjustment with a Human Face.* Oxford: Oxford University Press.

COX, HARVEY
1995   *Fire from Heaven: The Rise of Pentecostal Spirituality and the Reshaping of Religion in the Twenty-first Century.* Reading, Mass.: Addison-Wesley Publishing Company.

CROSSLEY, MICHAEL
1998   "Ideology, Curriculum and Community." In Laura Zimmer-Tamakoshi, ed., *Modern Papua New Guinea*, pp. 297–314. Kirksville, MO.: Thomas Jefferson University Press.

CURTIN, TIMOTHY
2000   "A New Dawn for Papua New Guinea's Economy?" *Pacific Economic Bulletin* 15(2): 1–35.

DAHL, GUNDRUN, AND ANNIKA RABO
1992   *Kam-Ap or Take-Off: Local Notions of Development.* Stockholm: Stockholm Studies in Social Anthropology.

DALTON, DOUG, ED.
2000   "A Critical Retrospective on 'Cargo Cult': Western/Melanesian Intersections." Special issue of *Oceania* 70(4).

DIAMOND, STANLEY
1974   *In Search of the Primitive: A Critique of Civilization.* New Brunswick, N.J.: Transaction Books.

DUBASH, NAVROZ K., AND COLIN FILER
2000   "Papua New Guinea." In Frances J. Seymour and Navroz K. Dubash, eds., *The Right Conditions: The World Bank, Structural Adjustment and Forest Policy Reform*, pp. 29–57, Washington, D.C.: World Resources Institute.

ERRINGTON, FREDERICK K., AND DEBORAH B. GEWERTZ
1990   "The Chief of the Chambri: Social Change and Cultural Permeability among a New Guinea People." In Nancy Lutkehaus et al., eds., *Sepik Heritage: Tradition and Change in Papua New Guinea*, pp. 309–319. Durham, N.C.: Carolina Academic Press.

ESCOBAR, ARTURO
1995   *Encountering Development: The Making and Unmaking of the Third World.* Princeton, N.J.: Princeton University Press.

FEINBERG, RICHARD
1995   "Introduction: Politics of Culture in the Pacific Islands." *Ethnology* 34(2):91–98.

FILER, COLIN
1998   "The Melanesian Way of Menacing the Mining Industry." In Laura Zimmer-Tamakoshi, ed., *Modern Papua New Guinea*, pp. 147–177. Kirksville, MO.: Thomas Jefferson University Press.

FINGLETON, JIM
1991   "The East Sepik Land Legislation." In Peter Larmour, ed., *Customary Land Tenure: Registration and Decentralization in Papua New Guinea*, pp. 147–161. Monograph 29, Institute of Applied Social and Economic Research. Boroko, Papua New Guinea: The National Research Institute.

FIRTH, STEWART
2000   "The Pacific Islands and the Globalization Agenda." *Contemporary Pacific* 12(1): 178–192.

FOSTER, ROBERT

1997   "Introduction: The Work of Nation Making." In Robert Foster, ed., *Nation Making: Emergent Identities in Postcolonial Melanesia*, pp. 1–30. Ann Arbor: The University of Michigan Press.

FOSTER, ROBERT, ed.

1997   *Nation Making: Emergent Identities in Postcolonial Melanesia*. Ann Arbor: The University of Michigan Press.

GARDNER, KATY, AND DAVID LEWIS

1996   *Anthropology, Development and the Post-Modern Challenge*. London: Pluto Press.

GEGEO, DAVID W.

1998   "Indigenous Knowledge and Empowerment: Rural Development Examined from Within." *Contemporary Pacific* 10(3): 289–315.

GEORGE, SUSAN, AND FABRIZIO SABELLI

1994   *Faith and Credit: The World Bank's Secular Empire*. Boulder, Colo.: Westview Press.

GEWERTZ, DEBORAH B., AND FREDERICK K. ERRINGTON

1991   *Twisted Histories, Altered Contexts: Representing the Chambri in a World System*. Cambridge: Cambridge University Press.

1999   *Emerging Class in Papua New Guinea: The Telling of Difference*. Cambridge: Cambridge University Press.

GIBSON, JOHN, AND SCOTT ROZELLE

1998   "Results of the Household Survey Component of the 1996 Poverty Assessment for Papua New Guinea" (May). Washington, D.C.: World Bank.

GREGORY, C. A.

1982   *Gifts and Commodities*. London: Academic Press.

GRIFFIN, JAMES, HANK NELSON, AND STEWART FIRTH

1979   *Papua New Guinea: A Political History*. Richmond, Victoria: Heinemann Educational Australia.

GRILLO, RALPH, AND ALAN REW

1985   *Social Anthropology and Development Policy*. London and New York: Tavistock.

GRILLO, R. D., AND R. L. STIRRAT

1997   *Discourses of Development: Anthropological Perspectives*. Oxford and New York: Berg.

HENWOOD, DOUG

2000   "*The Nation* Indicators: Health and Wealth." *The Nation*, July 10, p. 10.

HOBART, MARK
1995   "Introduction: The Growth of Ignorance?" In Mark Hobart, ed., *An Anthropological Critique of Development: The Growth of Ignorance*, pp. 1–30. London and New York: Routledge.

HOGBIN, IAN
1935   "Trading Expeditions in Northern New Guinea." *Oceania* 5(4):375–407.

HUBER, MARY
1988   *The Bishop's Progress: A Historical Ethnography of Catholic Missionary Experience on the Sepik Frontier.* Washington, D.C.: Smithsonian Institution Press.

HYNDMAN, DAVID
1994   *Ancestral Rain Forests and the Mountain of Gold: Indigenous Peoples and Mining in Papua New Guinea.* Boulder, Colo.: Westview Press.

JACOBSEN, MICHAEL
1997   "Vanishing Nations and the Infiltration of Nationalism: The Case of Papua New Guinea." In Robert Foster, ed., *Nation Making: Emergent Identities in Postcolonial Melanesia*, pp. 227–249. Ann Arbor: The University of Michigan Press.

KIRSCH, STUART
1997   "Indigenous Response to Environmental Impact along the Ok Tedi." In Susan Toft, ed., *Compensation for Resource Development in Papua New Guinea*, pp. 143–155. Monograph No. 6, Law Reform Commission of Papua New Guinea. Canberra: Research School of Pacific Studies and National Centre for Development Studies.

KNAUFT, BRUCE M.
1996   *Genealogies for the Present in Cultural Anthropology.* New York: Routledge.
1999   *From Primitive to Postcolonial in Melanesia and Anthropology.* Ann Arbor: The University of Michigan Press.

LAKAU, ANDREW
1997   "Customary Land Tenure, Customary Landowners and the Proposals for Customary Land Reform in Papua New Guinea." *Anthropological Forum* 7(4):529–547.

LARDNER, JAMES
1998   "Deadly Disparities: America's Widening Gap in Incomes May Be Narrowing Our Lifespans." *The Washington Post*, August 16, p. C1.

LARMOUR, PETER
1991   "Introduction." In Peter Larmour, ed., *Customary Land Tenure: Registration and Decentralization in Papua New Guinea*. Monograph 29, Institute of Applied Social and Economic Research. Boroko, Papua New Guinea: The National Research Institute.

LAWRENCE, PETER
1964   *Road Belong Cargo: A Study of the Cargo Movement in Southern Madang District, New Guinea.* Manchester, Eng.: University of Manchester Press.

LEA, DAVID
2000   "Dependency Theory and Its Relevance to Problems of Development in Papua New Guinea." *Pacific Economic Bulletin* 15(2):106–120. National Centre for Development Studies, The Australian National University.

LEAVITT, STEPHEN C.
2000   "The Apotheosis of White Men?: A Reexamination of Beliefs about Europeans as Ancestral Spirits." *Oceania* 70(4):304–316.

LINDSTROM, LAMONT
1990   *Knowledge and Power in a Pacific Society.* Washington, D.C., and London: Smithsonian Institution Press.

LONG, NORMAN
1992   "Conclusion." In *Battlefields of Knowledge: The Interlocking of Theory and Practice in Social Research and Development,* pp. 268–277. London and New York: Routledge.

MACINTYRE, MARTHA
1998   "The Persistence of Inequality." In Laura Zimmer-Taṃakoshi, ed., *Modern Papua New Guinea,* pp. 211–228. Kirksville, MO.: Thomas Jefferson University Press.

MANNING, MIKE
1997   "Developments in Papua New Guinea: 1997." *Pacific Economic Bulletin* 12(2):1–16.

MAUSS, MARCEL
1967   *The Gift.* New York: W. W. Norton and Company.
[1925]

McWILLIAM, SCOTT
1991   "Smallholder Production, the State and Land Tenure." In Peter Larmour, ed., *Customary Land Tenure: Registration and Decentralization in Papua New Guinea,* pp. 9–32. Monograph 29, Institute of Applied Social and Economic Research. Boroko, Papua New Guinea: The National Research Institute.

MURPHY, MICHAEL D.
1988   "The Culture of Spontaneity and the Politics of Enthusiasm: Catholic Pentecostalism in a California Parish." In George R. Saunders, ed., *Culture and Christianity: The Dialectics of Transformation,* pp. 135–158. New York: Greenwood Press.

NADER, LAURA
1991   "Harmony Models and the Construction of Law." In K. Avruch, P. Black, and J. Sci-
        mecca, eds., *Conflict Resolution: Cross-Cultural Perspectives*, pp. 41–59. Westport,
        Conn.: Greenwood Press.

THE NATIONAL (Boroko, Papua New Guinea)
1995   "Scrap Duty on Imported Tinned Fish." November 8, p. 18.

O'FAIRCHEALLAIGH, C.
1992   "The Local Politics of Resource Development in the South Pacific: Towards a General
        Framework of Analysis." In S. Henningham and R. J. May, eds., *Resource Develop-
        ment and Politics in the Pacific Islands*, pp. 258–289. Bathurst: Crawford House Press.
        Cited in Colin Filer, 1998, "The Melanesian Way of Menacing the Mining Industry,"
        p. 157, in Laura Zimmer-Tamakoshi, ed., *Modern Papua New Guinea*, pp. 147–177.
        Kirksville, MO.: Thomas Jefferson University Press.

PAPUA NEW GUINEA POST COURIER
1998   "Home Brew Liquor a Threat to Peace." February 16, p. 11.

PAPUA NEW GUINEA POST COURIER ONLINE
2001   "Wewak Cannery To Be 'the Biggest.' " March 28.

PARRY, JONATHAN, AND MAURICE BLOCH
1989   "Introduction: Money and the Morality of Exchange." In Jonathan Parry and Maurice
        Bloch, eds., *Money and the Morality of Exchange*, pp. 1–32. Cambridge: Cambridge
        University Press.

POKAWIN, S.
1982   "Papua New Guinea: Aftermath of Colonialism." In *Politics in the Pacific Islands: Mela-
        nesia*. Suva, Fiji. Cited in Alexander Wanek, *The State and Its Enemies in Papua New
        Guinea*, p. 51. Richmond, Surrey, U.K.: Curzon Press.

ROBBINS, JOEL
1997   "666, or Why Is the Millennium on the Skin?: Morality, the State and the Epistemology
        of Apocalypticism among the Urapmin of Papua New Guinea." In Pamela J. Stewart
        and Andrew Strathern, eds., *Millennial Markers*, pp. 35–58, Townsville, Australia:
        Center for Pacific Studies, James Cook University of North Queensland.
2001   "Introduction: Global Religions, Pacific Island Transformations." *Journal of Ritual
        Studies* 15(2):4–12.

ROBBINS, JOEL, PAMELA J. STEWART, AND ANDREW STRATHERN, EDS.
2001   "Charismatic and Pentecostal Christianity in the Pacific." Special issue of *Journal of
        Ritual Studies* 15(2).

RODATZ, HANS
1907   "Report by District Officer of Eitape, 1907." Trans. John J. Tschauder. Cited in Lorna Fleetwood, *A Short History of Wewak*, p. 10. Wewak, Papua New Guinea: Wirui Press, 1984.

SAHLINS, MARSHALL
1994   "Goodbye to Tristes Tropes: Ethnography in the Context of Modern World History." In R. Borofsky, ed., *Assessing Cultural Anthropology*, pp. 377–395. New York: McGraw-Hill.

SCAGLION, RICHARD
1983   "The 'Coming' of Independence in Papua New Guinea: An Abelam View." *Journal of the Polynesian Society* 92:463–486.
1996   "Chiefly Models in Papua New Guinea." *Contemporary Pacific* 8(1):1–31.

SCHWARTZ, THEODORE
1962   *The Paliau Movement in the Admiralty Islands, 1946–1954.* Anthropological Papers of the American Museum of Natural History 49.
1968   "Cargo Cult: A Melanesian Type-Response to Culture Contact." Paper presented at DeVos Conference on Psychological Adjustment and Adaptation to Culture Change, Hakone, Japan, 1968, and the Eighth International Congress of Anthropological and Ethnological Sciences, Tokyo.
1972   "Distributive Models of Culture in Relation to Societal Scale." Paper prepared for Wenner Gren Foundation for Anthropological Research Burg-Wartenstein Symposium No. 55, July 31–August 8, 1972.
1973   "Cult and Context: The Paranoid Ethos in Melanesia." *Ethos* 1(2):153–174.

SILLITOE, PAUL
1998   *An Introduction to the Anthropology of Melanesia: Culture and Tradition.* Cambridge: Cambridge University Press.
2000   *Social Change in Melanesia: Development and History.* Cambridge: Cambridge University Press.

SMITH, MICHAEL FRENCH
1982a   "The Catholic Ethic and the Spirit of Alcohol Use in an East Sepik Province Village." In Mac Marshall, ed., *Through a Glass Darkly: Beer and Modernization in Papua New Guinea*, pp.271–288. IASER Monograph 18. Boroko, Papua New Guinea: Institute of Applied Social and Economic Research.
1982b   "Bloody Time and Bloody Scarcity: Capitalism, Authority and the Transformation of Temporal Experience in a Papua New Guinea Village." *American Ethnologist* 9(30): 503–518.
1984   " 'Wild' Villagers and Capitalist Virtues: Perceptions of Western Work Habits in a Preindustrial Community." *Anthropological Quarterly* 57(4):125–138.

1985   "White Man, Rich Man, Bureaucrat, Priest: Hierarchy, Inequality and Legitimacy in a Changing Papua New Guinea Village." *South Pacific Forum* 2(1):1–24.

1988   "From Heathen to Atheist on Kairiru Island." In George Saunders, ed., *Culture and Christianity: The Dialectics of Transformation*, pp. 33–46. Westport, Conn.: Greenwood Press.

1990a   "Catholicism, Capitalist Incorporation and Resistance." In John Barker, ed., *The Ethnography of Christianity in the Pacific*, pp. 149–172. Association for Social Anthropology in Oceania Monograph No. 12. Lanham, Md.: University Press of America.

1990b   "Business and the Romance of Community Cooperation on Kairiru Island." In Nancy Lutkehaus, Christian Kaufman, William E. Mitchell, Douglass Newton, Lita Osmundsen, and Meinhard Schuster, eds., *Sepik Heritage: Tradition and Change in Papua New Guinea*, pp. 212–220. Durham, N.C.: Carolina Academic Press.

1994   *Hard Times on Kairiru Island: Poverty, Development, and Morality in a Papua New Guinea Village.* Honolulu: University of Hawai'i Press.

1995   "The Cultural Politics of Cooperation: An American Corporation and a Papua New Guinea Village." *Ethnology* 34(3): 191–199.

STEWART, PAMELA J., AND ANDREW STRATHERN
2001   "The Great Exchange: Moka with God." *Journal of Ritual Studies* 15(2):91–104.

STRATHERN, ANDREW J.
1991   "Struggles for Meaning." In Aletta Biersack, ed., *Clio in Oceania: Toward a Historical Anthropology*, pp. 205–230. Washington, D.C.: Smithsonian Institution Press.

STRATHERN, MARILYN
1988   *The Gender of the Gift: Problems with Women and Problems with Society in Melanesia.* Berkeley and Los Angeles: University of California Press.

TAUTEA, LAUATU
1997   "Human Resource Dilemma: The Missing Link?" In *Papua New Guinea: A 20/20 Vision*, pp. 176–187. Canberra: The Australian National University National Centre for Development Studies; Boroko: Papua New Guinea National Research Institute.

TERRELL, JOHN
1986   *Prehistory in the Pacific Islands: A Study of Variation in Language, Customs, and Human Biology.* Cambridge: Cambridge University Press.

THOMAS, NICHOLAS
1991   *Entangled Objects: Exchange, Material Culture, and Colonialism in the Pacific.* Cambridge, Mass.: Harvard University Press.

TOFT, SUSAN
1997   *Compensation for Resource Development in Papua New Guinea.* Monograph No. 6, Law Reform Commission of Papua New Guinea. Canberra: Research School of Pacific Studies and National Centre for Development Studies.

TURTLE, CHRIS
1991   "Administrative Reform and Land Mobilisation." In Peter Larmour, ed., *Customary Land Tenure: Registration and Decentralization in Papua New Guinea*, pp. 87–100. Monograph 29, Institute of Applied Social and Economic Research. Boroko, Papua New Guinea: The National Research Institute.

TUZIN, DONALD
1997   *The Cassowary's Revenge: The Life and Death of Masculinity in a New Guinea Society.* Chicago: University of Chicago Press.

WALLMAN, SANDRA
1977   *Perceptions of Development.* Cambridge: Cambridge University Press.

WANEK, ALEXANDER
1996   *The State and Its Enemies in Papua New Guinea.* Nordic Institute of Asian Studies Monograph Series, No. 68. Richmond, Surrey: Curzon Press.

WARD, ALAN
1991   "Time to Make a New Start." In Peter Larmour, ed., *Customary Land Tenure: Registration and Decentralization in Papua New Guinea*, pp. 177–193. Monograph 29, Institute of Applied Social and Economic Research. Boroko, Papua New Guinea: The National Research Institute.

WATANABE, TETSUO
1995   *The Naval Land Unit That Vanished in the Jungle.* Ed. and trans. Hiromitsu Iwamoto. Palmerston, Australia: Tabletop Press.

WEINER, ANNETTE B.
1992   *Inalienable Possessions: The Paradox of Keeping-While-Giving.* Berkeley: University of California Press.

WESLEY-SMITH, TERENCE, et al.
1996   "Melanesia in Review: Issues and Events, 1995." *Contemporary Pacific* 8(2): 409–442.
1998   "Melanesia in Review: Issues and Events, 1997." *Contemporary Pacific* 10(2): 424–455.

WEWAK PATROL REPORT
1946–   "Wewak Patrol Report No. 3." Port Moresby: Papua New Guinea National Archives.
1947

WHITE, GEOFFREY M., AND LAMONT LINDSTROM
1997   *Chiefs Today: Traditional Pacific Leadership and the Postcolonial State.* Stanford, Calif.: Stanford University Press.

WIVELL, RICHARD
1981   "Kairiru Grammar." Master's thesis, University of Auckland, Auckland, New Zealand.

WOLCOTT, HARRY F.
1995   *The Art of Fieldwork.* Walnut Creek, Calif., London, and New Delhi: Altamira Press.

WORLD BANK
1995   *Papua New Guinea: Delivering Public Services.* Volume II. Report No. 14414–PNG. Washington, D.C.: The World Bank.
2000   *Papua New Guinea: Country Assistance Evaluation.* Report No. 20183. Washington, D.C.: The World Bank.

WORSLEY, PETER
1968   *The Trumpet Shall Sound: A Study of 'Cargo Cults' in Melanesia.* New York: Schocken Books.

YALA, CHARLES, AND THEODORE LEVANTIS
1998   "Recent Economic Events in Papua New Guinea: A Continuing Drought in Development." *Pacific Economic Bulletin* 13(2):1–16.

ZIMMER-TAMAKOSHI, LAURA
1998   "Introduction." In Laura Zimmer-Tamakoshi, ed., *Modern Papua New Guinea*, pp. 1–16. Kirksville, MO.: Thomas Jefferson University Press.

Index

Australia: as colonial government, 8, 60–61; development pattern set by, 62, 187n; Mormon missionaries in, 16–17

Austronesian languages, and chiefs, 152–153

autonomy: beyond the village, 165, 175; and charismatic Catholicism, 168; and identity, 165; opportunities for in village, 165; restrictions on in village, 117, 165, 169

bigman/bigmen, 87; authority of, 111–112, 154–155; challenges to, 157–159; chief of Kragur and, 153; education and, 157–159; nostalgia for, 153–154; sorcery and, 54. *See also* leadership

business: as collective endeavor, 145–146, 174, 189n; experience with, 50, 54; and the Good Way, 144; harmony and, 54, 144; individualism and, 146, 174; land resources and, 44, 169; market gardening as, 70, 139, 141; obstacles to, 50, 139–140, 162; record keeping in, 50, 139; returns from, 140; as small-group endeavor, 145–146, 174, 189n; townsmen's efforts in, 143–144, 161; among villagers, 70, 89, 138. *See also* copra; money; tourism

capitalism: commodity exchange and, 40; land and, 43; as metaphor, 40–41; as model for development, 7–8, 64; as taken for granted, 13

cargo cults, 51–52, 136–137; charismatic Catholicism and, 138; Christianity and, 52, 186n; cultural context of, 51–52, 186n; irrational element in, 52, 186n; Lalau incident, 51, 186n; literature on, classic, 186n; literature on, recent, 186n; millenarianism and, 52, millenarianism, American and, 186n, millenarianism, Christian and,186n

Catholicism: acceptance of, 26–27; bureaucratization of, 125–126; cargo cults and, 52, 136–137; changes in aims of, 21; as collective endeavor, 121, 122; complicated relationship of villagers to, 17, 184n; domestication of, 31; in East Sepik Province, 16; European wealth and, 27; faces of, 121; generosity and, 55; harmony in, 121; individualism and, 134–135; leadership of in 1970s, 22, 122–123; and leadership opportunities in 1990s, 125–126; money and, 47, 49–50, 135, 136; moral worth, assertion of in, 17, 31; relaxation of, 123, 125; social unrest and, 121, 134–135, 168; sorcery and, 154; at St. Xavier's, 20–21; as taken for granted, 123. *See also* charismatic Catholicism; Virgin Mary

charismatic Catholicism: America and, 126–127, 129; autonomy and, 168; cargo cults and, 138; conflict and, 130–132; in the East Sepik, 127; generational conflict and, 129, 131–132; God and, 131, 132; individualism and, 135; leveling tendencies in, 189n; origins of, 126–127, 188n; in Pacific Islands, 188n; in Port Moresby, 127; risks of, 131–132; speaking in tongues in, 76; training in, 127–128;